HALLUCINABULIA

THE DREAM DIARY OF AN UNINTENDED SOLITARIAN

By Thomas Wictor

For those of us who've seen the elephant.

Abulia (ă-bū'lē-ă) n.
1. Deficiency of will, initiative, motivation, or
drive; inability to make decisions.
2. Reduction in speech, movement,
thought, and emotional reaction.

CONTENTS

ACKNOWLEDGEMENTS

Many thanks to the people who helped me out. I couldn't have done it without you.

Thanks to my brother Tim for his designs and support and for being source material.

Thanks to Carmen and Scott, my former ghosts and forever-muses.

Thanks to Joe Cady for his interpretative skills. It's good to know for sure that I'm utterly off my rocker. *Whew!*

Thanks to Mark McCann for reading, praising, sharing news of the perfectly symmetrical, and wearing funny glasses.

Thanks to Tom Pickel, the proofreader with the eyes of a kestrel.

Thanks to everyone who appears on these pages.

And thanks to Michael, if that really was you.

INTRODUCTION

Most of my dreams were nightmares. Some were so bad that I wrote them down. I wasn't sure why I bothered; preserving them to read over again wasn't the goal. Instead, I think I simply wanted to get them out of my system. And by capturing them, I caged them. My nightmares often made me wake up screaming. Putting them on paper helped me cope with the thoughts and emotional hangovers they produced. Sometimes my nightmares ruined the entire day. The worst came in 1989, 1994, 1995, and 1996. They form the bulk of this diary.

Beginning in 1997 my waking hours became an unending nightmare, as my greatest fears were realized one after another over a period of five years. I walked among aliens with whom I could never communicate, I lost the ability to build scale models due to failing eyesight, I discovered that no other woman would ever compare to the Cardinal Ghost "Carmen," I failed utterly as a music journalist, and I finally admitted to myself that I couldn't play the bass guitar anymore because of osteoarthritis. It no longer served any purpose whatsoever to record the torment, weirdness, and humiliation that my brain manufactured as I slept. The days and nights were indistinguishable, so I stopped keeping the dream diary.

From 2002 I wrote terrible novels and very good books on military history. I wrote all day, every day, morning to night. There was no opportunity to resume the dream diary. I also found different tools—psychotherapy and medication—to cage my nightmares. Though my dreams remained as vivid and lingering as movies, the horror shows diminished. I used to hate going to bed, because my nights were usually a journey into hell. But I gradually lost my fear of sleep.

Hallucinabulia is the third volume of the *Ghosts* trilogy. It joins *Ghosts and Ballyhoo: Memoirs of a Failed L.A. Music Journalist* and the novel *Chasing the Last Whale.* All explore the theme of conquering a profoundly traumatic past by converting anger over loss into gratitude for what once was. The feedback I've gotten from *Ghosts and Ballyhoo* prompted me to publish this extremely private document, since it provides context to the memoir and serves the same function: It banishes and entertains. Not everything in this book is negative. Some of it will make you laugh. *Hallucinabulia* also documents the psychological and emotional state in which I existed until October of 2011, when I was diagnosed with Meniere's disease and junked the last of the rage that had eaten me alive my entire life.

By reading my dreams, you'll be able to see for yourself how far I've come. I'm proud of that achievement, as well as the fact that I kicked the drugs and booze and never took out my rage on others. Making public what was inside me for so long is also my way of bearing witness. It's a chronicle of disaster, no different from a diary kept during the Black Death, for example. I've edited some of these dreams, removing details and changing specific nouns and verbs. What you'll read is nowhere near as hideous as the nightmares actually were. It's my prerogative to withhold, and besides, my intent in publishing *Hallucinabulia* isn't to exploit my history or seek your pity. It's simply to create another art project. I wrote 90 percent of this diary in longhand, filling several notebooks, and then I transcribed it onto my computer. It deserves to be published if for no other reason than the sheer time and work that went into it. Also, I think some of the imagery is outstandingly odd and hilarious.

There's great freedom in being housebound and solitary. I'm now indifferent to so much that worries others. Topping the list of things I no longer care about is how people perceive me. Make of my dream diary what you will. If there *is* a message in the *Ghosts* trilogy, it's this: *You are not alone.* Plenty of us know what you're going through, since we've gone through it ourselves. I kept thinking that things could not *possibly* get worse, but I was wrong. There's no bottom to reach, no "bad as bad can be." Bad is not finite. As bad as you can imagine your life can become, reality has a way of topping you.

And yet...

The person who had these dreams is now happy. He's achieved clarity, and gratitude has allowed him to weather far worse storms in the past six months than he did in the fifty years that came before. Clarity and gratitude saved his life.

As long as you're alive, there's hope.

Thomas Wictor
August 2013
Los Angeles

CHAPTER ONE
A NIGHTMARE'S GIFT

I worried how to start *Hallucinabulia* because the first nightmare cluster is truly unpleasant. It set a tone I didn't like, but there seemed to be no other option. I simply couldn't figure out how to structure the book except in the way I had, so I resigned myself to beginning with material that risked turning people off right from the start.

Then I was given a gift.

A nightmare from my past contacted me on July 2, 2013, and expressed its desire that I die soon. It threatened to expose my history to the world, said I had a way of making people want to punch me, and called me whiny, merciless, paranoid, self-pitying, judgmental, pathetic, cruel, poisonous, a fucking son of a bitch, an emotional retard, a perpetual loser, a self-important snob, a moron, a stable boy, a baby, and a hypocrite.

"When you die," it finished, "if I'm still around to hear of that glorious day, I'll have a party."

What was amazing to me is that this nightmare hadn't changed one iota in seventeen years. Several oceans' worth of water had flowed under the bridge that the nightmare and I crossed together. We'd both experienced deaths, but the nightmare had also married, become a mother, joined the Topanga Canyon

1

jet set, and inherited a fortune. I, on the other hand, had lost almost everything and had been transformed into a dizzy, cloistered vomiter who has his brother and four close friends—one in France, one in Russia, one in Australia, and one in Northern California. I haven't seen the France-based friend in ten years, I've never met the Russian or the Australian in person, and the fourth is a musician who simply doesn't have the time to communicate with me except sporadically.

But I'm happy, while the nightmare remains consumed by the psychotic rage that compelled it to try and make me kill myself. Time has stood still for the nightmare. It turns its rage outward, while I internalized mine. I was finally able to give up my rage on October 7, 2011. Today, the nightmare is as full of hate as it was when I last saw it in 1996. I haven't heard its voice in seventeen years. After we broke up, it would call and deliver strange, slow messages in a low-frequency roar, like a death-metal singer reading flashcards.

"You. Will. Be. Sorry. Do. You. Hear. Me. I. Will. Make. You. Pay. You. Have. Ruined. My. Life. Nobody. Fucks. Me. Over. I. Will. Get. You."

I could never understand why the nightmare hated me so much. We dated for only a month, and—as it pointed out—I was just a fat loser, a pitiful runt, and a failure who was terrible in bed. Wouldn't *everyone* prefer to be rid of a creature such as me?

Well...no, apparently, because when the lightbulb finally went on over my fat, runty-yet-outsized baby-head, and I realized that I should skedaddle, the nightmare ascended to heights of frenzied savagery that ended only when my brother Tim intervened. Though the nightmare held me in contempt, it was afraid of Tim. The nightmare was crazy, not stupid.

So I wondered what to write on my Website. That was how the nightmare contacted me on July 2, 2013. There was no question of engaging the nightmare directly, since I'm not the person I was in 1996. I now have no qualms about saying or doing whatever it takes to defend myself. A confrontation would've quickly escalated out of control. I might've posted a detailed description of the photo I found hidden under the nightmare's bedside lamp, for example. It was ghastly, irrefutable confirmation of what I'd suspected.

The nightmare has a husband and two daughters. They saved the nightmare. For their sake and theirs alone, I didn't do any of the things I could easily have done. By "easily," I mean it wouldn't have taxed me physically, emotionally, or logistically. Not in the least. But to spare a man and two small children who I don't know and will never meet, I refrained.

Don't take that the wrong way. Ask an Australian Web designer what happened to her when she tried to rip me off. I warned her, she didn't listen, and now she knows I wasn't kidding. My ability to destroy people gives me no pleasure. It's just a necessary tool, unfortunately. I hope none of you need this tool in your shed. If I had my way, *I* wouldn't need it either. But I do, and I use it without hesitation. The day the assaults stop, I'll put my tool back in the shed forever. I'm pretty sure the assaults won't stop until I'm dead. That's fine. The nightmare can have its party, and my tool will rust into a quaint artifact. Most importantly, the melodrama will finally be over.

When faced with unpleasantness, I turn to art. It always has an answer. Music, paintings, film, and poetry are part of my salvation. Because of the nightmare, I found one of the best poems ever written, which I posted without explanation on my Website.

The poet is Josephine Preston Peabody (1874-1922). Her poem is all my dreams. You don't even have to read this book. Read Ms. Peabody's stunning work of art instead.

And thank a nightmare for drawing it to your attention.

* * *

"Wolf, Wolf-stay-at-home,
Prowler, — scout,
Clanless and castaways,
And ailing with the drought,
Out from your hidings, — hither to the call;

3

Lift up your eyes to the high wind-fall!
Lift up your eyes from the poisoned spring;
Overhead, — overhead! The dragon Thing,
    — What should it bring?
    — Poising on the wing?"

"Wolf, Wolf, Old one, I saw it, even I.
Yesterday, yesterday, the Thing came by
Prowling at the outpost of the last lean wood,
By the gray waste ashes where the minster stood;
And out through the cloister where the belfry fronts
The market-place, and the town was once;
High, — high above the bright wide square
And the folk all flocking together, unaware,
The Thing-with-the-wings came there.
    Brother Vulture saw it
    And called me, as it passed:
    'Look and see, look and see, —
    Men have wings at last.'

"By the eyeless belfry I saw it, overhead,
Poised like a hawk, — like a storm unshed.
Near the huddled doves there, from the shattered cote,
I watched too.... And it smote!

"Not a threat of thunder, — not an armèd man,
Where the fury struck, and the fleet fire ran. —
But girl-child, man-child, mothers and their young,
Newborn of woman, with milk upon its tongue;
Nursling where it clung.

4

"Not a talon reached they, yet, the lords of prey!
But left the red dregs there, rent and cast away;
Fled from the spoils there, scattered things accurst:
    — It was not for hunger.
     It was not for thirst.

    "From the eyeless belfry,
    Brother Vulture laughed:
    'This is all we have to see
    For his master-craft?
    — Old ones, and lean ones,
    Never now to fast,
    Men have wings at last!'

"Brought they any tidings for us from the Sun?"
    "No, my chief, not one."
"Left they not a road-sign, how the way was won?"
    "No, my chief, none."
But girl-child, man-child, creature yet unborn,
Doe and fawn together so, weltering and torn,
Newborn of women where the flagstones bled;
(Better can the vultures do, for the shamèd dead.)
Road-dust sobbing where the lightning burst —
    It was not for hunger;
    It was not for thirst."

"Brought they not some token that the stars took on?"
    — "No, my chief, none."
"Never yet a message from the highways overhead?"
    — "Brother, I have said."

"Old years, gray years, years of growing things,
We have toiled and kept the watch with our wonderings;
But to see what things should be, when that Men had wings.

"Sea-mark, sea-wall, — ships above the tide;
Mine and mole-way under-earth, to have its hidden pride; —
Not enough, not enough, more and more beside!

"Bridle, for our proud-of-mane, — then the triple yoke;
Ox-goad and lash again, and bonded fellow-folk!
Not enough; not enough; — for his master-stroke.
Thunder trapped and muttering, and led away for thrall;
Lightnings leashed together then, at his beck and call;
Not enough; not enough; — for his Wherewithal!

 "He must look with evil eye
On the spaces of the sky:
 He must scheme and try! —
While all we, with dread and awe,
Sheathing and unsheathing claw,
 Watch apart, and prophesy
That we never saw. —

"Wings, to seek his more-and-more
 Where we knew us blind;
Wings to make him conqueror,
 With his master-mind;
Wings, that he out-watch, — out-soar,
 Eagle and his kind!

"Lo, the dream fulfilled at last! — And the dread outgrown,
Broken, as a bird's heart; — fallen as a stone
    ....What was he, to make afraid?
      — Hating all that he had made?
      — Hating all his own.

"Scatter to your strongholds, till the race is run.
Doe and fawn together, so, soon it will be done.
Never now, never now, Ship without a mast,
In the harbors of the Sun, do you make fast!
      But the floods shall cleanse again
      Every blackened trail of Men, —
      Men with wings, at last!"[1]

---

1 Josephine Preston Peabody, "Men Have Wings at Last," in *Poems of the Great War,* selected by J. W. Cunliffe (New York: The MacMillan Company, 1918), pp. 207-211.

CHAPTER TWO
THE FIRST NIGHTMARE CLUSTER

When I met the Cardinal Ghost Carmen in November of 1987, I recognized and remembered her. She was as familiar to me as a sibling or best friend. Something clicked into place, and I was finally whole. I never believed in love at first sight, destiny, or soul mates. All my relationships had been farcical wipeouts; my exes can testify to that. Meeting this small, beautiful, freckled woman with her pale skin, dark eyes, and black hair instantly changed my entire perception of reality. I didn't fight the sense that I'd known her many times before. I knew it was true, the way I know that I'm left handed. Meeting her again made me understand how lonely I'd been without her. I'd missed her terribly.

A very intelligent friend once said to me, "Even if you're lucky enough to find your soul mate, it doesn't mean that both of you will be ready for each other at the time."

For about eighteen months, Carmen and I had an extremely turbulent, on-again, off-again relationship characterized by endless fighting, deception, and titanic drinking. Although I knew in my bones that I was supposed to be with her, it finally got to be too much. I simply wasn't equipped to handle the emotional highs and lows of the most intense happiness and the worst pain I'd ever experienced.

After I left Carmen in June of 1989, I began having indescribably horrible nightmares every time I went to sleep. These are the ones I wrote down. There were many more; usually I didn't have time to record them, since in those days I used a pen, a difficult task since childhood. I had to shower and get to work—generally hung over and still stoned on hashish—so most of the dreams in this cluster eluded my cage.

Carmen and I got back together in July of 1989, and the nightmares stopped for the most part, until she drove me away in 1993.

*   *   *

JUNE 10, 1989

I lay on my stomach across a table, my feet on the floor and my sweaty head cushioned on my folded arms. My friend Steiv Dixon's girlfriend Yumi stood behind me, stabbing me slowly and deeply with a long-bladed knife. I wasn't restrained, but I knew I couldn't move. Doing so would only make the pain worse. Even lying perfectly still, it was excruciating. Spears of agony lacerated my guts. They penetrated all the way up to my heart.

Yumi chuckled. "There. That's not so bad, is it?" she murmured. "Now, you *know* you're not supposed to move. You *know* that."

Her voice was affectionate—teasing and jocular. It sounded much deeper than normal. Since she couldn't speak English, I wondered if she were possessed.

Though she was behind me, I could somehow see her face. She looked like the *Madonna Litta,* her head cocked forward with an indulgent almost-smile and her eyes half-closed as she leisurely, rhythmically stabbed.

I knew it would soon be over. It never lasted very long, so I held my breath, gritted my teeth, and waited it out.

HALLUCINABULIA

JUNE 14, 1989

My teeth suddenly became loose in my jaw. I put my fingers in my mouth
to see how unstable they were. The lower-left incisors, cuspid, and bicuspids
seemed to be held in place by strings, the way my baby teeth felt right before
they fell out. Using my tongue, I could probe the undersides of the teeth. They
had the same jagged hollow under the crown as I remembered from my childhood, and when I used my tongue to push saliva into them, they produced the
same squishy sounds.

My newly loose teeth panicked me because it meant that something was
seriously wrong. Without knowing why, I pulled the teeth from my jaw, examined them, and dropped them on the floor. They were amazingly long and
white, like a wolf or dog's teeth. The third or fourth tooth I removed had a bit
of jawbone stuck to it. This really upset me, but I kept on plucking out larger
and larger pieces.

The jawbone was made of wood, and the teeth were attached with rusty
iron screws. I was terrified and outraged that this junk had been in my mouth
all these years, and I'd never noticed it. God knew what sorts of diseases it
had caused. Finally, I yanked out a chunk of bone almost four inches long and
studied it.

Below the rotted, corroded sockets where the teeth had been, my mother's
name—Cecilia Wictor—was burned into the wood. There was a date beside
her name, comprised of a day, month, and year ending in either '66 or '68, but
I couldn't read it. I felt incredible anger at my mother for making me such a
cruddy, dangerously fragile jaw. It was unbelievable that she'd been so uncaring and thoughtless.

JUNE 19, 1989

I was a Chinese peasant living under the Mongols. Thousands of us had gathered in Peking to witness a public execution. A Mongol noble was carried

10

through the crowd on a sedan chair, his guards hacking their way through the masses with swords.

The noble stopped in front of me, and guards cleared an empty circle on the cobblestones about thirty feet in diameter. A bound prisoner was brought forward. He giggled and shrugged as though he liked being the center of attention.

After guard knocked him down, two executioners approached, carrying poles with curved, toothed blades on the ends. They began sawing at his thighs and abdomen, ripping him open. The teeth of the blades caught on the material of his clothing and his muscle fibers, cartilage, and sinews. It sounded exactly like a bread knife sawing through cardboard.

As the executioners butchered him, the prisoner made a grisly chattering noise: *"Ah-ch-ch-ch-ch-ch-ch! Ah-ch-ch-ch-ch-ch-ch!"*

Nobody around me reacted, and the Mongol noble seemed bored. What I watched was evil beyond comprehension, but there was nothing I could do. If I screamed or protested, they'd do the same to me.

JUNE 21, 1989

A small, coal black Ethiopian child lay on the ground in front of me. He was emaciated and had the bloated belly of starvation. I kicked him as hard as I could. He stared up at me with large, faintly sad eyes that squeezed shut at each blow. I couldn't see the rest of his face.

My heavy, steel-toed boots tore the skin on his sides, spraying blood in all directions. My mind was completely blank as I did this. I felt nothing whatsoever.

The child and I were illuminated by what seemed to be an overhead spotlight. Outside the cone of light, everything was dark. We were on a dirt floor, maybe in a cellar, and I knew there were other children lying just beyond my vision. An unseen audience surrounded us, and I did this for their delectation.

They watched with a cold passion, entertained but not showing it because that would be gauche.

I became a member of the audience and now watched a grainy film of me kicking the child. It reminded me of the European documentaries made in the seventies that showed Third Worlders committing terrible atrocities, the filmmakers presenting genuine suffering as entertainment but disguising it with phony moralizing. The movie of me killing the Ethiopian child had the same air of rationalization, of utter corruption cloaked in false sobriety and didacticism.

Then I was simultaneously watcher *and* participant. The camerawork became more frantic, focusing on my caked boots and getting close-ups of the ragged, smashed-in torso of the child. After I'd destroyed his body, I began stomping on his head, crushing his face and jumping up and down on him until his skull broke open. His brains, teeth, and deflated eyeballs caught on the tips of my boots, flew into the air, and spattered down into my hair.

Eventually, I stopped and stood blankly beside what remained of the child. He now looked like a pile of brown, black, and red rags—just an empty skin with damp, darkened dirt surrounding it. The watcher-me was as unmoved as the perpetrator.

JUNE 22, 1989

Asleep on the futon on the floor of my apartment, I began floating up off the floor. I turned over onto my belly as I rose, allowing the quilt to drop off. With my knees bent and my arms spread, I came to rest against the ceiling in the position I assumed when I lay on the floor to ease my back pain. My body was completely weightless, affected by the faintest of eddies in the air as I lay looking down on the room. I was so insubstantial that I could blow away at any second. If the ceiling hadn't been there, I would've kept floating until I went into outer space.

After a while I had to come down. Floating was very uncomfortable; my head thrummed as if an electric current ran through it. Through sheer will-power I managed to descend until my feet barely brushed the floor, but as I settled I was transformed into a hunchback. My body was bent double, and I had a gnarled hump between my shoulders. I wanted to see what I looked like, so I pointed my toes like a ballerina and delicately pushed myself along the floor toward the bathroom, skimming for a few feet before I had to push again. As I approached the bathroom mirror, I kept my eyes fixed on the front door of my apartment to avoid seeing myself until I was ready.

Hovering in front of the mirror, I slowly turned my head. I was backlit by a powerful spotlight; all I could see of myself was a silhouette. My skull was narrow and pointed, with no more than a dozen long hairs sprouting from it. As I kept turning, my profile came into view. I had a hooked nose, a prognathous lower jaw with protruding teeth, and old-man ears shaped like bullhorns.

Facing the mirror head on, I saw more details as my vision adjusted. My glistening pop-eyes were at dramatically different levels, and the skin of my face was deeply lined. I seemed to be wearing a medieval cotte with a hood pooled on my shoulders. Apparently, I was a freak from the Middle Ages, a court jester or deformed street beggar.

When I tried to speak, I could produce only thick moans.

"Eeyuh. Mmmuh. Uhnnuh! Mmuhmuh."

I was appalled at what I'd become and furious at the unfairness of it.

What've I gotten myself into now? I thought.

JUNE 26, 1989

As I lay on my futon in my apartment, trying to sleep, I felt a catastrophic urge to urinate. I leaped up and raced to the bathroom, thinking I wouldn't get there in time. It was as if the urine were a living creature, trying to force its way out of me. I reached the tiny bathroom and yanked down the waistband of my boxer shorts with my right hand, gripping my penis with my left. Relaxing, I experienced the glorious relief of letting go.

Within a few seconds, I realized that I couldn't feel the urine stream in my penis. The fingers of my left hand didn't register the usual rushing sensation. However, I could hear liquid splashing into the toilet. Overcome with terror but knowing what I'd discover, I let go of the waistband with my right hand and turned on the bathroom light, looking down at my groin.

The stream of urine came from a ragged hole in my groin to the right of my penis. This new opening looked as if it had been abraded into the skin, or maybe the urine had burst through under the immense pressure. The hole didn't look like a puncture.

Urine poured out of me with no sign of letting up, as if I were full to the brim. The ragged, fleshy edges of the hole flapped in the stream, spraying droplets. Obviously I was fatally ill with some horrible disease, because holes didn't just appear unless someone was already far gone in illness. I began screaming hysterically.

JULY 6, 1989

The streets of Tokyo were deserted. I had no idea where I was, and the night got steadily darker the longer I walked.

When I turned a corner and almost ran into a young Japanese man, I tried to say, "Excuse me, but I'm lost. Can you please tell me where I am?" All that came out was a series of low groans. My mouth was paralyzed. The young man's eyes widened, and he hurriedly backed away.

"Wait," I tried to say, but it came out a zombielike roar. The young man turned and ran. I kept walking until I saw a young Japanese woman. She didn't wait for me to speak but fled immediately, shrieking. I remembered reading somewhere that the astral body was housed in the right hemisphere of the brain, and the speech centers were located in the left hemisphere. Maybe I was an astral projection, which was why I couldn't speak.

That didn't explain why people bolted from me on sight. I may have been transparent, like a ghost.

I began feeling weaker and weaker, until finally I nose-dived onto the paving stones. As soon as I fell, people appeared from everywhere and began going through my pockets, taking my wallet, keys, and coins. I lay on my back, unable to move.

After the crowd stripped me of valuables and left, three dogs bounded up and began eating my face. I could feel their hot breath, their teeth scraping against my bones and yanking off strips of flesh. It didn't hurt. One of them clamped onto my tongue and pulled it out by the roots, and another devoured my eyes. Even though I felt no pain, I was nearly insane with horror at being so defenseless, being torn to shreds while still alive, and being shunned, robbed, or abandoned by every single person I'd come across.

JULY 9, 1989

The courtyard was in the center of a Chinese-style building, open to the sky. It was a square about fifty yards wide, four walls made of immense stone blocks. The floor of this square was black dirt as dry, light, and soft as talcum powder. It was night, and torches in sconces lined the walls. There was no sound at all. I stood outside a large circle of about twenty weathered, cylindrical stones that resembled gray footstools. They were knee high, deeply pitted and cracked.

Cold dread oozed through me from the top of my head down to the ends of my toes. I turned and faced a large double door set into the wall. It was covered in padded, dark green leather inlaid with golden dragons and other designs. A stone arch surmounted the rounded tops of the doors, and the entire wall was painted bright red.

Somewhere out of sight, a crowd of men and women laughed and loudly spoke an Asian language I didn't recognize. I then knew that a man would come through the door and attack me with a knife. He'd kill me in the center of the ring of stones, doing so repeatedly for all eternity. I heard more laughter, and the right-hand door in the red wall flew open. A small man who looked Burmese or Vietnamese burst through and sprinted toward me with a big, toothy smile. He wore a golden-white turban and a dark green jacket and trousers. In his right hand was a curved, shining scimitar that reflected glimmers of torchlight. His bare feet sent up puffs of dust from the ground. It was absolutely silent again, like a film with the soundtrack cut, as this man ran at me with insane speed.

I turned to escape. Though I tried to avoid the circle of stones, I was physically compelled into the center, as if pulled by a giant magnet. The brown-skinned man pounced on me to the accompaniment of crashes, music, shrieks, hisses—a deafening cacophony that I knew was every sound in the universe. He stabbed me right under the breastbone, the blade piercing my heart, but I felt nothing.

At that instant I found myself climbing a stairway that lay along the four walls of an immense wooden building. There was no center to the structure, just empty blackness, like an elevator or mine shaft. I climbed endlessly, outside myself and watching from above. The white railings on the stairs starkly framed the yawning black square in the center.

Eventually, I emerged from the shaft and entered a public restroom the size of a football field. The lights had been turned off, but I could see row upon row of green toilets, urinals, and bathtubs, stretching off into the darkness. All the fixtures were enclosed by chrome railings of the kind seen on toilets for the handicapped. The low-ceilinged room was filthy, with piles of yellow-brown excrement everywhere. I walked out of the restroom up another rickety flight of wooden stairs, this one leading to an attic. The stairway was well lit with oil lamps, but outside the circles of light thrown on the walls it was pitch black. Climbing along, I went from light to dark to light again.

At the top of the stairs was a loft shaped like the letter *A,* the two ceilings sloping sharply almost to the floor. At the far end of the room, a picture window showed a sunny New England fishing village, with hovering seagulls, pointy church steeples, and white clapboard houses.

Cots with lumpy, stained, sheetless mattresses lined the walls of the loft. About twenty old men gathered around one man who'd just died. He lay in bed propped against the wall, his mouth hanging open. The old men mumbled in agitation, trying to catch the attention of a fat, middle-aged man who sat in a booth overlooking the room. He wore horn-rimmed half-spectacles and fiddled with a clipboard. When some of the old men climbed the stairs to his booth, he shook his head and waved them away. I got the impression that this was a homeless shelter. After the old men came back down from the booth, I went up the stairs to ask the fat man where I was.

He was an administrator, the booth his crammed office. It had a desk, an electric heater, and several pornographic photos on the walls that showed sleek, naked blonde women. Though they were no different from any other soft-core nudie images I'd seen, they struck me as so vile that I wanted to vomit. I felt trapped and jittery, so when the administrator beckoned silently for me to follow, I obeyed. We went through a door in the back of the booth and passed a small kitchen in which a young woman and three small children sat at a table eating bowls of porridge or oatmeal. There was a poster of a spread-eagled nude woman on the wall, surrounded by several smaller pornographic pictures. The administrator paused and blew a kiss to the people in the kitchen, fluttering his fingers at them. They quickly looked back at their bowls.

The fat man pointed me to a door, which I went through. I found myself in an old university, its hallways filled with students. They all had deathly white skin and looked famished. I went into a small room, trying to escape the hubbub of babbling voices and footsteps. Inside, a very tall girl with wildly disarrayed hair spoke to another girl, her books clutched to her chest. She turned to include me in the conversation, but her speech was completely incoherent, a jumble of random sounds. Her cutoffs revealed revolting, malformed legs covered with satchels of dimply cellulite.

"You may not believe it from looking at me," she said, "but I actually have a tendency to run to fat." Her expression was distant and stunned.

The other girl shrieked with laughter and blew a long raspberry, her tongue sticking out about ten inches. Attractive and heavily made-up like a TV aerobics instructor, she made horrible animal noises—growls, grunts, and short barks. I'd had a nagging urge to flee since I'd come into the building; these two girls were the final straw. Seeing another door, I ran to it, yanked at the knob, and blindly dashed through.

Outside was the dirt-covered, torchlit courtyard with the circle of cylindrical stones. Terrified, I burst into tears. When I turned to go back into the school, it was gone. The double door in the wall opened, and a smiling middle-aged Chinese woman came out, dressed in a blue Mao suit. Her sleeves were rolled up, and she had a long, slim carving knife in one hand. She was fifty yards away, moving very slowly, but the second I glanced away from her, I was in the center of the ring of stones again, and she slammed into me. I felt her knife slip into my back, between two ribs. As it punctured my heart, I heard the same confusing roar of voices and noises as before.

Then I was in a car at night, on my way to California. There'd been a disaster, and the highway was filled with refugees. They trudged hopelessly through the beams of my headlights, wearing backpacks and carrying long staffs. I had to get home to see my family for Christmas, but the increasing foot traffic forced me to slow down. Finally, I came to a complete stop, the car engulfed in fleeing people. I got out, ready to run if they tried to steal my wallet, but everybody ignored me.

An old man in a green hooded raincoat walked past with his head down. A younger man with short black hair and glasses came up behind him and grabbed him by the back of the neck. Afraid that the younger man was a robber, I raced over and spun him around by the shoulder. He whirled so fast I thought he was going to hit me; I flinched and raised my hands. His yellow face was as round as the moon, and he had big, slack lips. He yanked one of my feet out from under me and put it against his crotch, chanting something. As I broke his grip and turned away, I realized what he said: "*Bum*-pump, *bum*-pump, *bum*-pump." He gave it the cadence of a heartbeat.

I tried to run, but I could move only in slow motion. Flitting like an insect, he slid in right behind me, up against me, and said in a calm, lucid voice, "It was just that I got used to it. Honestly. That's all. Spending all that time with them, I had to get used to doing it their way. You should try it. You'll get used to it too. Here."

He pulled a small harmonica from his pocket and blew a note on it. Three or four howling, foaming Doberman Pinschers appeared. They ran at me and bit my buttocks, ripping them open and trying to mount me. The moonfaced man hovered around, laughing maniacally. The bites and mountings were hideously painful, as if I were being disemboweled. Fighting off the dogs was impossible. They were all over me, and their strength was phenomenal. I was like a rag doll or an infant. Knocked to the ground, turned inside out, and penetrated, I died and came back to life in the same walled courtyard again, facing the same double door and ring of stones.

The door opened. Several dozen brown-skinned Malays or Cambodians poured through dressed in golden turbans and green pants and jackets. They carried an amazing array of edged killing instruments: swords, knives, axes, two-handed scythes, throwing stars, scissors, and darts. Led by the man who'd attacked me the first time, they closed in slowly. Though I tried running in several different directions one after another, I kept ending up in the center of the stones. All the men were impassive, but the leader laughed uproariously. A dagger appeared in my hand; I turned to face the laughing man. As I did so, the people behind me rushed in. I spun to defend myself against them, and the crowd in front charged. Every time I took my eyes off a group, it moved in swiftly.

Surrounding me, the men began cutting and slicing. Each blade driven into me made a solid *thunk* of impact, and pieces of my body fell off onto the ground. I felt no pain, only a staggering, beyond-stratospheric level of fright. Despite fighting desperately, I couldn't reach any of them. A small girl of six or seven stabbed at my legs. When I grabbed her up to use as a shield, there was a loud shout of dismay. The mob stopped their assault and angrily shook their fists or wagged their fingers.

As if a TV channel had been switched, I was in my house in Los Angeles. It *wasn't* my house, even though it was. I lay on the living-room couch, next to the French doors. It was night, and the streetlights shone foggily through the window. Tense and restless, I thrashed around on the sofa in this unfamiliar house that I somehow knew. Since it was clear that I'd never fall asleep, I got up, lit a cigarette, and paced. I discovered that I could float like a soap bubble. In joyous disbelief I tested myself, flying around the room and dodging furniture with ease.

My happiness ebbed, and I finally understood that I was only dreaming. I went out into the back yard and saw a small pond filled with slime, gunk, and unidentifiable water creatures. They resembled frogs crossed with slugs, their eyes on stalks and their rear ends tapered into glistening points. These disgusting mutants bothered me so much that I retreated to the living room and turned off the lights to try and sleep, aware that I was already asleep. The idea of trying to sleep in a dream terrified me. Looking out the window, I saw a smooth, semihuman reptilian thing crawling over the hedge, illuminated from behind. It realized that I'd seen it and froze, half on and half off the hedge. I fumbled for the switch on one of the lamps but couldn't find it in the dark. Suddenly, I knew that the thing on the hedge was in the room with me. Now all the lamps themselves had disappeared. I jumped off the couch and blundered around, sobbing and knocking over tables and chairs. The reptile-thing watched and waited. It enjoyed my fear.

I remembered that I could fly, so I jetted into the kitchen, where I surprised my sister Carrie coming through a doorway. Tall and dark haired, she didn't look anything like Carrie. She glared at me.

"Jesus," she said. "You always cause so much trouble whenever you come home."

With no idea how to respond, I went to the bathroom. I could see my mother through the glass of the shower stall, her outline indistinct because of the steam. A bloated, white mass like an albino walrus, she sang in a croaking, rattling voice that drove me back into the living room. My sister stood there, her arms at her sides.

"This is all just a dream," I said. "You're not Carrie. I really want to wake up now."

She pointed to the floor. "Look at these cats I had imported from Japan."

Two fig-shaped kittens lolled like round-bottomed toys at her feet. They had tiny heads and scrawny, vestigial limbs. When I picked one up, it humped my hand and moaned. I flung it down, fell onto the couch, and started crying.

"I'm sick of all this imagery!" I screamed.

Then it was Christmas morning. My brother Pat came into the living room. He was about a foot tall and so loathsome that I wanted to kill him.

"The fucking loser's back," he said.

I bent down and grabbed him around the waist. My father and mother rushed over.

"Leave him alone, you bastard!" Dad shouted.

Everyone surrounded me, backing me into the Christmas tree. When I saw that Pat changed into a wooden toy soldier, I dropped him. My mother and father de-aged until they were in their early thirties. Dad looked like a stereotypical Madison Avenue executive from the sixties, with side-parted hair, black horn-rims, a black suit, and a skinny tie. Mom was blonde and fat. My two older brothers Tim and Paul became chain-smoking laborers with shaved heads and blocky muscles.

"Hey! You leave *Tom* alone!" they yelled at my father, but they also laughed at me. A group of black women came in, wailing and keening. They were part of the family too. Every aspect of my house and family—down to the smallest detail—was twisted, perverted, and so distorted that I was beyond hysterical. When calliope music began to play, I completely lost control and ran outside screaming. I was like a rocket, traveling at a tremendous, effortless speed.

From far behind me, one of my brothers called, "Sure, man. It's okay. I understand."

None of my real brothers would ever address me as "man." My dream-brother chuckled, then laughed, then began roaring and howling like a crazed beast, the sound following me as I ran through darkened streets filled with people. I came upon a nocturnal fair or a music video being filmed—whirling couples under spotlights, voices squawking though loudspeakers. Men had fistfights and kicked down concession stands. As I ran past, a few tried to talk to me, their sweaty faces looming monstrously out of the crowd.

"I'm dreaming! I'm not even here!" I screamed at them, but now I was sure that I'd died and gone to hell. At any second I'd appear in the ring of stones in the courtyard again, where I'd be chopped to pieces by ravening Asiatics, and this would go on forever.

CHAPTER THREE
HAGGING AND PLANE CRASHES

The "old hag syndrome" or "hagging" is a form of sleep paralysis that may be caused by a short circuit in the brain's system for preventing you from acting out your dreams. When you enter REM (rapid eye movement) sleep—the dreaming stage—neurons release chemicals that produce atonia, or muscle paralysis. It's likely that the old hag is the result of you waking up out of REM sleep while your brain still has you in a state of muscle paralysis. It's a hideous phenomenon that I've experienced more times than I can count. The paralysis is always accompanied by awful sounds, voices, and demonic presences.

Many believe that the old hag has nothing to do with biology and is entirely a supernatural phenomenon. I tend toward the scientific explanation, although I also think that demons and malefic spirits probably do exist. My own opinion is that evil is volitional. If there *is* such a thing as possession, one must consent to it. People can't be "led astray" or tricked. If you read religious texts, it's all about choice. Evil seduces rather than fools.

For most of my life, I was also absolutely convinced that I was destined to die in an airplane crash. It's been twenty years since I've flown. I grounded myself voluntarily, but now flying is out of the question because of the Meniere's disease. I haven't had an airplane-crash dream in well over a decade. No matter how statistically safe I knew it to be, and even though I knew death in an airplane crash would almost certainly be swift and painless, there was something about flying that scared me more than anything else.

A quick side note.

Tim and I once flew over the North Pole in a TWA Boeing 747. The turbulence was the worst we'd ever experienced. We could see through the windows that the port engine pods and wingtip all bounced and flapped at different rates, as if the aircraft were made of rubber. The cabin shook violently, dropped, pitched, and buffeted for hours. I've never been in an airliner that was knocked sideways hard enough to wrench my lower back. Six miles below was a desolate expanse bestrewn with crumpled-looking mountains, everything dazzlingly, antiseptically white. In the airport gift shop, Tim had picked up a copy of *Crisis in the Skies,* by Joseph Laurence Marx, a book about…airliner crashes. Yes, they sold a book about airliner crashes in the airport gift shop. Big deal. What matters is that *airline passengers bought it.*

Chugging double Screwdrivers and Bloody Marys, Tim described the book's best crashes to me as the ship bucked and jolted.

"Oh my God, listen to *this!* The plane went straight into the ground, and all the passengers ended up crammed into the nose, so it was just this tube full of *cooked meat!* They couldn't even separate the bodies, so they just buried the *whole thing!*"

Since I was still too young to drink, I'm astounded that I survived that flight. While my brother laughed and whooped, I consoled myself with the fact that when the jet disintegrated in midair, I'd immediately lose consciousness from lack of oxygen. If the worst happened and the wing or tail tore off, we'd be wide-awake as we rode the bastard down to the ice, screaming all the way. Everyone except for Tim, that is. He'd keep on reading, drinking, and laughing until his molecules were dispersed across the glaciers. I know that for a fact. During the Northridge earthquake, our house went into convulsions. Every single surface was in frenetic motion. I thought we were seconds from becoming paste under tons of wreckage. The heater grate flew up and down out of the floor, *DANG-DANG-DANG-DANG-DANG.*

"*Tim!*" I screamed into his darkened bedroom. "*Earthquake!*"

"Yeah, yeah," he growled. "I *know.*" He was just annoyed.

It's strange that despite everything I now believe, I'm still afraid of flying. The idea of getting on an airliner gives me butterflies. Thrashing, refrigerated butterflies as big as eagles. This one fear seems to be unconquerable.

My hagging and plane-crash dreams were so similar that I've decided to publish just the standouts. These represent about a tenth of the dreams I remember having.

* * *

JUNE 18, 1982

The living room couch in my grandmother's house was very uncomfortable. Thrashing around on the lumpy, coarse material of the cushions, trying to find a position that didn't hurt, I heard a cacophony of voices chanting, muttering, and blathering in a foreign language. A continuous sound like a Tibetan prayer, it filled me with terror.

My body became completely paralyzed; I couldn't even open my eyes, a blessing because I didn't want to see whatever entities were all around me in the living room, chanting away. A massive body lay down on top of me, pressing me into the sofa cushions. It was hot, bloated, and flabby, so heavy that I couldn't breathe. A pair of wet, bulbous lips pressed against my right ear.

"This is a kiss," a cracked voice whispered.

The lips pulled away, leaving whistling and roaring like a hurricane in my ears, and then the lips came down on mine. They squished and writhed with a disgusting sinuosity as they pressed my own lips flat against my teeth. I screamed, my voice muffled and echoing, as if I were shouting into the empty bottle of a water cooler. My body felt as rigid as iron. The kiss went on forever.

Just as I thought I couldn't take anymore and would lose my mind, it stopped, as did the roaring and the chanting.

I yanked myself free and sat up. The living room was empty.

AUGUST 23, 1984

The airliner flew only about thirty feet off the ground. I sat in the last row. My cabin section had only three seats, but they were padded armchairs covered in red leather, furniture that belonged in a private club for millionaires. The entire rear of the plane was made of glass, like a greenhouse. I could see all around me except for directly in front, where a steel bulkhead cut off my view.

As the airliner careened between mountains and tall trees, I knew that there was no one else onboard. The pilot was crazy, dead, or had somehow abandoned ship, leaving me helpless inside this out-of-control monster. I shouldn't have gotten on the jet in the first place, so I had only myself to blame.

The airliner entered a city and dodged skyscrapers, the cabin floor tilting sickeningly. I held on and waited to collide with a building. People on the ground and in the windows of the offices went about their business as I flew by. Nobody reacted to a jet airliner roaring right past their faces or over their heads. They didn't care what happened to me, and I hated them for it.

DECEMBER 17, 1985

I became paralyzed in my bed and heard the usual roaring of wind and babble of voices, but this time I saw an image in the air as I strained and grunted, trying to break the grip of the old hag, my head vibrating like a tuning fork.

The image appeared to be a painting. There were two figures on a black background that had a white grid, the type used to depict perspective. The squares of the grid were wider at the bottom than at the top, and the grid ended about a third of the way up the image. If the viewer had been inside the painting, the ground would've been black with white lines forming large tiles as far as the eye could see.

On the left sat a small boy in shorts and a T-shirt, hugging his drawn-up knees. He gazed up over his left shoulder with an expression of total exhaustion and surrender. Though he was only about seven, he looked old and worn out.

The figure on the right—the object of the boy's attention—was the Grim Reaper. He wore a hooded black robe and carried a scythe, and he had a skeleton's face and hands. An hourglass hung from the rope belt around his waist. He held his scythe in his left hand and extended his right to the huddled child, who showed no fear. Somehow the artist had made it clear that the boy was about to accept the hand.

Since most of the canvas was black, the Reaper's robe had been rendered in dark grays and blues. The medium appeared to be pastel or chalk. I couldn't help admiring the amazing technical skill and artistry, even as I struggled.

AUGUST 8, 1986

A group of friends and I chartered a small twin-engine turboprop to fly over Greenland, Canada, or Alaska. We were only about a hundred feet off the ground, herds of reindeer and elk running from us across the foggy tundra.

All my life I'd been afraid of flying, because I knew I was destined to die in a plane crash. I told myself if only planes flew really low, I'd be able to handle it. Now I realized that flying low was even worse than flying high. I could see every blade of grass, every hair on every elk, and every piece of lichen on every rock. I knew we were going to crash.

The plane had six seats; I sat on the starboard side, right behind the passenger in the cockpit who spoke to the pilot. The overcast sky was so bright that it made the interior of the plane too dark for me to discern anybody's face. I could see out the windshield, between the pilot on the left and the front passenger on the right.

The person sitting next to the pilot wore mirrored sunglasses and spoke loudly over the droning engines. I couldn't understand him. Everyone was happy and excited, while all I felt was terror.

Up ahead a runway appeared in the fog. As we headed toward it, both engines cut out, and the plane nosed into a dive.

"*Goddammit! Shit!*" the pilot shouted, frantically throwing switches and pulling levers.

I braced my feet against the base of the seat in front of me and gripped my armrests, but I knew it wouldn't make any difference. Through the windshield, I saw the runway tilt and rush toward us.

Everyone in the aircraft said, "Whoa. Whoa! *Whoa!* WHOA! *WHOA!*" until they were all screaming. The plane met the runway with no sound or sense of impact, and everything went black.

OCTOBER 14, 1987

The airliner crash-landed in the ocean. I was both a passenger and an outside observer. Once the plane touched down, it became wingless. The observer-me watched the silver fuselage slowly roll over in water that was yellow and somehow gelatinous. The participant-me was inside the aircraft, waist-deep in foam and churned-up slime from the bottom.

There was no noise or panic. I seemed to be the only person aboard. The lights flickered on and off, plunging me into intermittent darkness. Though I was terrified—one of my greatest fears was drowning in the dark—I was also indifferent. What was happening was preordained. I always knew I'd die in an airliner, buried in warm filth. Coming unglued about it was a waste of energy.

NOVEMBER 30, 1987

I spent the night in Carmen's Tokyo apartment, sharing a futon with her on the floor. Suddenly, there was a flurry of pounding on the front door. A male voice screamed, *"Caaaarrrrmen! Caaaarrrrmen! Caaaarrrrmen!"* as if begging her to save his life. I couldn't move, but I could speak.

"Carmen!" I shouted. "Wake up! Somebody's outside the apartment! I think it's Hazim!"

She didn't answer. Fighting as hard as I could, I slowly turned my head to look at her. She lay on her back, completely still. In the blue light, she was like a statue.

The pounding and screaming moved from the front door, up the side of the apartment, across the wall that faced the street, down the wall next to the neighbors' apartment, and to the sliding glass doors. It sounded as though a dozen fists slammed the apartment simultaneously, the scream of *"Caaaarrrrmen! Caaaarrrrmen! Caaaarrrrmen!"* never ceasing.

My fear was total. The sliding glass doors boomed, thudded, and seemed about to shatter. Then the noise ended instantly as though the pounder and screamer dematerialized. The second the noise stopped, I was able to move again. I sat up and tried to wake Carmen, shaking her and shouting at her, but she seemed dead or unconscious.

JULY 18, 1990

The jumbo jet careened all over the sky. It banked so violently that people who didn't have their seatbelts on fell across the width of the fuselage and piled up against the windows on the opposite side of the aircraft. Then, when the jet banked violently in the opposite direction, these people fell back to the other side of the fuselage. They screamed in rising and falling waves, like roller coaster riders.

Since I knew we were all going to die anyway, I decided I might as well try and get to the cockpit and land the airliner myself. I unbuckled my seatbelt and staggered up one of the two aisles, dodging flying bodies and luggage falling out of the overhead bins.

The jet began porpoising, climbing and diving, the engines roaring deafeningly. When it dove, I leaped forward and traveled twenty feet at a time, as though I were on the moon. During the climbs, my weight tripled, and I groaned under my own crushing mass.

I finally made it to the cockpit and opened the door. The pilot was a teenager wearing a tank top and cutoffs. He steered the jet with his bare feet.

"*What the fuck are you doing?*" I roared at him.

He tilted back his head and looked at me over his right shoulder. His blond beard and mustache were like wisps of cotton.

"Settle down, man," he said. "We're cool. Just...*chillin'* here."

The cockpit was full of pot smoke. When I lunged for the yoke, the pilot pushed it forward as hard as he could, laughing at me. I smashed into the ceiling and stuck there, flattened out and spread-eagled, completely helpless as we headed for the earth. The airspeed indicator read 980 miles per hour. I heard the wings come off with a thunderous, rending, metallic *waboom,* and then there was silence, since all the engines had gone with them. Through the windshield, I saw the ground spinning like a giant roulette wheel.

"Uh-oh," the pilot said. "I think I fucked up." He giggled nervously and gave me an embarrassed little wince, like, "Oopsie!"

MARCH 9. 1992

Lying next to Carmen in our double bed, I realized that I couldn't move. A strange, whining rattle came out of my mouth and nose. It felt as though I were being electrocuted, my head buzzing and my skin tingling.

With great effort, I turned my head to the right. A squat man about three feet tall waddled through the door into the bedroom. Almost perfectly square, his head as wide as his body, he swayed from side to side like a refrigerator being walked a short distance by movers.

His skin and clothing were the same dark blue, as though he'd been spray painted, and he wore what resembled an Egyptian pharaoh's nemes headdress. He had no neck, his head growing straight up out of his chest. Although he didn't seem aware of me, the sight of him gave me a jolt of pure terror. He'd brought evil and disaster to our home.

JUNE 17, 1995

The room was huge, the walls to the right and left of me disappearing into the gloom. It was a messy enclosure, packed with junk. Clothes lay everywhere, and the scene was bathed in a bluish-gray light. I lay in bed, totally paralyzed.

Gradually, I became aware that my lower body stood straight up off the bed, my legs pointing at the ceiling. Since my shoulders and upper back were still pressed onto the mattress, my body had achieved a ninety-degree bend at mid-chest. My legs and feet were clad in thigh-length, fur-lined leather boots, like those worn by World War One aviators, and they felt as light as balloons.

I tried to speak but could produce only sludgy moans. Electricity shocked my jaw and the muscles of my face into tingling rigidity; my head vibrated like a cell phone. I discovered that I could grab my right leg and bend it all the way over my right shoulder, twisting it to the left so that my knee touched the back of my neck. There was no pain, only a feeling of insubstantiality, as if my leg were made of crumpled newspaper.

A small, flickering, red figure appeared on the other side of the room. Featureless and bright like a Keith Haring drawing, it was Satan, trying to gain access to my soul. It darted back and forth, hid behind piles of junk, and changed color from bright red to black and back to red again.

Overcome with rage, I mentally dared it to try and get me. I made the Sign of the Cross in the air beside me, my leather-wrapped legs still pointing straight up and my body folded in half at the chest.

The little red Satan retreated, though I knew it still posed a threat.

CHAPTER FOUR
THE SECOND NIGHTMARE CLUSTER

In August of 1993, I went to Los Angeles so Carmen and I could have some of that luscious "time off" to "take stock." She immediately found someone else. When Tim and I picked up my things from the apartment in San Francisco, Carmen had completely changed her appearance. During our five years together, she always wore sweaters, leotards, sneakers, baseball caps, and no makeup. The day I moved out of her life, she cheerily greeted me in a black blouse and miniskirt, high heels, and heavy makeup.

Her new relationship didn't work out, and in May of 1994, she asked me to come visit her. I thought it was the beginning of reconciliation, but it was actually my execution. She spoke to me as if she hated me so much that she couldn't bear the thought of me being alive. Just knowing that I still existed somewhere—even completely cut off from her—was so unacceptable that it made her nearly foam at the mouth. I responded in kind and drove back to L.A. in what I've since learned was a state of post-traumatic psychosis. The diagnostic entity is "post-traumatic stress disorder with secondary psychotic features" (PTSD-SP). Think of it as an endless anxiety attack peppered with dissociation, paranoia, and brief audio-visual hallucinations.

It's no exaggeration to say that I depended on Carmen for my very sanity. When I lost her, I lost my sanity for a year or so, even though I carried on as a music journalist. I hid my mental collapse quite well. My interview subjects didn't know that a full-fledged madman sat across from them. Nobody—not even my family—was aware of how tenuous my grip on reality became. For any psychiatrist reading this, I can tell you that it's possible to come back from total derangement without medical intervention. I have no clue whatsoever how I did it. Maybe willpower and my inherent desire to improve. Or maybe I had help. The dreams in Chapter Twelve might be relevant; I really don't know. Despite my recuperation, I can't recommend the route I took. Watch the movie *Jacob's Ladder*. That's what it was like.

Here's a thought: Maybe I didn't recover at all, and I'm just hallucinating my happiness and current literary achievements. I could be the actualization of Ambrose Bierce's short story "An Occurrence at Owl Creek Bridge." Maybe on my trip back to L.A. in May of '94, I drove off a cliff, and I'm still in the air, about to hit the ground and burst into flames. If that's the case, why didn't I use my death's door imagination to make myself a mentally sound, billionaire playboy with a twenty-nine-inch waist? What the hell was the point of constructing two decades of failure, rage, and weight problems?

I can't do anything right.

Well, let's assume for the sake of continuing this book that I'm actually here.

After I returned to L.A., Carmen began writing to me, explaining why she'd driven me away. The letters accused me of things I hadn't done, such as dominate her, criticize her, and control her. What I'd *tried* to do in my inept way was explain why her actions were killing me. She also said I felt sorry for myself and believed I was worthless. Guilty on both counts. I can freely admit to *those* failings, since I was the one who confessed them. Carmen and I often revealed to each other the darkest aspects of our self-conceptions. It was a sign of trust. I never imagined that it would come back to bite me in the can.

Most baffling was a letter in which she said in the same paragraph that I rejected the real her, *and* she hated me for knowing the real her. In a total break from my usual destructive idiocy, I did the right thing and immediately gave up. I didn't vent my bloodthirsty anger or yield to my hankering for revenge, and I didn't try to win her back. For whatever reason I spared us both more pain.

In 2009 I found a poem by Stephen Crane—The Poet Who Saved My Life—that allegorized what I chose to not inflict on Carmen and myself. My good sense was very uncharacteristic. Unique, even. I still can't tell you why I accepted the loss of the person who was everything to me. In the past I'd always groveled and then bombarded my former intimates with pissy notes, cards, and memoranda.

Anyway, the Crane poem.

> *I saw a man pursuing the horizon;*
> *Round and round they sped.*
> *I was disturbed at this;*
> *I accosted the man.*
> *It is futile," I said,*
> *"You can never—"*
>
> *"You lie," he cried,*
> *And ran on.*[2]

Carmen sent letters regularly. Back then I couldn't understand her motivation. Each time I saw an envelope in the mailbox with her beautiful, rounded handwriting, it made me relive the day I moved out of our apartment. It called

---

2 Stephen Crane, "XXIV," *The Black Riders and Other Lines* (Boston: Copeland and Day, 1896), p. 25.

up the agony of our last year together, when I tried so hard to reach her, and all she wanted was for me to be gone. It widened and deepened the hole in my life. It brought back our final confrontation, a Bizarro World version of our lives, in which we were mortal enemies.

My relationships were always horrendously dysfunctional. Carmen fit into my pattern for eighteen months, but then we were able to connect and experience three years of complete mutual happiness that ended because of a single conversation.

In July of 1994, Carmen wrote that she'd met someone. I didn't reply. She continued mailing me friendly and impersonal missives that I found impossible to believe came from the brilliant, funny, exceptionally talented goofball I'd known over several lifetimes—the other half of me, who I'd found by sheer luck. Occasionally, I'd dash off an insipid commentary on music, dumbfounded that we'd been reduced to this after how much we'd once loved each other, after all the outlandish conversations we'd had in bed, laughing our heads off at how strange and happy we were. In August of 1995, she announced that she and her boyfriend were engaged. I stopped responding to her letters, and soon she stopped sending them.

Since childhood almost everything scared me. And yet the one fear I never had was that I'd lose Carmen. We were destined to be together forever. She was the only element of my life I was absolutely sure I could always count on. After she drove me away, it was three years before I stopped thinking I'd wake up and tell her that I'd just had the nightmare to end all nightmares.

*   *   *

JUNE 14, 1994

Tim's old friend "Noreen" reappeared after years in exile. She looked like a different person. Now her hair was blonde—a cheap, honey-colored dye job that made her look like an Istanbul streetwalker. Also, her face had changed to a wincing, haggard fox's mask, with a long nose resembling a muzzle. She tried to warn Tim and me about something or someone, but she was incoherent and skittish. When we approached she'd dance away.

"You'd better be careful," she'd mutter.

Since she was a waste of time, I left her and Tim out on the street and started for home, a New York brownstone. I walked up the stairs into the foyer; one of the frosted-glass doors stood open, revealing a group of six or seven young women sitting on the floor or pacing back and forth.

They were in their early twenties and dressed in the latest grunge and alternative fashions, with ripped jeans and either flannel shirts or XXXL T-shirts. Though all were extremely attractive, they gave me a spasm of terror. When they saw me, they smiled broadly and nodded at each other. The seated ones got up, and I knew that they were the lesbian murderers who'd been marauding the area. They walked toward me, smiling and chanting, "Breeder. Breeder. Breeder," in a soft, jokey tone absolutely full of menace. I sprinted down the stairs.

Out on the street, I discovered that I could run like the wind. The women strolled along behind me, in no hurry. Even so, I couldn't increase the distance between us. My arms and legs pumped up and down so fast that I couldn't see them.

Pretty good for a smoker, I thought, but I didn't make any headway. My pursuers chatted and giggled in self-conscious, hair-tossing breeziness that made me furious and even more terrified. They were going to murder me for no reason except to please ridiculous arbiters of taste. I'd die because they wanted badly to be accepted by abominable fashionistas and status whores.

Suddenly, I was in an airport. Lines of heavily laden passengers snaked everywhere. I'd befriended a Middle Eastern guy who was alternately three years old, then an adult, then retarded, then not, then two feet tall, then of average height. He constantly changed. The airport itself was at times packed full of people all whining about the delays, and at other times it was deserted. My mission was to catch a terrier that had a plastic soldier in its mouth.

I passed a kiosk stocked with books, newspapers, magazines, cigarettes, and candy.

"That's where I spent my gold sovereigns," I said. It was a lie.

After I meandered aimlessly for hours, a blonde, buck-toothed airport security officer approached.

"Do you need help, sir?" she asked.

"Yes," I said. "I'm looking for my friend."

"Oh, does he look like this?" She leaned back and shambled grotesquely, kicking her legs out in a sort of low goose step and yelping, *Duh! Duh!*"

"Yes, that's my friend. But I don't think I can get past all the security gates."

"No problem," she said. "Just go on through."

So I did. I walked right by the miserable, complaining, ugly passengers waiting in lines that stretched for miles down corridors. They had suitcases, birdcages, and rolled tarpaulins balanced on their shoulders. I went through the security checkpoints, carrying the plastic soldier I'd somehow recovered from the terrier. Nobody challenged or even seemed to see me, and I felt superior to them all.

JUNE 19, 1994

From my vantage point in the second-story window of a house, I saw that a storm had just ended. The street and lawn were under about four inches of water. Cloudless and bereft of stars and moon, the night sky was tinged with red at the horizon.

I looked down onto the lawn and watched Carmen talk with her ex-boyfriend "Wayne." They chatted and laughed, hugging occasionally. Carmen sometimes pirouetted, as if she couldn't contain her joy.

They had an arrangement whereby Wayne would come see her once a week. The meetings took place on the front lawn, and I was never introduced to him. I'd sit in my window, bubbling over with resentment, but I felt that I didn't have the right to interfere. Since I'd been away for a long time and this had started in my absence, it was my fault for neglecting Carmen. Still, she'd taken it too far. Her actions negated me, as though I didn't even exist.

Wayne and Carmen leaned forward to kiss each other on the lips, standing on their tiptoes, their bodies far apart and their arms held out behind them like birds' wings. I'd seen that pose in old magazine advertisements for toothpaste or chewing gum. After their kiss, they laughed and embraced. They knew I watched; their display was to demonstrate their contempt for me.

That's the last straw! I thought. *Now I gotta do something!*

In my head the two lines sounded scripted and fake. I started downstairs and met Tim, who'd shaved off his beard. He looked ridiculous, a Nazi caricature of a Jew. His nose was like a puffin's beak, and he had no chin.

"Don't I look better without my beard?" he asked.

"Yeah, much better," I said and went out onto the wet front lawn.

Carmen and Wayne tickled each other and grinned like flirting teenagers. Wayne was very tall, slim, and blond, a Kevin Bacon lookalike. That was strange because I knew he was Japanese-American. He was superficially affable yet deeply hostile toward me. I opened a pack of cigarettes and put one in my mouth.

"Gimmie that!" he said and snatched it in a playful, mock-aggressive way.

After I lit it for him, he bounded off in triumph, having made me look like an idiot.

"Okay, I'll get it," Carmen said to him. She turned to go into the house, and he nodded absently. I tried to catch her attention, but Wayne came over. He felt entitled to engage me because we shared the same woman.

"So whattaya do?" he asked. Then he blew a cloud of smoke in my face.

"I'm a writer," I said. As Carmen walked away, I called, "Could you come over here, please? I'd really like to talk to you." I tried to keep my voice pleasant but firm.

She stared at me with dislike. "I have to *get* something," she half shouted, flapping her arm and shaking her head.

I was immediately enraged. "Just come over here. I'd like to talk to both of you."

"Why don't you just forget about it, huh?" Wayne said. "Just leave well enough alone."

His phony reasonable tone didn't mask the unmistakable threat.

"No," I said. "I need to tell you guys something."

Carmen returned, and the three of us splashed across the lawn into the flooded street.

"When I sit up in my window and watch you two," I said, "I think, 'Wow, I'd like to have a girlfriend like that,' and then I remember that I *do* have a girlfriend like that. Carmen is my girlfriend, but the way you two act makes me forget."

My words made no sense. They were as canned and false as my thoughts of a few minutes earlier, but I spoke earnestly and calmly, trying to reach them.

Carmen unleashed her braying laugh at me: "WAAAAAA AH AH AH AAAAHHHH."

Wayne got visibly angry and walked across the street.

"Nothing happened," he said. "Nothing *could* happen. It's all dried up between us."

I followed, about to contradict him. He abruptly sat on the curb.

"Look," he snarled, "you shut your fuckin' mouth before I dump you *and* her both in the fuckin' ditch. Shut your mouth or I'll cancel your fuckin' publication."

He opened his eyes very wide as he spoke. I remembered Carmen telling me that he got violent when he drank, so I realized he must be drunk. His boozy machismo and weird, over-amped, Hollywood tough-guy words made me even angrier.

"Ooh, I'm *scared!*" I jeered. "Look at me *tremble!* Look at my *legs shake!*" I flapped my legs like the early Elvis Presley.

"Yeah? Yeah?" he yelled, reaching into the pocket of his sweat pants and pulling out a pistol. "How about *this?*"

He fired at me, a cottony, popping sound.

Oh shit, I thought. *He's going to shoot me. It's really going to happen.*

I ran. He fired several more shots, and I felt a violent blow on the back of my head. Simultaneously, I saw a flash of light and tasted a gush of warm saltiness in my throat. There was a gigantic stab of pain deep inside my skull. The pain was so great that I knew it was mortal; it faded to numbness immediately.

This is it, I thought as I collapsed. *Here I go.*

Everything faded to black, and all sounds receded, as though I were falling down a deep well. I was dead.

JUNE 22, 1994

My brothers Tim and Paul and I were invited to take part in an experiment that would test new emergency exits and safety devices for buses. A bus was to be suspended by a swivel device attached to its center axis, so that it could be rolled out over a deep trench filled with water and tilted either way, submerging the front or back of the vehicle. The trench looked like a larger version of the concrete troughs used to dip sheep.

A man in a white lab coat was in charge of the experiment. He looked like Terence Stamp and was introduced to us as "Doctor." We were given a tour of the bus and shown "air-curtain exits" on the sides, as well as shatterproof windows that would pop from their frames so that passengers could climb out. Everything looked to be in order, except I noticed that the carpeting was littered with discarded pairs of red swim goggles small enough for babies. I was suspicious, but when we met two other passengers, I recognized them as current Australian swimming champions. They made me feel better about the whole thing.

The bus was loaded up with people for the demonstration. It was driven out over the trough and began to tilt rearwards, the end sinking slightly into the water. A voice explained over a loudspeaker that this was done to give us a feeling of danger, the only way to adequately test the safety devices. Everyone on board was calm, smiling at each other and enjoying themselves. They nodded and *ooh*ed and *aah*ed as we tilted. I got up and went over to the air curtain exit, simply a plastic sheet hanging in front of an open window. Not knowing why, I hopped out of the bus onto the cement.

As soon as I disembarked, the bus reared up, and the back end plunged violently into the dark green water, which was several thousand feet deep. The people left inside screamed, tumbling over the seats and landing in a big pile in the rear. I looked for my brothers and saw that Tim had gotten out on the other side. I called him several times, but he never even glanced at me.

The bus now stood vertically and pogoed up and down like a runaway piston, full of green water, white froth, and swirling bodies. It began to gyrate even more violently, spinning on several axes and smashing the sides of the trough as it went in and out of the water. Several people hanging halfway out the windows and exits were crushed into smeary pulp between the bus and the concrete sides of the trough. The shatterproof glass broke into large, jagged pieces that flew in among the passengers and chopped them up like chainsaws. Faces, feet, arms, and legs all churned around in a horrible, bloody mess.

Someone switched off the power, and the bus stopped. Emergency crews appeared on the scene and began cutting apart the vehicle with pneumatic shears, peeling back the metal like paper. Most of the people inside were dead, and many had lost their clothes. I recognized a few as fellow exchange students who'd gone with me to Japan when I was in college, but I felt nothing.

I wonder if they'd be embarrassed to be seen naked in public, I thought.

My brother Paul lay under a pile of corpses, and again I had no response. He was pale and looked dead. One of the emergency workers pulled the other passengers off his naked body and punctured the side of his chest with a narrow blade. Water ran out of his chest and mouth, and he revived.

"Doctor. Doctor," he called, coughing.

I came out of my trance, swamped with relief. The doctor was on a flight of metal stairs, heading for his office, a clipboard in his right hand.

"*Doctor!*" I thundered.

He turned, his face expressionless. I slowly pointed my finger at him. My hand shook, but I was faking. It was just a cheap show for everyone there.

"*Don't. You. Even. Think. Of. Doing. Something. Like. Putting. A. Bullet. Into. Your. Head,*" I said, spacing out the words and emphasizing each one, my voice trembling and hissing with rage.

I was appalled at my hokey, melodramatic acting job. My dialog was utterly absurd, worse than anything in a Grade-Z soap opera. I could tell that my shitty performance fooled nobody; they just thought I was ridiculous and bizarre, exploiting a tragedy to get attention for myself. Dropping my finger, I saw my mother.

"Are you going to sue?" she asked, bright and cheerful as a child.

"No," I said. "I would've if we'd lost Paul, but since he's going to be all right, I don't think I'll bother."

Now I was calm and content, as if nothing had happened.

JULY 14, 1994

Back in Japan I traveled with a group of people whose faces I couldn't see. Some of them may have been cast members of the TV series *Seinfeld*. We were in an underground train station that was like the Cologne Cathedral. It had extremely high, vaulted ceilings and dim lighting.

I was full of confidence because I knew exactly what to do, and I was eager to show everybody. This was my element, the happiest period of my life. As soon as I took charge, our trip became a fiasco. Japanese writing had changed during my absence. When I tried to read the name of the station, the characters were like twisted, wrought iron vines and leaves.

We went to an automatic ticket dispenser with a map of the rail system above it, and I was at a total loss. I had no idea what any of it meant. Beside the ticket dispenser, a young American woman spoke to a Japan Railways employee, asking him how the machine worked. The railway man was bearded and had a ponytail.

"The Japanese train," I said to the woman, "I mean *transportation*...I mean *mass transit* is the best in the world." I wanted to impress her and the rail employee.

He gave me a contemptuous glance and answered the American woman's questions. As she fished in her purse, he turned to an elderly couple beside her and shouted in a thick Bronx patois, "Anything else? 'Cause I gotta go!"

My traveling companions had departed. The American woman—who looked like Sally Field—was still unsure. I offered to help her buy her ticket, since I had to get my own. Looking at the dispenser, I couldn't figure out where she or I were going or how much it cost, because the chart stating the ticket prices kept changing. It also spun, like a wind-driven turbine vent. Sally and I went to a different machine, and I inserted several bills totaling hundreds of thousands of yen; what looked like a long supermarket receipt came spooling out. I had to take this to the first machine and feed it in, which would then give me our tickets.

Sally chatted happily, asking me what I did for a living. I felt increasingly embarrassed and unsure of myself.

"I'm a bank president," I said.

Her clothes kept changing from casual to a trench coat and fedora and then back to casual again. We tried to feed the supermarket receipt into the first machine, but it wouldn't go. I struggled endlessly, and then the machine gobbled up the receipt and spat out a one-yen ticket. The price of a ticket to go even one stop was one thousand yen, so I realized that we'd have to keep going back to the other machine and get more receipts to feed into the dispenser. It would take several hours for us to get our tickets.

Panicked, I suddenly understood that I could buy the tickets with cash. I pulled out my wallet and saw that it was stuffed with dollars, not yen. My brain shut down, and I stood immobile in front of the machine, pondering the problem for several minutes before figuring out that it wouldn't work. I knew that somehow I could change dollars into yen, but I couldn't remember how or where. The whole time, Sally stood next to me, smiling and talking, apparently unaware of how I screwed up absolutely everything.

Since the people behind me had gotten impatient, I moved out of the way. After an interminable period of thought, I remembered that some Japanese comic books included train tickets. I found a kiosk and picked up a book. It was a pornographic comic that included pictures of a naked young woman standing on her head at the beach. Her legs were spread, and several other young women surrounded her, putting their mouths on her from all angles.

"I've got to buy this so I can *masturbate* with it later!" I said.

As I turned the pages, I saw a flash of train tickets housed in a clear plastic binder. I took another peek at the beach-going lesbians and then tried to find the tickets again, but they were gone. Though I went through the entire book over and over, the tickets had disappeared. Sally had abandoned me too. I was left alone in the murky station with my pornographic comic book—frantic, unable to figure out how to buy train tickets, and not even knowing where I wanted to go.

JULY 23, 1994

I'd been in the bare, wintery forest many times. The trees were leafless and dark, but there was no snow on the ground. I knew it was winter by the yellowish-gray light, which was oppressive and beautiful. Everything was familiar, both reassuring and frightening.

My car was old and dilapidated and kept changing into a red, double-decker London bus. I looked up at the trees from my car, then down at them from the bus, then up at them, then down at them.

On the floor beside my seat was either a large doll or a corpse. It was thin and repulsive, like a mummified alien. Its eyes were tightly shut and its mouth gaped. I stole glances at it as I drove, hating it and wishing I could throw it out the window.

A car appeared from behind and kept trying to pass on the right shoulder, despite the fact that the road was totally empty. I got more and more angry at the driver, a fat, middle-aged blonde woman. She looked exhausted and bitter with defeat.

For several miles she honked her horn and tried to roar past me. I blocked her each time. Finally, she zoomed by on the right, cut in front of me, turned off the road on the left, and pulled into the yard of the sweetest little Hansel and Gretel cottage I'd ever seen. She puffed out her cheeks in relief as she turned off her engine, not getting out of her car.

As I drove past, I stuck my head out the window.

"Hey, you fat cunt!" I screamed. *"Where'd you learn how to drive?"*

She ignored me.

I kept going through the bare forest in the yellow-gray light, my car alternating between a sedan and a double-decker London bus, the doll or mummified alien lying on the floor beside me.

AUGUST 4, 1994

The church service was held in Alabama or Georgia, in a low-ceilinged basement room lit by candles and yellow bug lights. There were no pews; hundreds of people milled around and talked while the preacher orated. Some congregants sang hymns, but each chose a different one, producing a demented cacophony. The basement was crammed with boxes, crates, shelves, barrels, and items hanging from the ceiling, as though the church doubled as a country general store.

I spotted "Billy Fisher" from Rice Elementary School in Tyler, Texas. We were in the fifth and sixth grades together. Though I hadn't seen him in twenty-two years, I recognized him immediately. I knew he'd have no idea who I was, since I was a pariah at the time, while he was one of the cool guys. He looked ancient, with sunken eyes, a basset hound's hanging face, and white hair. I had to talk to him.

During the service he spoke to several young soldiers in camouflaged fatigues and Kevlar helmets. At one point Billy himself was uniformed in a combat jacket and helmet, but when I looked away for a second and then back, he wore civilian clothes again. After the service the congregation headed for the door. I struggled toward Billy, who'd donned a wide-brimmed Panama hat and slung a rucksack over his shoulder.

"You're Billy Fisher, aren't you?" I said.

He glanced at me sideways and muttered something.

"Are you Billy Fisher?" He was obviously crazy, and there was absolutely no reason for me to speak to him. It was a theatrical, self-aggrandizing whim that mystified me. We made our way up a flight of stairs and left the church.

I asked him again, "Are you Billy Fisher?"

"Uh...yeah," he finally said, nodding his head in quick little bursts. "Yes. Yep. Yah." He avoided looking me in the eye and walked as fast as he could toward a decrepit pickup truck.

"Well, look," I said in a brisk, professional voice that I hoped would impress him. "I know you don't remember me, but you and I went to fifth grade together in Tyler, Texas. You showed me how to play American football. When I first got there, I was just this dumb, innocent kid from Venezuela, and when the coach made us play football, I had no idea how it was done. You showed me how. And I always remembered that. I've always been grateful for your help, and I just wanted to thank you."

As I listened to myself talk, I was horrified. I used phrases that would never pass my lips in real conversation, I expressed cornball sentiments I didn't feel, and everything I recounted was a lie. Billy hadn't taught me how to play football—nobody had. I'd floundered around horribly in school, not having the slightest idea what to do, but I couldn't stop sucking up to Billy now, even though he revolted me, and I could see that he was completely insane. His truck had no tires, and another vehicle had hit it so violently that it was crescent shaped.

He put his rucksack in through the shattered driver's side window and stood motionless, mumbling, "Oh. Hmm. Uh-huh. Ah. Well. Yes," as I spoke.

I could tell that he was on another planet, but I kept on talking until I ran out of steam.

After we stood there silently staring at each other for ages, I went back to the church to tell my sister that I'd reconnected with Billy. As I walked toward the wooden building—which looked like a grain-processing plant in the Midwest—I was struck by a sudden and excruciating urge to defecate. I ran inside, entering a warren of hallways lined with stalls that sold produce, cheese, meats, spices, and kitchenware. After an eternity of racing through the warped, uneven passageways, the pain and pressure in my middle growing more and more acute, I found a bathroom.

Throwing open the door, I entered a stall, pulled down my pants, and sat on the toilet. As I relieved myself, I saw too late that there was another toilet in the same stall, facing me. A man occupied it, his own pants around his ankles and his knees touching mine. I became horribly embarrassed, my face so hot it felt as though it were in flames. The man finished, stood up, and flushed; I forced myself to not look at him. As he exited the bathroom, he left both the stall and the bathroom doors open, exposing me to everybody who walked by in the hallway. I couldn't reach the stall door, so I just sat there in abject mortification as people eyed me with curiosity.

An Indian or Pakistani doctor came into the stall and sat down to use the toilet. I was so self-conscious that I looked around on the floor for something to read or fiddle with. It took me forever to finish, and I was beginning to panic when I saw the doctor cross his legs, even though I avoided looking directly at him. I realized that he sat on the toilet with his pants on. He was there to observe me as part of a scientific study.

Then I was inside a car at night, going down a country road in the rain. There were several people in the car with me, but I couldn't see them. Ahead of us was an electric car that skimmed along with a low humming sound, the rain deflected away from it. A dark green, 1940s-type vehicle, it was the wave of the future. I was excited and afraid as it sped through the night, taking its own dry space with it wherever it went.

We arrived at a complex of tunnels and bridges that led us to an amusement park, where suddenly it was daytime. After we got out of the car, my companions kept moving just out of my line of sight, their faces right at the edge of my vision. We walked through the park, which was somewhere in the South, and I began feeling a terrible need to get out of there.

A malevolent figure followed me, and the park had a smarmy, sinister, ersatz-Christian theme, with crosses, an ark, a manger, and steepled buildings. Everything was made of mossy, stained concrete, and all the guests were obese freaks. As I trudged up a curving cement track, a blonde female guide joined me. She pointed out which spots to avoid.

"You don't wanna go over there," she drawled, pointing to a stagnant moat in which swam what looked to be a cross between a bear and a raccoon.

"No, I don't," I agreed.

I went into an airy cafeteria decorated in a garish, fifties motif. There was a checkerboard floor, lots of chrome, neon, exposed pipes and ducts on the ceiling, and big windows. A fat, uniformed guard directed me to a door marked "Exit." I opened it and saw a narrow, vertical shaft filled by a spiral staircase painted red. There was another door on the other side of the staircase. To get out, I'd have to squeeze through the space between the staircase and the wall. Though terrified of getting stuck and dying, I was about to do it when I realized that I carried something long and awkward. I couldn't tell if it was a camera tripod or a set of fishing poles. It prevented me from taking this exit, but I couldn't leave this whatever-it-was behind.

A different guard came over and directed me to a normal-looking stairway.

"Just go out this way," he said. "You're not supposed to, but no one will stop you."

I worried that the evil person following me would draw the guards' attention, and we'd both be caught. At the same time, I wanted him or her to escape with me. The stairway took me to a room as big as Grand Central Station, with metal detectors, uniformed security people, and youngsters dressed like airline ticket agents in shirts and ties or blouses and skirts. Nobody paid attention to me as I slowly walked through the crowd. There were signs everywhere, warning, "Wrong Way" and "No Exit."

Above the metal detectors was a large sign that read, "Body Cavity Search." The ticket agents knelt in front of people who hiked up their skirts or pulled down their pants. Each agent put his or her arm into the guests' various orifices all the way up to the elbow. There were X-ray screens above the metal detectors that showed color images of the patrons' viscera being squished and jiggled around. The agents' hands produced mushy slurping sounds, like someone kneading a bowl of oatmeal. Both agent and guest watched the screens calmly.

As I walked past this disgusting scene, I saw to my right a group of deformed children lined up behind a divider rope covered in red velvet. They served as a display. One teenage girl was in the process of either giving birth or having sex with a midget; it was impossible to tell. Her legs were twisted and vestigial, curled uselessly like rams' horns. All of the children looked clean and earnest yet so phony that I wanted to scream. They seemed totally corrupt. I finally moved past them and threw open the gate to the outside.

AUGUST 8, 1994

My fingers needed surgery. I went to a veterinarian's office, even though I knew it was an inane decision. The vet looked like a taller, thinner version of Rod Steiger, with a small, gray mustache and rimless glasses. His lower lip quivered, and his chin trembled the entire time I was with him.

"Ve'll do ze operation rrrright here in ze office," he said in a thick German accent.

After he took me over to a desk and had me lay my left hand on a computer mouse pad, he pulled out a carving knife and sliced off the tips of the first two fingers, down to the first joint. There was no blood, but I felt extremely sharp, stinging pain, like a paper cut. The wounds were ragged, as though a gnawing rodent had made them. Within seconds the stumps grew over with skin and new fingernails sprouted. Now the first two fingers were much shorter than the others and had only one set of joints past the knuckles.

"Zair," the veterinarian said. "Ass you can see, ze surgery vas a sooksess. Now ve go on to ze next phase."

His white lab coat had changed to a stained, white coverall, like those worn by employees of meat-processing plants. The next phase of the operation would consist of the vet amputating the second joint of the same fingers. He told me to put my hand on the computer mouse pad again, but I refused.

"If you think I'm going to go through *that* again, you're crazy," I told him. "Nah-ah. No way. Absolutely *not!*"

Despite my words I was absolutely indifferent to what happened to me. The emotion I expressed was completely false. My goal was to milk it for all the melodramatic impact I could, but my phrasing and delivery embarrassed me. They were so cheesy.

Two FBI agents in fedoras and dark suits appeared next to the veterinarian. They looked at me with kindness and concern, shaking their heads sympathetically.

"*Of course* you don't have to go through that again," one said. "*Nobody* should have to."

I loved them deeply in a fawning, unctuous, utterly revolting way. Everything I felt and conveyed was fraudulent. It was clear that the FBI men knew I was trying to mislead them; their concern was as fake as my play-suffering, but I didn't care.

The vet looked on, his entire head trembling in suppressed rage and fear. His lips were compressed in frustration, and he seemed to physically shrink.

AUGUST 12, 1994

After wandering the world for years, I'd gotten word that Carmen was ready to take me back. I found her in a gloomy apartment that seemed to be made of one unbroken, vacuformed sheet of plastic. Everything was dark green, aqua, or black, and there were clothes piled everywhere. Carmen looked stunning, and when I first saw her I was so happy I thought I'd drop dead from sheer emotion. She greeted me at the door naked, holding a towel in front of her against her breasts. It hung down and covered her waist, hips, and thighs. She was expressionless, and through my immense joy, I felt remorse. She'd still not opened herself up to me. Even after all we'd been through, together and apart, she still wouldn't let me know her.

The thought of her just barely tolerating me—never to smile or joke around or be genuinely happy to see me—was horrifying. Getting back together with her was an inexcusable mistake, but I couldn't help myself. I caressed her; she seemed rounder, her flesh more dense, than I remembered. As I reached out to take off her towel so I could fondle her breasts, I suddenly understood that she had several videotapes containing moments in which I'd suffered total blackouts. During these episodes, I'd savagely beaten her. I had no memory of doing this, but I knew she had the tapes to prove it.

"You're a batterer," a chorus of women's voices said. I looked around and saw nobody.

The women were there, unseen, watching closely yet dispassionately.

"Yes, you did do it," they said. Though they sounded sympathetic, even friendly, I knew that I deserved no mercy if it were true.

"Turn her around," the voices suggested.

I gently grasped Carmen's warm shoulders—the touch of her making me ache with desire—and turned her. Since she was naked under the towel, I could see that her buttocks were scarred and covered with bruises. I wasn't responsible for the fresh marks because we'd been apart for so long, but I was appalled. After we'd split up, she'd found someone even worse than me, so it was my fault after all. I'd made her accustomed to being abused.

When I turned her to face me again, she stared into the distance with total disinterest. Her utterly blank look convinced me once and for all that we'd never get back together emotionally, even if we did physically. I therefore left the apartment and walked the dark streets, wishing I had the courage to kill myself. Eventually, I went to Tim's house. I was exhausted and had no idea what I'd do; I felt worse than I had before I'd gotten back with Carmen, because now I knew I was an abuser.

At Tim's place, I saw a photo album lying on a coffee table. Tim approached looking wary and uncomfortable. He sat me down.

"Listen, Carmen's gone," he said very gently. "She went away for good."

I was unable to respond.

"She left this photo album," he went on. "She said she wanted you to see how happy she is. It has pictures of her family."

He handed me the album, which had a bright aqua vinyl cover. I opened it to snapshots of a baby boy. He was dead, the autopsy incision on his chest sewn up with heavy black thread. His blue eyes had withered in their sockets, giving him the dry stare of a pig's head in a butcher shop. The baby's whole body looked shriveled and leathery, as if it had been preserved in formaldehyde. Whoever had taken the photos had propped the corpse against walls, next to a wadded-up towel, in a crib, and so on. The baby's arms and legs were drawn up against its body, and its mouth was twisted into a smile. Its orangish hair stood up in an ugly tuft.

Looking at the photos, I felt such shame and sorrow for what I'd done to Carmen that I knew I was going insane. It was too much to bear. On the next page, the photos were even worse.

"This is her husband," Tim murmured.

These pictures showed the mummified remains of a man sitting upright in a chair. His eyes had swollen into black plums, and the skin of his face had been sliced away, exposing the musculature and cartilage underneath. Like the baby, he had a ghastly smile on his lipless mouth, his teeth exposed like those of a rat. He looked as if he'd been heavily varnished with polyurethane. Since I knew that I was responsible for this abomination too, I got up and hurried outside. I began running down twisting brick paths, sobbing uncontrollably. The faster I went, the stronger and more physically fit I felt. I knew I'd never see or touch Carmen again, that I'd ruined her life, but now my body felt better than it had when I was a teenager.

Coming to a stairway set in the path, I saw a middle-aged woman loom up in front of me. She had long, gray hair and was dressed for gardening in shorts, a purple sun hat with a wide brim, and dark glasses. I slammed into her, knocking her over backwards. Her head-over-heels tumble down the stairs made me feel guilty, but I knew she deserved it. I launched myself into space and gazed down at the stairs that now dipped away from me, several hundred feet below. Flying was easy; I'd always known I'd someday be able to do it, once I'd achieved the proper mental state. Being airborne at last was incredible. I was free, clean, and blameless.

As I arrived at the first peace of mind I'd felt in years, a man abruptly shot like a rocket up from the ground and whooshed right into my face, making me cringe. His hair was dark and tightly curled, his nose was enormous, and his eyes were little slits.

"Remember, now," he whispered. "Don't tell anyone."

I was about to reveal the secret of directional flight to the other people floating aimlessly around me in the sky. My desire to tell them how to achieve control meant that I no longer merited the knowledge. I lost my buoyancy, sinking slowly down to the ground and feeling dirtier than I had after seeing Carmen's terrible photos.

AUGUST 17, 1994

The hospital was a Soviet-style behemoth of dirty concrete and green-tinted glass. Though I was there as a visitor, I was also a patient. The visitor-me was with a group of older men, none of whom I knew. We all sat in the hospital room, visiting the patient-me while a film crew scurried around recording it.

In my group were two obese, middle-aged men dressed like Andy Devine, in flannel shirts and coveralls. One was in a wheelchair, and when the film crew trained their camera on them, the two men giggled and blushed like Japanese schoolgirls. I was alternately in a cot on the floor and standing by the window, sometimes both at once. Outside there was a flying exhibition or air show taking place, with lots of T-6 Texans modified to pass for Mitsubishi Zeros. One pilot caught our attention by making his plane shimmy and shake like a dancing bee telling the rest of the hive where the flowers are located. He flew closer and closer to the hospital until the T-6 filled the entire window.

"He's gonna hit!" someone screamed. *"All that av-gas!"*

The aircraft exploded through the window and froze in midair. Although everything now looked like a still photo, I felt a slow sensation of heat engulf my body. I knew it was the flaming aviation fuel, but I was also aware that I'd been killed before I could feel any pain. My body had been flash-fried in an instant. After a moment of blurriness in my vision, Patrick Swayze leaned over me with a grim expression as he shoveled something into a cart.

"What's going on?" I asked.

"You're dead," he answered.

"No I'm not!"

He lifted a gray, ashy section of human torso from the floor and crumbled it in his hands, staring at me pointedly. Then he picked me up and set me on my feet.

"Do you get it now?" he asked as he dusted off my shoulders. "You're dead."

He was right, and though at first I felt a rush of exhilaration at being free, I soon saw that nothing had changed. I tried walking around and sneaking up on people, but everyone could still see me. Disappointed, I went into the room next to the one hit by the aircraft, where my mother was on the telephone.

"I'm dead, you know," I told her.

"Yes, yes," she said impatiently and went back to her conversation.

When I ambled out into the hallway again, I ran into some people I knew from the music industry.

"What's it like to be dead?" one asked.

"It's a rip-off," I said "My back still hurts. My shins still hurt. I'm hungry. I'm big and fat and clumsy. Nothing's changed. Can you tell me where I can find some food?"

They were shocked. "You shouldn't eat food for the living!" somebody said.

That was so stupid I just sneered. Eventually, I found a big platter of white cake slices and ate several pieces while everyone around me expressed their disapproval. Full, I went outside and walked down concrete steps toward the beach behind the hospital. Here I discovered the only change that came from being dead: I could fly.

Flying involved the same tensing of chest muscles that allowed you to hold your breath. The sensation was very similar and was accompanied by the knowledge that unless I devoted all my attention to it, I'd fall out of the sky. It was a combination of muscle power in the chest and sheer determination. I amused myself by flying around the hospital grounds for a while, and then I landed on the beach. When I looked up at the window where the plane had crashed, I was gratified that the side of the building was scorched, and the glass was blown out.

An old man stood next to me.

"See?" I said. "There's the evidence that it really happened. There's the proof that I'm really dead."

"There's your vindication, all right," he said. We gazed at it in silence for a few minutes.

I went down to the beach. The surf was violent, with slow-moving waves that turned the surface of the ocean into a series of hills and valleys several hundred feet deep. Since I was dead, one of the things I could do now was to tie myself to an old army tank and be dumped into the ocean. I could ride the tank all the way to the black depths and find out what things were really like down there. The thought of being among sharks and other sea creatures hundreds of feet long—miles and miles from the nearest human—paralyzed me with horror, and I quickly turned away from the ocean.

Suddenly, I hated being dead. A stab of panic and loneliness made me gather my energies and fly into the sky to try and cheer myself up.

The next thing I knew, I was on a tree-lined street at night, walking beside my friend Steiv from Japan. The warm, orange glow from the streetlights comforted me as I explained what it was like to be dead. Steiv was now younger than I was. He cocked his head like an intelligent squirrel, very interested in what I said. To put on a demonstration of my flying ability, I gave myself a running start and just barely got off the ground. It worried me greatly that I seemed to be losing the only nice thing about being dead.

Then I was in a room sitting on the top mattress of a bunk bed. I worked on a plastic model tank; when I needed a sharper hobby knife, I saw I'd have to fly from the bunk bed over to the desk to get it. Reluctant to squander my diminishing resources, I held my breath and just managed to make it to the desk. While I hovered I heard a crash and saw that the model tank had fallen off the mattress and lay on the floor. It wasn't damaged, but I was disgusted with myself. I ruined everything I touched. My entire life was an unbroken string of failures.

With that thought I was outside again, alone in the night, standing at the foot of a towering, dark mountain that reared up into the sky and plunged down into the ground. It was both a mountain *and* a chasm, dotted with thousands of lights carried by people traveling over and through it. I wanted badly to join them. They were my brothers and sisters. It would be a great adventure, and I'd finally be free.

AUGUST 19, 1994

The building resembled the high-ceilinged school I attended in Holland. It had long, gray hallways and lofty doorways leading into classrooms furnished with wooden tables and desks. Everybody I encountered in the crowded hallways was my age of thirty-three.

"Brigitte"—the First Ghost and my first great love—approached. She looked extremely bizarre, with a wizened head twice the normal size and a shriveled, midgety body.

"Hey, I'd like to ask you something!" she said cheerfully.

I stopped.

"Why'd you steal my wallet? Why are you stalking me?" she asked, suddenly angry. I was completely shocked—not at the accusation, because I knew I hadn't done anything, but that she'd discovered *it,* whatever *it* was. She knew what I was doing, even though I myself didn't know what that was. Spluttering and frantic, I searched my pockets for my own wallet. When I found it, I held it out to her.

"See?" I said, hoping that since I had my own wallet, she'd think I wouldn't need hers.

Her lip curled in epic contempt, as though she couldn't believe how ludicrous I was.

I fled into a classroom. All fifty or sixty students fell silent as I walked in. I found a desk and sat down, and a second later a woman in a harlequin outfit came in, holding a dozen or so helium-filled balloons on strings.

"It's your *birth*-daaaay," she said to me with a taunting lilt. She'd been sent from some birthday-greeting agency, presumably hired by someone who cared about me, but my classmates regarded her with no pleasure. I was horribly embarrassed, sure that everybody thought I'd arranged this myself, the action of the biggest possible loser on the face of the earth.

The woman went up to the blackboard and began to write out a genealogy, with names in boxes connected by vertical and horizontal lines.

"Now, this is how it all started," she said.

Since it was going to be a long-winded, meaningless lecture about my birthday that would make my classmates despise me even more, I stood and interrupted her.

"Look, I already went through this once today," I said. "I have to appear in court in about an hour. I'm sorry, but I have to cut you short and leave."

As I walked out of the room, I was furious at myself for concocting such a transparent lie. All it did was make me look even stupider.

The hallway had changed into a tiny, cylindrical subway car stuffed with people. It lurched through a tunnel, the windows occasionally lighting up from electrical flashes as the train went from one circuit to the next. The ceiling of the car was so low that I had to squat. I ran into Brigitte again, who'd shrunk down to about eighteen inches tall. She perched like a doll on a bar stool, watching me. I squeezed in beside her.

"Why'd you steal my wallet?" she asked again. "Why are you stalking me?"

While I tried to think of an answer, more and more women wedged themselves in around us. They stared at me, expressionless but somehow conveying their intense dislike. Soon the tiny car was crammed full, five women pressing against me. I lost my temper and violently shoved past all the hostile faces. Since I hadn't done anything to them, they could all go fuck themselves. I went the length of the train to the dining car at the end. Along the way, women stared and shook their heads, whispering to each other after I'd passed.

In the diner I ordered champagne. There were no seats, but hundreds of leather hand straps hung from the ceiling. The interior of the car was bright pink, the air filled with a constant fall of confetti and paper streamers. A waiter gave me a handful of telegrams, most of which were from people I'd known in Japan. The first I read was from Steiv, though he'd signed it "Steve."

"Congratulations!" it said. "Five Frenchwomen all at once! Unbelievable!"

He thought I'd had an orgy with those scornful women squashed up against me in the tiny subway car. His obliviousness really hurt; he had no idea how badly I wanted those women to understand me. In his mind that dismal, bitter physical contact was recreational sex. The other telegrams were the same, nothing but vapid praise for my studliness. After reading just a few, I crumpled them all up and threw them away, hoping that the women watching would see and be impressed with my sincerity.

I left the diner and went into a long dormitory car. A tall, dark-haired woman in a purple evening dress and long white gloves stood in the aisle. She put clothing and papers into a backpack that sat on the top mattress of a bunk bed. I approached her, recognizing her as a famous porn star.

She glanced at me, went back to what she was doing, and said, "You know it's not going to work, don't you? Everyone knows. *Everyone.* You're not going to get away with it."

There were thousands of beds in the dormitory car; from each, a woman stared silently. In an instant they were all laughing at me, thousands of roaring voices, the sound as primordial and frightening as newsreels of the Nuremburg Rally.

The porn star was the only one who didn't laugh. She stopped packing and leaned against the bunk bed to study me. I knew she felt sorry for me, but she still wanted me to go through whatever was about to happen to me, because I deserved everything I got.

I hated them for making me see how worthless I was.

CHAPTER FIVE
MURDERS

Over the past forty-four years, I've had several nightmares in which I committed murder. The three in this chapter are different in that I thought they'd actually occurred. For several minutes or much longer, I was absolutely sure that I'd murdered people. Words can't express how these nightmares made me feel about myself.

"Damned" comes close.

"Irredeemable."

"Utterly and eternally forsaken."

I expunged many dreams from this diary because there's no reason to publish them. They're allegorical representations that would distract from my purpose, which is to document the state of mind I was able to overcome by jettisoning the chronic rage that characterized my personality.

From reading books and listening to interviews, I've learned that there are experiences—real or imagined—that simply can't be conveyed in the way the author intends. Specific responses to certain information seem to be hardwired into us. Any attempt to bypass our biological programming is bound to fail. A writer may create short-term buzz by leaving nothing to the imagination, but tsunamis of ghastliness inevitably erode the readership. It's possible for an author to burn out a career with only one book; I've seen it happen many times. And in the end, what purpose did it serve? Did people really learn anything? Were any lives saved? Did anybody read the book and say, "You know what? I'd better not do that thing that I knew was wrong anyway"?

As awful as some of my dreams may be to you, they're nothing compared to the ones that will never be made public, except maybe posthumously. I may leave behind something as a testament to what I carried around inside my head. As Tim told me, I should publish those dreams only when I've decided that I don't want to write anything else. For now, I *do* want to write, so I keep the worst of my nightmares to myself. It's why I don't publicly discuss my past. Exposing some things—outside the psychiatric or ecclesiastical realms—automatically defeats the purpose for doing so. In my case it's brought me nothing but grief. I no longer have the urge to share, because it's not anything that one *can* share. It may not be something one *should* share, except with a few loved ones and those in the mental health and spiritual professions. The former group is problematic. If I had this life to live over again, I'd exclude my loved ones from knowing. Telling them cost me everything.

Back to the murder-dreams.

These three nightmares did the most damage, I believe, in that they made me think I was capable of committing the ultimate transgression. They demolished my self-image. When I woke from them, I could easily have killed myself to escape the maelstrom they unleashed in my head and heart.

I was seven years old when I had the first dream. It was so realistic that I had to get up in the middle of the night to make sure that my brother was still alive. Forty-four years later, I can still see the imagery in all its gory detail. Although I'm not sure, I think I had this nightmare more than once. Going over it in my head as an adult, I realized that the roof of the back patio was too low for us to use the poles that we swung at each other. Even now I'm relieved at coming to this inarguable conclusion. I feel much better knowing that physically I couldn't have carried out that nonexistent crime.

On June 25, 2013, I told Tim about the dream. It was the first time I mentioned it to anyone. He confirmed that we had no such poles, and though he's a mechanical genius who knows just about every piece of hardware ever made, he couldn't identify the sockets. I drew them for him, but he said he'd never seen anything like them and explained why such a design wouldn't work. Again, a load off my mind.

The second dream gave me several minutes of intense, heart-pounding fright after I awoke. I lay in the lower berth of the bunk bed, listening for Pat's breathing above me, and I didn't hear a sound. Also, the door was open. We always shut the door when we went to bed. I knew I had a history of sleepwalking; in fact, I may be one of the only people on the planet who's had a lucid sleepwalking episode.

A few weeks before the second dream, I clearly remember waking up at around midnight and going downstairs to the living room, where I encountered Tim.

"I have to call Brigitte," I told him.

"Why?" he asked. He sat on the sofa in front of the window, reading a magazine.

"Because I have to tell her when Nuisance and Charlie get up."

Nuisance and Charlie were our cat and dog, respectively.

"Well, I don't think you have to do that," Tim said. "Why don't you go back to bed?"

It was extremely important that I tell Brigitte when Nuisance and Charlie got up. It frustrated me that Tim couldn't understand, even though I also knew that something was *very* wrong with my thinking. I seemed to have gone insane, so I reluctantly went back to bed.

The next morning I asked Tim, "Last night did I come downstairs and tell you I had to call Brigitte to tell her when Nuisance and Charlie get up?"

"*Yes* you did!" he boomed, swinging up his head on the *Yes* and sounding like an old-time radio announcer reminding the listeners to tune into next week's zaniness.

Has anybody in the history of the human race ever gone sleepwalking, been totally aware of it at the time, and then remembered it? Because *I* have. It happened only that one time, but it scared the hell out of me. So when I had the second dream listed below, I was absolutely certain that it was real.

The third dream is without a doubt one of the worst in my life. Not only is the dream itself absolutely brutal and detestable, but the Toy People in question then disappeared for two weeks. I saw them only in church, and for two weeks after the dream, they didn't come to Mass on Sunday.

There was no question that I'd murdered an entire family. For two solid weeks, I lived in a pit of chips-are-down, twilight-of-the-gods, clincher-guilt. I made up my mind that if the Toy People weren't at church after three weeks, I'd tell my parents what I'd done and turn myself in to the police. Norway didn't have capital punishment, but from what I knew of Norwegian prisons, I could easily kill myself. I'd have to; the knowledge of my unforgivable crime consumed me like cancer. My work at the shore-support base suffered. Loading and unloading supply ships that serviced oil platforms in the North Sea was exceptionally dangerous, to which my many permanent injuries can attest. Distraction was lethal. Since I thought I was a murderer, I also couldn't eat or hang out with my unrequited love "Jennifer," the Second Ghost.

On the appointed Sunday, my family and I went to church. As we walked in, I saw the Toy People sitting in a pew, and I nearly burst into tears and toppled to the floor. I've never experienced such an emancipating reprieve, such an effusion of gratitude, not even when I was told that I didn't have multiple sclerosis after all.

If I had to choose between being a murderer and having multiple sclerosis, it would be no contest.

Bring on the sclerae.

* * *

1969

On the back patio, Paul and I hit at each other with long wooden poles that had metal sockets on the end. The sockets were made of two stamped-steel halves held together with nuts and bolts threaded through semicircular protrusions on the edges; the four bolts in each socket were about three inches long.

Tea colored and shiny with shellac, the poles were well over six feet long. Paul and I gripped them with two hands and swung them downward like kendo practitioners or lumberjacks chopping wood. We weren't actually fighting; it was a game we'd agreed on, knowing how dangerous it was and how much trouble we'd get in if our mother caught us. The bolts in the sockets were like nails in medieval clubs.

Although the patio roof was very low, we managed to swing the poles down at each other. Neither of us blocked the other's blows, but we didn't connect. All we did was stand there and swing, not hitting the ceiling, the floor, or each other.

After a very long time and countless swings, I hit Paul right in the center of his scalp. The impact was both hard and soft. I imagined that breaking an ostrich egg with a hammer would feel like that. Paul dropped his pole and closed his eyes, holding his bleeding head and kicking his legs out to the side like a sailor dancing a hornpipe. He screamed, a high-pitched, flutelike note.

Feeling nothing, I swung the pole down as hard as I could, hitting him on the head again. He kept dancing and screaming. I got nervous that Mom would hear him and come to investigate, so I hit him a third time. He fell on his face and didn't move.

I picked up his pole as blood began to pool on the cement around his head. It spread incredibly quickly, like spilled milk. I had to hide the poles so that Mom wouldn't know what I did. As long as I wasn't in the area when she found Paul, I'd be all right.

After checking for blood on my pole and finding none, I entered Dad's shop and concealed the poles under some planks piled up at the base of one wall. The sun had begun to set, so I went into the house, leaving Paul's body on the patio floor next to one of the bamboo chairs. Seeing the chair reminded me of the song "Me Ol' Bamboo" from the movie *Chitty Chitty Bang Bang.* Paul had been terrified of the film's Child Catcher. He wouldn't have to be afraid anymore. I wondered if killing him with a bamboo staff would've felt any different than using the pole with the strange metal socket on the end.

Inside, I went to the room I shared with Tim and Paul, got into bed, pulled the covers up to my chin, and turned off the light.

MAY 18, 1977

It was night as I walked through our row house in Rijswijk, the Netherlands. I was agitated to near-hysteria. None of the light switches worked, and the house seemed utterly dead, engulfed in a tomblike silence pregnant with menace. The air actually seemed to have weight, like a thick, invisible fog.

I went up the steep staircase to the second floor and looked around for my family. There was nobody in the room I shared with my brother Pat, and my parents' bedroom was also empty. In both rooms the bedclothes were crumpled on the floor, as if the occupants had leaped out of bed or had been yanked out. I went up the second set of stairs and looked into Tim and Paul's room. There was nobody there either.

Finally, feeling so much dread that I could barely move, I entered my sister's room. She lay on her bed naked, and she'd been decapitated. The ragged stump of her neck looked like a raw roast of beef, with the same reddish juices and rim of white fat. Her pale body was spread-eagled on its back, her hands and feet hanging over the edges of the bed. The sheets were soaked with blood. I turned to stone, my hair standing on end. Whoever had done this was still in the house and now stalked me.

Although I was too afraid to go down the stairways into the blackness, it was the only way out of the house. As soon as I took my first step, I knew that

I was the one who'd murdered my sister. I'd killed the rest of my family too. Their bodies were hidden all over the house. I'd done it in a trance state; they'd had time to know what I did, because I woke everyone up individually before I murdered him or her with a butcher knife. A quick stab to the heart, and they were dead. Neither parent in the same bed nor brother in the same room had heard a thing.

I was able to walk down to the second floor, but since I'd murdered my entire family, I didn't deserve to live. With nowhere to go, I got back into bed and pulled the sheet and blanket over my head.

NOVEMBER 29, 1980

It was a very cold night as I plodded down the street in Stavanger, Norway. Though I had a specific destination, I couldn't remember what it was. I'd recognize it when I got there. My breath puffed out in visible clouds, and I wore a heavy coat, a scarf, gloves, and a knitted cap.

My vision registered strangely in my brain. There was a subtle distortion, the same effect produced by a few hits of hashish. It was as though I saw through a camera instead of my own eyes. My mind didn't feel drugged, just blank. I was both in control and impelled by some outside force. My arms swung and my legs rose and fell with a machinelike regularity. I was a voluntary robot. If I'd wanted to, I could've broken out of my trance.

Ahead of me I saw the place where I was supposed to go, an apartment complex. I marched around it until I found a side entrance to the underground garage. Opening a door, I went into the large, cement-floored enclosure, which was brightly lit by fluorescent tubes hanging from the ceiling. In the center of the garage, a family of four packed the trunk of their car, getting ready to go on vacation. I recognized them as the Toy People; we called them that because they were small, cute, innocuous, and always impeccably dressed. The bearded, bespectacled husband and his chubby wife were exactly the same tiny height, and their two small daughters wore identical soup-bowl haircuts and sweet miniature dresses.

They couldn't see me, apparently, even though I made no attempt to be stealthy as I clumped toward them. I looked down and watched my left hand pull a Bowie knife from my belt, and then I walked up behind the father, grasped his forehead in my right hand, and cut his throat, right to left. Bracing his body against my hip, I pulled the knife as deeply as I could into his neck. The blade grated across his vertebrae, producing a gritty, wet, scraping sound. He immediately collapsed, a fountain of blood spraying from his neck.

The two little girls and their mother burst into horrified screams, their eyes popping and their hands clutching the sides of their faces. I felt absolutely nothing. Advancing on them, I held the knife out in front of me.

Then I was driving the family's car. I realized that I'd killed them all, though I had no memory of it. Still vacant and robotic, I drove the car to a nearby lake. The family's bodies were in the trunk, where I'd stuffed them. I'd first removed the luggage and placed it in the back seat. My knowledge of having done all this seemed to have come from an outside source, as if someone had told me about it or I'd read it somewhere.

When I arrived at the lake, I drove to the water's edge, stopped the car on the shore, and got out. I stood next to the car, staring at the wavelets breaking at my feet. After a few minutes, I released the parking brake and let the car roll into the lake, where it sank. I knew there was a steep falloff only a few feet out, the reason why the force that controlled me had chosen this site for the disposal.

Somehow I saw the car turn over in the darkness and plummet to the bottom, landing on its roof as water rushed into the passenger compartment. I turned and marched home in the same robotic, mechanical way that I'd used on my way to the apartment garage. It was necessary for me to walk like that, to satisfy the entity dictating my actions. Performance and style mattered. I thought about what I'd done but felt absolutely nothing.

After several hours, I arrived back at my house. I went down the outside stairs to the basement and entered my room. In the dark, I undressed and got into bed, pulling the covers up to my chin and lying motionless, not sleeping. Though I wondered vaguely why I'd murdered a family, I couldn't summon any emotions about it one way or the other.

It was done. That was all I knew. I'd go to hell for it, but I didn't care.

CHAPTER SIX
THE THIRD NIGHTMARE CLUSTER

This nightmare cluster began soon after Carmen told me in late August of 1995 that she was engaged. Another likely factor is that in September, I met "Roger" and "Dolores," my guides in the debauched, depraved, unimaginably depressing Los Angeles entertainment world. They told me stories and took me to parties, where I met thousands of former humans.

In October Tim and I went to work at a bookstore. Our boss was an ancient flim-flam man who ripped off everyone in as many ways as he could. He surrounded himself with loons, including a whiskey-voiced witch seven feet tall, a Samoan who sounded like a flushing toilet when he spoke, a clucking chicken-woman, a tiny gun maniac with rat eyes, and a homeless smiler. The smiler was the scariest, because his happy-face immediately vanished when he thought you weren't looking. His habitual expression was one of sly calculation and appraisal.

A few weeks before Tim and I were almost murdered at the store, I began seeing little black blobs at the edges of my vision, like cats that ducked out of sight when I turned my head. I had no idea what to make of them. In Kurt Vonnegut's *Galápagos,* the character Siegfried von Kleist waits his entire life for the first signs of the hereditary madness he has a 50 percent chance of developing. By late 1995 I'd recovered from the post-traumatic psychosis I suffered after Carmen drove me away, but I was fairly sure that someday I'd lose my mind permanently. I thought the black blobs were introductory hallucinations that would grow into busty Sasquatches, terrestrial squid, or talking pools of oil.

The very afternoon I'd decided to tell Tim that I probably needed to be locked up, he turned to me as we loaded up a shelf.

"This is going to sound totally crazy," he said, "but are you seeing little black things out of the corners of your eyes?"

Panicky thankfulness isn't one of the more commonplace emotions. We decided to stay, which was stupid. In our defense we actually thought we could save our boss's store, and he'd promised to hire us as his permanent staff. We could have real careers!

November of 1995 was the first time we saw the black blobs. We've seen them since, and they never herald good news.

A rule of thumb: Black blobs at the edges of your vision mean you need to either see an eye doctor or brace yourself for oncoming catastrophe.

* * *

SEPTEMBER 2, 1995

The party was held in a room on the top floor of a two-story motel. It was to celebrate the parole of the Yuppie Murderer. I lay on the bed in a room next to the party, which was filmed by the local news station and broadcast live on TV. The partygoers were young, white, college-age men and women; they were all naked, hundreds of them crammed into the small space.

Amidst falling paper streamers and confetti, the Yuppie Murderer's supporters lay on the bed or floor. Tanned and smooth, they writhed all over each other. Periodically, the camera swung back to the Yuppie Murderer sitting like a king in his armchair. He bawled incoherent things at the audience and looked like a homeless person, with long, greasy hair and filthy polyester clothes. In his youth he'd been clean-cut and handsome.

Some sort of contest took place on the bed. A naked man would lie on his back and prop his body in the air with his elbows, bracing his lower back with one hand. He'd furiously pedal his legs as if he were on a bicycle while violating himself with a small gold crucifix and grinning inanely. When the man was done, a woman would take his place, pedaling and using the crucifix on her vagina. I watched with revulsion and faint arousal at the sheer lack of inhibition.

"Look at that!" I said out loud when the camera showed the leering Yuppie Murderer. "This bastard hasn't learned a goddamn thing!"

My words were histrionic and fraudulent, spoken for the benefit of people I hoped would overhear and admire me for my uncompromising strength and ability to fearlessly speak the truth.

The bed-cyclists on the screen changed into twisting, spread-eagled women who sighed and giggled as they caused their labia to flap open and closed like swimming bivalves. I was appalled and increasingly excited.

There was a knock on my door. Opening it, I saw that the party had spilled out onto the landing. Clothed and nude people milled in a crowd, out of which came a thin, dirty black man with stringy hair, a gigantic nose, and a sparse goatee. He stepped through my doorway and held up a glass of dark beer or tea.

"C'mon 'n join the pawty," he said.

Disgusted and afraid, I put my hands on his chest and tried to shove him away, but he was too heavy to move.

He leaned into me. "Aw man. C'mon. Doan be like that. Sheeyit."

I managed to push him out and shut the door. A plastic scale model kit of a jet airplane lay on the floor in the middle of the room; I sat down and opened it. Though it was missing several pieces and wasn't even the model depicted on the box top, I was excited to finally have it in my hands.

Then I was outside on the paved street of an Italian village with ancient row houses, piazzas, and tiered sidewalks. With me were John Kobylt and

Ken Champeau of *The John and Ken Show* on KFI AM 640, Los Angeles. They regaled me with tales of their sexual prowess. Kobylt looked awful. He wore bellbottomed denim coveralls held up by narrow straps and had an elderly woman's low paunch. His head was abnormally tall, about eighteen inches, topped with a blond crew cut. As he jabbered incessantly, I knew he had some form of retardation. I felt sorry for him, but he also repulsed me.

Champeau was tall and thin, with a lined face, a gargantuan nose, fat lips, and long hair. He wore a *Miami Vice* linen suit that was crumpled and dirty. Though I tried to like him, he struck me as phony and sinister. The plan as they described it was for them to go to the top of a tiered sidewalk and enter a widow's home, where young nubiles waited for them. They'd have to don women's clothing to pull it off. I walked with them up to the house, chatting about nothing and marveling that these two famous radio personalities would be so open and indiscreet with a perfect stranger about their illicit dalliances. We entered the dwelling and found it full of young women in baby-doll nighties, teddies, and filmy wisps of lingerie. When I looked over at John and Ken, they'd changed into women's clothes and were surrounded by girls who stroked, rubbed, and caressed, slipping their hands into the men's panties and squeezing.

I got very uncomfortable and walked out of the room into a two-story hallway that had ornate wooden handrails on the second floor. There were apartments and small stores along both floors of the hall, and a wide stairway led to the second story. A young woman stood at the foot of the stairs, calling out something incomprehensible. A prayer or incantation, it was answered by a beautiful, rich, feminine voice from above. The young woman ascended the stairs, and I knew that Mother Theresa was up there. She was more than a thousand years old and would grant a person's wish if given a donation and addressed in the correct manner.

I went to the foot of the stairs and tried to repeat the prayer, which had the line, "Oh Great Mother, hear me..." Though I couldn't remember anything else, I decided to go upstairs anyway. On the second floor, I found Mother Theresa's apartment. She wore the white sari with blue borders adopted by the Missionaries of Charity and looked exactly like the young Orson Welles. Shocked at my presence, she circled me warily, grabbing random items and stuffing them into a handbag.

"I really need your help," I said. "Please. Can't you stop for a second?"

She wasn't listening. That made me very angry.

"Where are you going?" I asked. "You can't go like this. You can't leave your things behind. Is it me?"

"Who are you to judge me?" she mumbled and then sprinted down an ornate staircase in the middle of the apartment floor. I was left alone with her belongings. Pleased to be the new owner of all these books, antiques, rugs, and valuables, I was also ashamed. I knew that Mother Theresa pulled this same scam in cities across the country; still, I regretted forcing her to flee.

SEPTEMBER 3, 1995

The nocturnal rainstorm was violent, flooding the streets and sidewalks. Water on the ground contained bacteria that caused instant psychosis in anyone who touched it, but falling rain was harmless.

A group of people and I searched for members of our team who may have become infected. One of them was a young Japanese boy of about twelve. We'd traced him to an abandoned brownstone, where he chattered and gibbered inside. I was scared to death that I'd be the one ordered to make contact with him. Carmen was on the team; although I was concerned for her safety, part of me hoped she'd contract the illness as punishment for what she'd done to me.

We were equipped with flashlights and some sort of weapon that I couldn't figure out how to use. As I feared, I was sent into the dark building to find our young Japanese colleague. I stumbled around, tripping on boards and debris, unable to see where I was going even with the bright beam from my light.

Everyone else on the team left, and now I was alone, abandoned in this tomb-like space with a homicidal child circling me in the blackness.

Then I found myself in a large brick courtyard, like the recess area of old East Coast high schools. It was pouring rain, and I was naked, floating on a blue vinyl gym mat in several inches of infected water. Every time I moved, one edge of the mat became submerged. I'd have to shift in the other direction to keep from being dipped. Since the raft was far too precarious, I somehow steered it over to one of the four brick walls. I grabbed onto a large drainpipe and pulled myself up. The gym mat sank as soon as I stepped off it. I climbed the pipe hand over hand until I was on the slanting roof high above the court-yard. Now I wore a soaking pair of boxer shorts or long underwear bottoms—I wasn't sure which.

Crouched in the torrential rain, I wondered what to do.

SEPTEMBER 12, 1995

My father led me over a concrete bridge that crossed a cement moat, like those found in the L.A. River. There was only a trickle of water at the bottom, and I could see large, wedge-shaped objects submerged in the green-ish stream. They looked like pieces of pie. My father had hidden them there.

He looked to be about seventeen, wearing coveralls and unbuckled galoshes that flapped and clinked as he walked. As he guided me to an old apartment block or strip mall, he babbled interminably. I understood nothing he said except for the final sentence.

"Bogart. *Bohhhhgaaaarrrrt.* That's what it's called."

The building was ugly and sinister because of its very blandness. It was a peachy, pastel color, a two-story cracker box with no ornamentation. I was desperate to avoid it.

Suddenly, we were behind the building in a combination of Tim's gar-den in California and an idealized Venezuelan jungle, with overgrown plants, vines, and leaves all jumbled together. An enclosure sat in the middle of the garden. It was a low, irregularly shaped cage with metal bars and frames, some of which had glass or acrylic panes in them.

My siblings were there, and they were all children again. I was my present age of thirty-three. We'd captured a tiny monkey about five inches tall and put it in the cage along with a small dog or pig on a chain. We wanted to see what would happen when the two were together. The monkey had red fur; it scampered around the enclosure, trying to escape. We had to block the various openings in the metal framework with bits of cloth, pieces of glass, and our bare hands.

Several times during the battle with the monkey, I went into the kitchen of the peach-colored building and rummaged through empty cereal boxes and heaps of stale food, looking for something but not knowing what.

"He's getting away!" someone yelled.

I grabbed a glass butter dish with its cover and ran outside. The monkey climbed through one of the openings and leaped out of the cage. I caught it in mid-air, the butter dish in one hand and the glass cover in the other. When I clapped them together, the edges of the cover crushed the monkey's hips and face; its legs stuck out, kicking. I felt terrible and gently tipped the monkey out into the cage again, where it lay on its back. It filled its cheeks with air—looking like Dizzy Gillespie—and emptied them in silent screams, over and over. I felt so guilty that I wanted to kill myself, but I was also amused and detached.

The monkey's face inflated like a balloon, and the crushed part filled out again so that it looked normal. It rolled over onto its stomach, stood, and clasped its lower back with both front paws, the cartoon posture of an old man. It still screamed soundlessly.

"He's going to be all right," I said, ashamed almost to the point of madness.

Paul smirked. "You crushed him. Look what you did! His back is broken."

Since he was just goading me and didn't really care about the monkey, I tried not to let it bother me. It didn't work. I hated Paul for drawing attention to my crime and mocking me for it.

The monkey recovered enough that it was able to slowly limp around. I told myself that it was just as good as new, a shabby and transparent lie. With a murderous expression, the monkey limped over to the dog-pig, grabbed the chain around its neck, and scrambled up one of the metal poles in the frame of the cage. The creature on the end of the chain was hanged, its tongue protruding and its eyes popping. It struggled and kicked for a few seconds before going limp. The monkey gnashed its teeth in triumph. I felt responsible for everything and was so sickened that I wanted to throw up, but part of me was indifferent. Instead of doing or saying anything, I simply stood like a statue and watched.

Then I was inside an old building, home to the people who worked on the *Queen Mary.* All were Mexicans. I hated them but also liked them and wished them well. A short, fat, middle-aged man with a black mustache pointed up a flight of stairs.

"That ees where we leeve," he said.

I went up the stairs onto a landing, which took me to another flight of stairs and another and another, until I was thousands of feet off the ground. At the top of the house, there were tiny, neatly kept bedrooms. The narrow beds were from the late nineteenth century.

As I walked over the wooden floorboards, they creaked and gave. The rooms charmed me, horrified me, and made me feel suffocated. They reminded me of the residence at the top of the Eiffel Tower, a cramped space like a ship's berth. The bedspreads were thin, the carpets were threadbare, and the small bookshelves had spindly, fluted legs and were packed with useless old tomes on the history of California, biographies of Catholic religious leaders, and in-depth studies of crystal and glassware. I had to get out or die, so I dashed back down the stairs.

SEPTEMBER 20, 1995

The rundown neighborhood was in the Northeast, and I knew it was sometime in the early sixties. Most of the houses looked abandoned, with grass four feet high in the front yard, shells of washing machines and refrigerators everywhere, and sun-faded plastic toys on the porches. A group of small children played on the sidewalk of one yard. Many were black or mulatto, with light mocha skin and blondish, frizzy hair. They rode Big Wheel tricycles and made a lot of noise.

On the porch of the house, a row of elderly black women sat in rocking chairs. They wore glasses, pearl necklaces, and veiled pillbox hats attached to their hair with long pins. All the women were toothless and held canes between their knees. They rocked slowly, mumbling to each other and occasionally letting loose with a loud, *"Mmm, mmm, mmm."*

I went up on the porch and was about to ask them where I was when I saw a dead child stretched out facedown on the concrete driveway, hidden in the tall grass that had grown up through the cement. He'd obviously been run over, because the top portion of his body and head were flat, one arm twisted around the nape of his neck. He was dried up like a squashed frog on a road. I turned away, feeling terrible guilt and the need to escape.

When I looked back, I saw that the child wasn't actually dead. He'd gotten to his knees, and he was trying to pull his upper torso and head from the cement, his body straining.

"He's alive!" I shouted to the line of women on the porch. *"He's still alive! Call nine-one-one! Immediately!"*

Despite my screaming, I didn't care about the child's welfare. I wanted him saved so that I wouldn't be held responsible for his death. Though my hammy, unconvincing performance telegraphed my indifference, none of the old ladies reacted. They all just sat there and stared ahead expressionlessly, infuriating me. My histrionics hadn't taken them in; now I'd be accused of killing the child.

He finally unstuck his head from the cement and stood upright, his eyes open and blinking in his flattened face. Since his left arm was still behind his neck, it looked as though he had two right arms. He tottered away, blue and stiff, headed for home.

I was glad that he was alive, but I knew he'd cause a lot more problems in his present condition than if he'd just stayed where he was, dead. As he disappeared, I watched with despair and disinterest. What had happened to him had nothing to do with me. If anybody asked, I could prove it.

OCTOBER 5, 1995

Our car cruised along at night as we searched for a place to park. Unsure if I drove or was a passenger, I didn't recognize anyone in my group, even though I knew them all. We were in an unfamiliar city that looked like the setting of a film noir. The traffic was ancient American cars with tail fins and rounded, fleshy curves, and the sidewalks were extremely crowded. Everyone wore overcoats and hats.

We found a parking lot that had a wooden sandwich board in front.

Park in the Marked Spot
and Win a Great Prize!
Records, CDs, All Sorts
of Cool Stuff!

Over to the side was an empty parking space with a metal sign above it that read, "The Marked Spot!" An arrow pointed downward, and the space had a big *X* in it. The doltish simplicity of the contest made us suspicious. Could it be a trap? We discussed it for what seemed like hours, going over the pros and cons again and again.

"What the hell," someone finally said. "Let's do it."

The instant we pulled into the space, a black dwarf in an orange zoot suit and a wide-brimmed fedora scuttled up.

"Hey, congratulations! You win!" he croaked in a *Fat Albert* voice. He handed us a stack of flyers, tickets, and coupons, pointed to his right, and said, "Just go down the street. You'll see where you can pick up your prizes."

We thanked him. On our way out of the lot, I noticed that several of the parking spaces were actually graves with headstones painted in luminous oranges, pinks, blues, yellows, and greens. I assumed it was a festival, like the Mexican Day of the Dead.

As we walked along the darkened streets, I got nervous. The sidewalks were wide but unnaturally dark. Streetlights cast circles of feeble yellow light about six feet in diameter. The passersby avoided the light and stayed in the deep shadows, whispering to each other as we passed. They watched us closely, most of them squat, broad dwarfs with fat lips and wide faces. I caught only glimpses of them.

The darkness prevented us from seeing the cage until we nearly ran into it. An enclosure of wood and chicken wire, it blocked the sidewalk and was full of whimpering, snarling dogs the size of ponies. They were packed in shoulder-to-shoulder, like cattle in a truck headed for the slaughterhouse. I knew then that the entire population of the town was insane and that this was where everybody kept their dogs.

We went out into the street to go around the cage. It was at least ten feet tall and about three hundred feet long. When we returned to the sidewalk, we immediately found another cage. This one was full of crouching, shivering humans. They were completely hairless, their skin smooth and featureless as neoprene. A line of cages stretched far into the distance in front of us, each containing something different. All around us, the townspeople stared at us silently from the darkness.

Without speaking, we hightailed it back to our car, forgetting about our contest prizes.

OCTOBER 9, 1995

The multistoried house had walkways and skyways going in all directions, like a skewed M.C. Escher lithograph. Urns, marble statues, and fluted columns were everywhere, and the place seemed to be half open space, as if there were no walls or roof. The building resembled a Hollywood version of an ancient Greek temple.

As I tried halfheartedly to find my way, young women kept running up behind me and throwing themselves onto my back. They flung their arms around my neck and gripped my hips with their thighs. They never wrapped their legs *around* me but squeezed instead. I knew they were dancers from their rock-hard muscles and viselike embrace. As soon as I pried open one woman's arms and dumped her off of me, another would zip up and land on my back. They moved as quickly as houseflies, even though each weighed about a hundred pounds.

When I turned, I'd see flashes of rolling eyes and grimacing mouths, as if they held on with great effort or fear. They were dressed in headscarves, filmy blouses, and harem pants, like Valerie Harper in the early *Mary Tyler Moore Show.* As they rode me, they chattered incoherently in my ear, their speech jumbled and urgent.

Since I couldn't make out what they said, and since their weight slowed me down, they annoyed me more than anything. They were trivial and weird, a silly encumbrance. I'd shake off one, be free for a couple of seconds, and then another would grab me.

I lost count of how many times it happened and became so exhausted that I could barely move. Though a tiny, decayed devil-doll stalked me through the house, I was ready to give up because I couldn't get rid of these ridiculous women attaching themselves to me.

Looking down at my legs, I saw that the flesh had become ancient, crumbling layers of newspaper that fell away from the bones in gentle, feather-light drifts. I felt vague unease at this phenomenon, but I was too tired and empty to care.

OCTOBER 13, 1995

My family and I were at the local Basque restaurant, trying to order beef dip sandwiches to go. The place was unnaturally well lit, like the set of a TV show. We sat at the counter, waving at the waitresses.

"Excuse me!" I called. "Could we please order?"

They ignored us. The menu was chalked on a green-painted board, but it was in a foreign language that looked like alien hieroglyphs.

Finally, a waitress took our order. As soon as she did, a fat, middle-aged women said to the rest of the staff, "Come on, girls. Let's go."

All the waitresses began to leave. One was only about three feet tall. When she walked by behind the counter, I leaned over to watch her pass. She looked up at me—her big, brown eyes deeply sad—and pulled the spaghetti strap of her blouse away from her shoulder, exposing one nipple. Another waitress was a trashy, fortyish woman in jeans and a tank top. She'd rolled her shirt up past her chest, displaying small, upward-pointing breasts with large, fleshy nipples. Embarrassed but excited, I was disappointed when the waitresses filed through swinging doors into a hallway and disappeared.

A group of men took over the restaurant, so we ordered our beef dip sandwiches again. After we sat quietly for what seemed like days, the waiters began dumping fried chicken on the counter in front of us. They brought no plates, utensils, or napkins. The piece of cold, greasy chicken I picked up was already half-eaten. I took a bite anyway. Though it was unbelievably delicious, I put it down because it wasn't what I'd ordered. Justice demanded that I get what I wanted. An hour or so later, a waiter came back.

"Look," he said. "I know you've ordered your hamburgers, but they're not *ready* yet and *won't be* for a *long time!*"

He was impatient and sarcastic, as if I were a child asking stupid questions he was tired of answering.

"We didn't order hamburgers," I said. "We ordered beef dips." I took a deep breath and screamed, *"We've already ordered them twice!"*

The waiter backed away, raising his hands. "Okay! Okay! I'll get right on it."

Both of us delivered our lines like fifth-rate actors in a crappy movie. I couldn't understand what motivated me to behave so strangely.

A man appeared by my side. I tried to look at him but couldn't, my head restrained by an invisible force that prevented me from turning. The only way

I could see the man was by bending my neck so far forward that I could peer at him from under my left armpit, lifting my arm out of the way. He was large, muscular, and blond, with a heavy mustache and a narrow, weather-beaten face. I watched out of the corners of my eyes as he shook hands with everyone in my family. When he reached out to me, I was able to snap my head out of the unseen grip and look at him.

"Why, you're Ricky Nelson!" I said, even though I knew he wasn't, and *he* knew that *I* knew he wasn't. My charade made no sense whatsoever and fooled nobody. Burning with self-mortification, I couldn't stop.

"Don't you remember?" I asked breathlessly. "You came over that time when I was, like, six, and I'd found an old, stamped-metal toy robot? I was trying to wind it up for you, and I turned the key too many times and ended up stripping all the gears, and it broke? Remember how I cried?"

Everyone in the entire restaurant had fallen into horrified silence, exchanging glances and clearing their throats. The blond man gaped at me.

"No, that's not right!" I shouted. *"You're* the one who broke the robot. Remember? You wound it and wound it until it broke with a big *sproing* sound, and I was, like, totally upset because I'd just found it, and then it was ruined after only a few minutes?"

He was utterly bewildered, speechless with disbelief. So was I. My deranged performance was just another of my incomprehensible fantasies that had collapsed under its own weight.

OCTOBER 21, 1995

Outside it was late afternoon, the golden hour, but inside our house, it was the middle of the night. I felt my way through the darkness and went into the kitchen. My father, Tim, and someone whose face I couldn't make out sat at the table, eating strange turkey sandwiches that were cylindrical like jellyrolls.

They hunched over their plates and gobbled frantically. The ambient light was so murky that the scene looked like a black-and-white movie. I watched them for a while.

"Are those from the commissary?" I asked. "Is this the commissary?"

Nobody responded.

After several minutes, my father looked up with an expression of virulent hostility. His mouth was crammed full, and he wore only his T-shirt and underwear.

"You gotta ask the priests," he said, glaring at me over the tops of his glasses.

I could barely understand him because he had so much food stuffed into his cheeks. The other two at the table pretended I wasn't there, and I saw that Tim was a child again.

My father's answer chilled me. I walked around the table toward the pantry door. A man dressed like a priest—in a short-sleeved black shirt, black pants, and a white dog collar—hovered by my side, but I didn't want to look at him. With mounting terror and confusion, I thought I'd been abandoned in Venezuela as a child and never given a chance to grow up.

I opened the pantry door. Men in white T-shirts and white pants were preparing food on the counter. They made me so sad that I wanted to die.

OCTOBER 28, 1995

The vast estate resembled Versailles. It was late fall or early winter, and the trees were all bare, the ground covered with dead grass and clumps of dried leaves. I walked until I arrived at an empty reflecting pool made of granite blocks. It was about a hundred feet long, fifty feet wide, and two feet deep. As I stood by the edge looking into it, a man appeared out of the woods. I recognized him as a Brit named Kelvin, a musician I'd known in Japan.

Kelvin sprinted toward the pool and fell in. While he was in the air, that end of the pool suddenly became thirty feet deep. He landed on his side in a running position and began making a horrible sound: *wo-AAK, wo-AAK, wo-AAK*. Since he was expressionless, I wondered if he might be a robot.

A crowd materialized and gathered around the pool, *tsk*ing and tut-tutting, shaking their heads. I realized that nobody was going to help Kelvin, so I went around to the other end—where it was still two feet deep—and jumped in.

"*No! Don't do that!*" several people shouted.

I ignored them and went to Kelvin. His face was half-buried in slime, and he still made that terrible noise, his eyes staring blankly.

The onlookers shrieked because the lion had been let in. I slowly turned and there it was, a full-grown male with a lush, dark mane. It stalked me, its eyes narrowing as it hissed and growled. I watched it with no emotion whatsoever, even though I knew that now I'd be killed. The lion circled me, waiting for the moment to pounce. I turned my back on it and knelt to help Kelvin.

Behind me, I heard the thumping of the lion's paws on the granite as it broke into a run.

NOVEMBER 9, 1995

While sitting at my modeling desk upstairs and working on a project, I noticed a tiny black spider descending from the ceiling. It played out a single strand of silk and headed for the floor next to my feet.

I didn't want to kill it, but I was afraid it might be a black widow or some other poisonous species. As soon as it landed on the carpet, I dumped a splash of rubbing alcohol on it from the bottle I kept next to the desk. It had no effect. I therefore poured about a cupful of alcohol on the struggling creature and went back to what I was doing.

After a few minutes, I looked down and saw that the spider still squirmed. Two other spiders—larger ones—emerged from the soaking carpet and crawled away. As I watched, the carpet began to foam slightly and more spiders came out, each larger than the last. When I saw that there were crickets too, I realized that the carpet was completely infested.

I pushed back the chair and moved my feet away from the spot, which now disgorged eight-inch centipedes, cigar-sized locusts, tarantulas, scorpions, and all manner of increasingly massive creepy-crawlies. There was nothing nearby I could use to swat them, which would've been futile anyway because the entire carpet heaved and pulsed from the movement of the creatures beneath it. They poured into the room by the millions, a clicking, scuttling, glistening, black torrent that flowed in all directions and disappeared. I was appalled at the damage I'd done and knew I'd be blamed for everything.

Squirrels, ferrets, cats, dogs, and Vietnamese potbellied pigs pulled themselves out of the foaming carpet. It was too much, some kind of elaborate hoax. That meant it wasn't my fault after all. Knowing I wouldn't be held responsible triggered a wave of nearly orgasmic relief.

As the procession of animals dwindled down to an occasional trundling bug, I saw that one of the pigs had left an envelope on the floor.

"That's for when she comes back," a voice said in my ear.

I picked up the envelope, scanned the blank face and back, and stuffed it into my pocket. Since it was sealed, there was no way I could figure out who it was for or how I could get it to her.

NOVEMBER 17, 1995

As I lay in my bed trying to sleep, it was nighttime in my room but the middle of the day outside my window. I was covered with sheets, a blanket, and a bedspread. When I started to drift off, a presence under my bed gave the bedclothes a tremendous yank. It terrified me, annoyed me, and left me indifferent.

With both hands, I pulled back as hard as I could. Something under the bed thumped against the wooden frame. I jerked the covers several times, causing the thing beneath me to bash into my bed over and over. With each impact it changed, from small and scurrying like a rat to the size of a human or larger and back to ratlike again. It also alternated between hard and soft, a giant beetle ricocheting off the floor and then a slab of quivering blubber.

I heard a noise outside my window and looked over to see Tim come out of one of the doors of the TV room. My window was open, so I shouted at him.

"Tim! *Tim!*"

His head was wrapped in a bright red scarf piled a foot high, the style worn by African women. He smiled to himself as he strolled around, ignoring me.

"Tim! Timothy! TIMOTHY!" I shouted. Though I felt increasingly desperate, part of me was amused. It was a ludicrous waste of time.

"Yes? What is it?" Tim finally answered in a middle-aged woman's pleasing, well-modulated contralto.

He was so calm and removed that I wanted to beat the hell out of him, but I sounded incredibly stupid even to myself. My situation was absurd.

"There's something under my bed," I yelled at him. "It's pulling off all my covers!"

As I spoke, the bedclothes were yanked even more violently; this time they were nearly snatched off. I pulled back as hard as I could, and a creature flew up into the air attached by its teeth to the edge of the blanket. It was small, black, round headed, and weaselly, like a demonic fetus. Still amused, I was also appalled at myself for not taking the situation seriously.

The thing landed in some cardboard boxes next to my bed and tumbled around on the floor for a few seconds, flopping like a carp out of water before slipping back under the bed. I was acutely aware that I should run out of the room, but instead I just lay there as this malign presence scrabbled around underneath me. I called out to Tim again. Receiving no answer, I looked out the window to see him watering his plants with a hose.

"Tim! *Tim!* TIM!" I yelled.

"Yes, I know," he answered placidly. "There's something under your bed pulling off all your sheets. I know all about it."

He still had that small, infuriatingly cool and distant smile, not even looking up at me as he watered. Suddenly, I found it impossible to look at him directly, my head refusing to turn as if it were held immobile by invisible hands. He abruptly seemed very indistinct, like a watercolor.

After an eternity of struggling and grunting, I was finally able to wrench my entire body into position to see his face. Nearly out of my mind with terror, I was also bored with the whole mess. I knew that whatever happened to me was my own fault for not leaving the room when I could've, so I'd lost interest in the situation.

As I opened my mouth to respond to Tim, the thing under my bed began hissing emphatically like an enraged goose: "*Hsh! Hsh!*"

It was horribly explosive and energetic, the sound of air brakes on an eighteen-wheeler. I knew I was really in trouble now.

That. Is. A. Terrible. Sound, I thought in slow motion. There was no question that I had to get out of the room immediately, but I also couldn't be bothered to rouse myself.

NOVEMBER 24, 1995

Something was lodged in my throat. It was soft, warm, and very long. I tried unsuccessfully to cough it up. Although I could breathe through my nose and mouth, the thing in my throat was irritating and oppressive.

When I felt it on the back of my tongue, I reached into my mouth and pulled out a rope of phlegm. It was the diameter of my thumb and had the texture of the rubber earthworms my father used as bait when he went fishing. I hauled out several feet that coiled on the ground.

There was no end to it. My mouth watered, and I began to feel nauseated as I frantically yanked phlegm out of me.

When I'd removed thirty or forty feet, I found a pair of scissors and snipped the rope. The part left inside snapped like a rubber band down my throat, and I no longer felt it. Even so, I knew it was there, poisoning me.

DECEMBER 1, 1995

The city was Tokyo or Pusan. Everything was gray and dirty, with miniature lakes of stinking water in the streets. I walked for ages and then had to urinate badly, so I went into an office building to use the men's room. There were several bathrooms, each door carrying a black plastic tag with white engraved lettering. I went into the one marked "Second Class Staff Men's Washroom."

The bathroom was jammed with men who milled around as though taking a coffee break. I remembered that it was rush hour, the end of the day; it was an awful mistake to go there at that time. The men were adult sized, but they were all about thirteen years old. They looked like children playing dress-up in their fathers' clothing. Each one glanced at me as he strolled by clutching his briefcase, pointedly avoiding my eyes when I looked back.

I realized that I was barefoot, and the bathroom floor was covered with puddles. The water was surely contaminated, so I tried to make my way to a stall by hopping from one foot to the other, avoiding the puddles. I made grunting noises of effort—*Ooh! Aah! Yuhng!*—that were completely idiotic, but I wanted people to pay attention to me and admire me for my courage.

When I realized that nobody cared, I left the bathroom, even though I still had to urinate. I made my way to a bookstore that was also a bank and diner. The customers had to sit at a bar and pass their orders for books, magazines, meals, or transactions to female clerks who wore red-and-blue uniforms that made them look like British Air flight attendants. Sitting at the counter, I gave my order for two copies of the current issue of *Bass Player,* which had my interview with Andy West in it. My perky, blonde clerk plucked the magazines from a stack, put them in a bag behind the counter, and took my money over to a large desk. The cashier was a fat banker with a cigar and a pince-nez.

There were dozens of clerks lined up to pay the banker-cashier, so I resigned myself to a long and pointless wait.

This is a really stupid way of doing business, I thought. Someone inside my head seemed to have spoken the words. Another clerk went over to the bag containing my magazines, fished one out, and handed it to a customer.

The clerk giggled and preened as though she thought she were adorable. She didn't even charge the customer, using my copy of the magazine to try and seduce him.

Though afraid of what would happen, I tried to get my clerk's attention.

"Hey," I said. "She stole my magazine. Make her give it back."

I sounded like a tired, old man feebly complaining about his lunch. To my surprise, the people around me took my side.

"Come on, lady! Help the guy!"

"Don't let that bitch get away with it!"

"Look what she's doing! Aren't you ashamed?"

My clerk looked inside my bag and went off to get me another copy of the magazine. As she passed in front of me, I shouted, "Duh! *DUH!*" at her. I didn't know why I insulted her; she was trying hard to make up for the other clerk's malfeasance.

When I finally got my hands on the magazine, I flipped through it to find my long and prominent article. It didn't seem to be there. In the table of contents, my name was badly misspelled: *Txyhrpobzlmvnajfrks Wvqidlkcftpzobmr.* I finally found the piece on page forty-eight. The editors had taken my photo of Andy West and superimposed his head on the naked, muscular body of a porn star fingering a happy nude woman sitting spread-eagled in a chair. Several other naked men crowded around, doing various things to her.

The interview had been changed from a narrative to a transcript. References to me "grinning slyly" or "chuckling nervously" had been inserted in parentheses before my questions. It was a disaster, the end of my career. I turned to the person next to me to express my shock and discovered that it was Joe Cady, my college roommate. He ignored my repeated attempts to show him what had been done to my article. Hurt and confused, I slid off my stool and prepared to leave.

"I'll give you a call later, and we can get together," I said.

He gave me a sideways glance. "Why would we want to do that?" After an emphatic pause, he shook his head and snorted, as if the idea were preposterous.

Fine. Whatever, I thought with a flare of rage and left the store, holding my worthless magazines and wondering how it had all happened. Outside, a fast-moving stream of water headed toward me on the sidewalk. I knew it came from a burst sewer line. Remembering that I was barefoot, I jumped into the street to avoid it. The entire neighborhood was under construction, and pedestrians had been told to walk in the middle of the muddy, half-demolished road. A construction worker in a white hardhat and orange coveralls gave instructions into a walkie-talkie. His face was wrapped in a towel, the way Japanese protestors hid their identities, but I could tell that he smiled mockingly at me.

Angry at him, I went in the opposite direction that he pointed. I crossed to the far side of the street where a crane squatted, the cab swinging around slowly as the machine lifted sections of pipe and metal plate. Ducking under the counterweight of the cab as it swung over my head, I intended to emerge on the other side. The counterweight expanded rapidly into a metal ceiling that stretched as far as I could see. Behind me, the masked construction worker howled with laughter, and the crowds of pedestrians joined in. I stumbled through soft piles of dirt and sand, trying to get out from under the crane, but wherever I turned, it was right there over my head.

I staggered and careened faster and faster, and I realized that the crane had changed into a bus or train. Spinning wheels hemmed me in as I flew down a road or bed of wooden railroad ties. I crawled on my hands and knees at hundreds of miles per hour. Looking back over my shoulder, I saw a wheel in the centerline of the vehicle above my head. If I stopped moving, this wheel would crush me. The wheels on either side were so close together that I couldn't slip between them fast enough to avoid being chopped to pieces. I had to keep crawling.

Up ahead, a low wall lay directly in my path. It blocked my escape from under the speeding train or bus. I understood with terrible sadness that I'd be killed, smashed between the wall and the wheel behind me. It wasn't fair, because I had so much more to give.

DECEMBER 5, 1995

I fiddled with a VCR in a very dark bedroom. Since I couldn't see, I was unable to put a tape into the machine or operate the remote. It didn't occur to me to turn on a light. The bedroom was in a hotel or halfway house; I knew I wasn't in my home.

As dark as the room was, I could still see that everything was new and expensive. There was plush carpeting; polished, dark wooden furniture; original paintings on the walls; and the combination TV, video, and stereo setup in front of me. What I was trying to do was a time waster, just putting off the inevitable, even though I didn't know what that was. I became more and more uneasy as I went through my meaningless motions. At some point I'd have to go out into the living room of this unfamiliar, sinister place, and I was mortally afraid.

Finally, I put down the VCR remote and went through the open bedroom door into the carpeted hallway. The living room floor was sunken about a foot, and as I walked toward it, I saw an open door that gave me a view into another dimly lit bedroom. Someone lay on a large bed, propped up by pillows; he was obviously sick or dying. His face was obscured by a nimbus of haze, like a cloud of cigarette smoke. I thought it might be Tim, but then I realized that it was nobody I knew. I turned away, and as I stepped down into the living room, I felt as if I were walking into a vacuum. The room was soundless and dead, a complete void yet suffused with a tremendous sense of imminence.

I suddenly knew that something absolutely terrible was going to happen, something so vile that I couldn't even begin to comprehend it. The room was terrifically evil. It made me feel such anguish that I wanted to die. A low thrumming began, a combination of sound and vibration, like the brass section of a marching band playing a deep, barely audible note. Something was coming, an event or entity beyond my endurance to face.

As the thrumming became more pronounced, I gave up and just stood there in the dark, waiting. I felt more passive, lost, and alone than at any point in my life. There was nowhere I could go and nobody I could turn to for help.

CHAPTER SEVEN
FAILURE, HUMILIATION, AND ILLEGITIMACY

To this day I have failure dreams. I'm sure I always will. They've drastically tapered off, though.

In my dreams I often make a complete fool out of myself, say and do the wrong thing, or present myself as a pathetic child expressing distorted emotions that just embarrass everybody. The worst of these nightmares are the ones that illustrate my fear of being perceived as showing off and craving attention.

The latter has one real-life counterpart. When my dorm floor in college had its first party—a mixer, I guess it would be called—I held forth on the job I'd had at the shore-support base in Norway, describing the danger, the stenches that produced instant projectile vomiting, and the circus-strongman Norwegians and Newfoundlanders who were my colleagues. The whole room was enthralled. When the party broke up, a bearded kid came over and asked my name.

"I wanted to meet you because you're such an interesting guy," he said.

It made me want to curl up in shame. That's the story of my life: I love to entertain, but I hate getting feedback for it. It makes me feel like a shabby attention whore. In my ideal world, I'd write and my former Collateral Ghost—Scott Thunes—would go out and promote my work for me. He can handle compliments. I can't.

Before each of my five books was published, I had dreams in which it was a debacle. I didn't record the dreams; I'd long since stopped keeping this diary. They were my typical author-failure nightmares, in that the books were printed on crummy paper or held together in some makeshift way or showed me to be an idiot who had no idea what he wrote about.

My failure and illegitimacy dreams don't bother me anymore. I now understand that I earned the right to have them.

* * *

1969

I suddenly realized that I was completely naked. Nobody in the classroom noticed, but as soon as the bell rang, I'd have to stand up, and then everyone would see.

As Miss Kuntzelmann wrote on the chalkboard, I tried to figure out how I'd cover myself. I had my folder and notebook, but if I held them in front and in back, everyone would see. There had to be a way to turn them into clothes before time ran out.

The folder had two pockets, one on each cover. Using my blunt little scissors, I cut off the bottom of the pockets and then slipped on the folder like a pair of shorts. It covered my rear but left the front bare. The bell rang. It was too late.

When everybody stood and made their way to the door, I leaped into the middle of the crowd, holding my notebook in front of my exposed genitals. It seemed to work; nobody said anything. The school day had ended, so the students in all the grades—first through eighth—were leaving. Outside, I walked the roofed, open-air corridors that connected all the buildings. Neither students nor teachers noticed me.

A motorcycle was parked in front of the school. It would be the fastest way to get home. When I jumped onto it, my folder pants fell apart, leaving me naked. The motorcycle seat was so much higher than the handlebars that I felt as though I stood on my head. I started the bike and took off, aware that everybody could now see up my bare rear as I sped past.

AUGUST 11, 1995

I wore a backpack, boots, and hiking clothes as I walked along the grassy bank of a narrow canal. Something was about to happen, but I didn't know what.

Ahead of me the canal branched out into the shape of a letter *T*, with a grassy hill on my left. I stopped and waited. From the right came a boulder about one hundred feet in diameter. It rolled over the canal at high speed and slammed into the hill, which recoiled and vibrated as if it were made of rubber. This was what I'd been waiting for, and I knew that the result of the collision of boulder and hill would be a tidal wave. I looked forward to experiencing it, even if it killed me.

All the water in the canal was suddenly sucked away to the left. At any second it would rush back in as a tsunami. I climbed down into the slimy canal bottom, where I met Bill Cosby and the cast of *The Brady Bunch,* all of whom were now blacks too. Cosby was businesslike, preparing the others for the tidal wave. He ignored me as he robotically issued instructions.

The tidal wave roared into the canal. It surrounded us and covered us without making us wet, due to some kind of force field that Cosby had created. When the canal was filled again, everybody began climbing around on the banks and wading in the water, looking for something. I saw a wooden bar stool floating upright in the canal, only the seat visible. The water around it began glowing like neon. I jumped onto the stool in a Swedish fall, supporting myself with both arms while the rest of my body and legs pointed stiffly into the sky.

"Look!" I yelled. "It's a miracle of God! *¡Es un milagro!*"

It wasn't a miracle, just some kind of weird, flooding-floating phenomenon that I tried to exploit so that Cosby and the rest would admire me. Nobody paid any attention, so even though my antics embarrassed me to death, I decided to amp them up by trying to support myself with just one arm on the stool. The glow in the water immediately went out, the equilibrium vanished, and I sank into the scummy, algae-topped water.

As my face submerged into the warm slickness, I realized what a stupid mistake I'd made.

AUGUST 24, 1995

The narrow laundry room in the rear of my house was a space about six feet wide by twelve feet long. I was part of a large crowd squeezed into it. Ironing boards, planks, and posts leaned against the walls; stacks of boxes and containers took up the rest of the space. Even so, hundreds of people were somehow in there with me.

As we stood in a compressed loaf of humanity, like passengers on the Tokyo subway, Oprah Winfrey gave a seminar. She narrated a montage from her shows, which she called *People Who Are Stuck in the 1950s*. There was a large-screen TV or monitor on one of the walls, and we were to watch and take notes. Oprah had an unfiltered cigarette and lighter in her hand; she used them to gesture at the screen as she spoke. Since her lecture and montage had nothing to do with the fifties, I lost interest, convinced that this was just a gimmick to get publicity for her show.

Behind Oprah, a shirtless, yellow-skinned man was stretched out on the floor. He was in his forties and looked utterly dissolute, with rheumy eyes, no teeth, and unkempt hair sticking out in all directions.

Oprah pointed at him. "Buddy Holly here is one of the people who knows what I'm talking about," she said.

The man got up, straightened out his pants, and squeezed past us to leave. He had a furtive, half-smiling expression that was very upsetting. I recognized the name Buddy Holly; I knew who he was, yet I also had no idea whatsoever who he was. His crapulous condition surprised me, but there was an air of deceit and falsehood about everything. He was a dangerous liar trying to trick me.

As Oprah droned on, I looked around for something to distract myself. Her monologue was painfully boring. I found a metal bucket on the ground and turned it over. Stuck to the bottom was a crumbling paper label, an advertisement for Vaseline petroleum jelly. It read, "Vaseline! The product that cares for you your entire life...and BEYOND!"

Beneath the slogan was a cartoon headstone; buried under it in the ground was the smiling corpse of a woman with crosses instead of eyes and a protruding tongue. The edges of the label were printed with doggerel such as "voon-voonoona" and "nooma nomoona."

I interrupted Oprah and showed her the underside of the bucket.

"Look how old and weird it is!" I said. "It's incredible!"

After staring at it for a long time, she looked me in the eye. "I don't think that's very funny at all," she said.

She lit her cigarette and turned back to the others, continuing her lecture.

I was crushed.

SEPTEMBER 19, 1995

Crouched on the wooden floor of a large, brightly lit room, I tried to attach two thick sheets of ice together. I used an electric drill to make holes in the ice and then ran metal bolts through them. Once the sheets of ice were together, I was supposed to sandwich them between two metal plates, using more bolts and nuts.

I had to work fast, because as soon as I put down the drill and fixed the bolts in place, the ice would melt, enlarging the holes. The bolts would then fall out. I'd drill another set of holes, and the same thing would happen.

My pulse thudded in my neck, ears, and fingertips as I started to panic. Soon I'd have no ice left. People came in and out the room, most of them laughing at me. I was going to be late for my John Taylor interview, but I couldn't stop.

Eventually, I was left with a handful of wet nuts and bolts and two metal plates, all the ice having melted into a puddle at my feet.

OCTOBER 11, 1995

The stationery store was also a veterinarian's office. Inside, there were a few stacks of typing and computer paper for sale, but the place was mostly empty. I was going to apply for a job, even though I knew I had no chance of getting it. Behind the counter was a large, angry-looking woman. She had a white lab coat and a pink bow at the front of her hair. I was afraid to talk to her because I knew my résumé was pathetic, and she looked impatient and very irritable. I approached her anyway.

She barely glanced at me as I explained my background and why I wanted to work for her.

"I was in Japan for five years," I said hopefully. "I did everything you could imagine! Then I worked in San Francisco! I'd totally devote myself to the job! I promise!"

Even though she tried to seem indifferent as she stacked things and put documents in drawers and filing cabinets, I could tell I'd won her over against her will.

"Well," she growled, "you can call me Mrs. MacLeish."

I understood exactly what she said.

"Madison?" I asked, giggling.

"No, no!" She gave me a terrible look. "MacLeish. *MacLeish!*"

I simply wouldn't repeat her name. There was no reason for me to do something so moronically self-sabotaging, but I couldn't stop.

"Uh...Anderson? Williamson?" I asked. I simpered, squirmed, and produced a repulsive *sh-sh-sh-sh* as my phony laugh.

"MacLeish!" the woman barked, furious now. She slammed her palms on the countertop and glared. I had one last chance.

Taking a deep breath, I said, "Marionson?"

The woman screamed like a locomotive steam whistle.

"MACLEISH! MACLEEISSH! MACLEEEEEIIIIISH!"

I ducked my head and chuckled. Though I'd destroyed my opportunity and was appalled at my actions, I felt that unseen observers would like me for being a really funny guy. I also knew that I utterly deluded myself. Anyone watching would be as disgusted with me as I was, but I still wanted to push the now-hysterical woman even further.

JANUARY 16, 1996

My brother Paul and I were law enforcement officers confronting shaven-headed Mexican gangsters in the muddy parking lot of a large store. Wearing my trench coat and armed with two chrome-plated automatic pistols, I felt strong and fit, able to run as fast as the wind.

The parking lot was covered with a thin, patchy film of yellow mud and big puddles, as if it had just rained. Paul and I cornered one of the gang-bangers, a sullen, fat, young man in a white wifebeater shirt. We arrested him but couldn't get any backup or a van to come take away our prisoner. I looked across the parking lot and saw the fat gangster's buddies standing around a parked car, talking. Their postures were menacing, and they seemed to be planning something, but Paul wasn't concerned.

"Where the hell is the backup?" I kept asking, but he'd just shrug.

"Don't worry about it," he'd say. "We're fine on our own."

The parking lot changed into a large field, and I saw that our prisoner was now in a barbed-wire pen attached to either an abandoned theater or a barn. He climbed up the side of the building, trying to get away. I watched with anxiety and amusement, afraid he'd escape but not really caring. When he got to the top of the structure, he jumped, fell twenty feet, and landed on his head with a loud crunch. I was horrified; it was entirely my fault.

He looked dead, his neck twisted at an impossible angle. I went over to him.

"All right," I said, "get up! I want you to sit on your butt and put your hands behind your back. NOW!"

Trying for a macho, TV-cop growl, I knew I was just a clown. The gangster sat up and clasped his hands behind his back. He seemed uninjured by his fall, his neck straight again, but I still felt incredibly guilty.

It was against procedure to let him put his hands behind his back; they had to be on top of his head, fingers laced together. I couldn't figure out how to tell him that. Also, I realized that for the past few minutes, my guns had been getting smaller and smaller, shrinking from forty-fives down to twenty-fives. The trigger guards began pinching me, so I held the pistols between my index fingers and thumbs. They became doll-guns, so tiny that they were useless. I was overcome by a horrendous sense of vulnerability. Paul and I were idiots.

"*Where's the goddamn backup?*" I shouted. He didn't answer or even look at me.

After an eternity of silently waiting for no reason, we walked our prisoner out of the field, which had two gates made of wooden beams and diamond-link fencing. As we were about to cross the street, a small European-style police car raced toward us, yellow lights flashing on the roof. The driver gripped the steering wheel with one hand and frantically signaled us to go back into the field, sweeping his free arm from side to side. His teeth showed in a panicked grimace.

When he came within ten feet or so, I recognized him as Edward James Olmos. Mildly surprised, I knew that he was only doing his job, unlike Paul and me.

FEBRUARY 1, 1996

John Taylor drove me in an SUV through Italy. It was nighttime, and he was grim and silent, not responding to my questions or acknowledging my presence. I felt stupid and out of place.

"Tell me about your divorce," I said. "What about all the drugs and groupies? What was it like knowing that people thought you were a shitty bassist? Are you a good father?"

I knew I behaved very inappropriately, but I was unable to stop. It seemed to be raining, and we drove with a sense of desperate urgency along narrow, winding roads that cut through the steep mountains.

Ahead I saw a miniscule village. Taylor pulled over and stopped in front of a tiny town hall right at the edge of the road.

"Take off your shoes," he said without looking at me.

He unlaced his own boots, so I took off my shoes and waited. When he got out, I followed. My socks immediately became soaked; I stopped to take them off while Taylor went into the town hall. The wet pavement was cold and amazingly intrusive against my bare feet, but I also enjoyed the sensation. It made me feel free and reckless.

Straightening, I found Taylor right in front of me, his arms full of cardboard shipping tubes and paper-wrapped packages. He shoved them at me, and I staggered back, managing to catch the entire load without dropping anything.

Taylor gripped my shoulders and spun me around to face an outdoor cafe. "See that cafe? Go wait over there."

As I tottered toward the cafe, a car door slammed behind me, and a motor started. I turned to see the SUV speeding away, and I realized that Taylor had tricked me. He'd left me alone and shoeless in this village where I didn't know anybody. Terrified, I looked at the cafe. A group of elderly Italian men sat outside with glasses of wine, watching me with amused contempt and hostility.

APRIL 22, 1996

It was time for my bass solo. I was onstage in a stadium that held several tens of thousands. As I raised my arms to salute the crowd, there was a deafening cheer.

You're finally going to do it! I thought. *Here's where you make a name for yourself!*

My drummer pounded out a funky rhythm, and I started to play. Instead of notes, there was a series of dull thuds, the noise of a distant construction site. I couldn't feel the bass strings under my fingers. Looking down, I saw that I wore heavy welder's gloves. I broke into a sweat, and the ocean of humanity in front of me fell completely silent.

The sky was glaring white, as if we were in the Gobi Desert. I felt suffocated despite my agoraphobia. The drumbeat died out; now the only sound was the muffled scraping of my gloves on the strings of my bass.

People began to exit the stadium in droves, and the other musicians filed off the stage, leaving me alone as I struggled to produce the music I heard in my head.

APRIL 26, 1996

The enclosed space was an open-air storage depot that covered hundreds of acres. My job was to stack empty picture frames against lines of earthen berms on the inside of the fenced-in property. They reminded me of the walls that surround the oldest buildings in China and Japan. The entire setting was a strange, unnatural beige, with splashes of washed-out brown and pale yellow.

As soon as I'd moved the thousands of picture frames into position, puddles appeared under them, and the berms began releasing small streams of water, as if from faucets. I knew I couldn't leave the frames in the puddles because they'd rot or mildew, but I couldn't figure out what to do. In a frenzy of distracted impatience, I paced the depot, trying to understand what was going on and how I could deal with it.

The puddles and streams of running water hadn't been there when I first arrived. They were some kind of sadistic practical joke, perpetrated by someone I didn't even know. And he'd get away with it, while I'd have to pay.

APRIL 27, 1996

My interview with Gene Simmons was published in *Bass Player.* The magazine was printed on pink and yellow paper towels stapled together in a brainless, asymmetrical hodgepodge, the edges of the pages unaligned and sticking out in every direction.

The photos of Simmons looked as though they'd been done with a rudimentary silk-screening process. All I could make out was a hulking male image. It could've been anyone from a businessman to a naval officer.

Although the photos filled entire pages, the article had been printed over them, directly across the faces. This made the images hopelessly indistinct and the writing illegible.

I was numb with shock, my big chance utterly ruined.

MAY 4, 1996

In the supermarket I stood in front of a pegboard wall filled with foil pouches of instant curries, the type I ate in Japan. They made me feel a wave of nostalgia for my time in Tokyo. I wanted to go back, even though I knew that I'd idealized the past. The real Tokyo era was nothing like what I wished it was, but these chicken and pork curries reminded me of Carmen. I still missed her, despite the cruelty and mercilessness she'd shown in driving me away.

I noticed that the "Japanese"-style cookies hung on the pegboard along with the curries were actually Mallomars or some other American confection that had nothing to do with Japan. Also, most of the containers had been opened and the cookies had been taken, leaving only crumbs. People had tampered with all of the pouches and containers, the foods either stolen or polluted somehow. The display now struck me as sinister and cheap, like something from a market in Lagos or Mumbai. I had to get out immediately.

Then I was on the living room floor of an unfamiliar house, stretched out on my stomach. Under the coffee table in front of me, an infant rode a tiny tricycle. He was no more than six inches tall, with a fleshy torso, broad back, and short arms and legs. His hair was thick and black, and he wore cartoon Baby Huey diapers with a big safety pin in front. He pedaled his tricycle so fast that his legs were blurred. Round and round he went under the coffee table, crashing through piles of foam-rubber toys and blow-molded plastic blocks and dolls.

Though I knew him, he was also a stranger; he may have been a relative. As he knocked the toys out of his way, I smiled and caressed his back. He whipped his head around and gave me a wary look full of intelligence and maturity, his face vaguely familiar. I held my breath.

After a few seconds, the baby went back to his game and I exhaled, swamped with guilt for what I'd done. I only wanted him to know that I cared about him, but he'd completely misinterpreted it. Even so, I understood his suspicion. I deserved it.

MAY 6, 1996

The school bus careened around the streets of a European city at night. I rode along with high school students and radio DJ Richard Blade. He'd brought a camera crew, which filmed while he narrated in his distinctive voice.

It was a cylindrical bus, the sides sloping so far downward that the people sitting at the windows had to either slouch low in their seats or lean toward the person in the aisle seat. The driver was a young blond guy with wire-rimmed glasses and a frizzy crew cut. He violently swung the steering wheel, panting with exertion.

Through the windshield I watched buildings, trees, lampposts, and parked cars whip past, as if we were in a low-flying airplane. The landscape was shades of green and black, the street lamps adding to the underwater gloom with their murky yellow cones of light. I realized that the driver exaggerated for the benefit of the camera. He made his work look much more exhausting than it really was, and he put us all at risk.

After several minutes of squealing tires and blurry vistas, I'd had enough.

"The driver's doing all this just for effect," I said. "He's not really having such a hard time. He's just making it look worse because we're being filmed."

Behind me, Richard Blade cleared his throat. "Uh, Tom? We're trying to get this on film. I'd really appreciate it if you wouldn't say things like that, because it makes us look bad."

He spoke with exaggerated patience, as though I were senile. My face burned and my skin crawled; I'd never felt like a bigger idiot. Without looking back at him, I raised my left hand and gave him what I hoped was a devastatingly sarcastic thumbs up. Everyone on the bus stared at me with the same disgust Blade had expressed. I slid down in my seat and tried to put a crooked, superior smile on my face, but I knew nobody was fooled.

MAY 15, 1996

I was back at Lewis and Clark College in Portland, Oregon, but the dorms had changed. They were much airier, the hallways and lounges like airplane hangers and Quonset huts. Billy Fisher—who was in the fifth and sixth grades with me at Rice Elementary School in Tyler, Texas—ran around the campus with a semiautomatic rifle. Nobody seemed to notice him. As he staggered under the glass-sided skyway that connected the two dorms, I watched from the second floor, trying to figure out how to tip off the police without him knowing it. I felt more amused than afraid; I couldn't understand why. Billy was a murderous lunatic. There was nothing funny about him.

After a lot of thought, I picked up one of the phones on the oaken desks in the dorm lounge. I dialed "A911" and a female operator answered, but she seemed to have picked up the phone in the middle of a conversation with someone else. Her unintelligible drone was overlaid by several other babbling voices, as if all the lines were crossed.

"If you have an emergency," she finally said, "state which you need: police, fire, or ambulance."

From her bored, robotic tone I knew that I could never get her to help me, so I just hung up. I went over to the window and looked out to see Billy standing on a concrete sidewalk, clutching his rifle and idly doodling in the dirt with the tip of one shoe. He'd changed back into a little boy, as he was when I knew him, but he was still incredibly dangerous. Somehow he sapped my will, making me slow witted and indecisive.

I returned to the phone, dialed A911 again, and heard the same babble of voices.

"You know you can't keep doing this, Mrs. Cross," the operator said. "This number's only for emergencies. You *know* that."

As she spoke I realized that I was an addled, elderly woman. My hair was dyed black, and I held the receiver with both trembling hands. I wondered querulously what I should do. The last few times I'd called A911, they hadn't taken me seriously. My problem was that everything—noises, people, strange cars—scared me and made me call. I also knew that unless I got off the phone immediately, Billy would notice and kill me.

No longer an old woman, I hung up and went to the window just in time to see Billy charging the building, his rifle carried at port arms and his teeth bared. He roared incoherently, and I knew he came specifically for me. I ran out the door, down the hall, into another lounge, and down the stairs to the outside, hoping Billy ran up the other stairway to the lounge I'd just occupied.

Circling the campus, I encountered several people.

"I need help! I'm in trouble!" I said to each one, but nobody reacted. They all ignored me.

At the edge of the campus, I noticed that I held a paper plate with a big, sloppy hamburger on it. I came across a tiny, well-kept cottage just as three young black men in wire-rimmed glasses came out the front door. They were upper classmen, students I knew very well. I ran to them.

"*Help!*" I shouted.

When they saw me, their shoulders slumped and they rolled their eyes at each other. Two of them moaned, "Aw, *man!*" They were utterly sick of me.

"No, no!" I yelled. "There's a guy with a gun running around campus! Call security! Call the cops! Get them to form a wall with their squad cars *right there!*"

I pointed to an inclined driveway on the edge of the campus, bordered by a highway loop that encircled the college. The three upper classmen suddenly looked scared. They ran back into their cottage, and I waited for the police, still clutching my hamburger. My hokey, nonsensical instructions embarrassed me, and I knew that I exploited the situation to try and cover myself with glory.

MAY 26, 1996

The large, old brick building was an embassy. Inside, several brown-skinned East Asian men looked to me for direction. Opposing forces massed in the city nearby, and there was only a short time before we'd be overwhelmed or taken into custody.

We went through large closets, looking for zippered vinyl clothing bags that held something that we needed. Whenever I looked away from the Asian men and then back, I'd see that they'd changed into Caucasian teenagers from the seventies, wearing Keds sneakers, chinos, and striped Hanes T-shirts. I'd look away and then back, and they'd be Asian men again. This happened over and over.

When we found the vinyl bags and opened them, we discovered that they were full of artifacts from my youth, including clothes, modeling tools, and items I no longer recognized. Looking at them, I knew that they were irrelevant now, and it was absurd self-delusion to try and assign them meaning. Though I'd never admit it, most of what was in the bags was junk that signified nothing.

Some of the Asian men squatted in front of a closet and pulled out a bag that held a black, floor-length, leather trench coat. They were excited, chattering in a foreign language and passing the trench coat around to feel its finish.

When they gave me the coat, I said, "Watch carefully. I'll show you how it's done."

I put on the coat and belted it tightly around my middle. As I did so, my hair became a slicked-back, blond brush cut. I now wore rimless glasses and hard leather shoes with three-inch spike heels. My face was transformed into a pop-eyed mask, with a thin-lipped little mouth. I was a Nazi Gestapo agent. Hands clasped behind my back, I rocked up and down on my new high heels.

The Asian men gazed up at me in adoration. I picked out one and walked toward him.

"Stand!" I barked.

He scrambled to his feet, and I circled him slowly, my locked face quivering with the stress of keeping it in its ugly grimace. Finally, I spoke to him in a thick German accent.

"Vat iss it you tink you are doing? Do you know vat ze penalty iss for zat, hmm?" I was mortified by my performance. It was utterly deranged. "*DO YOU?*" I screamed.

All the Asians nodded to each other in comprehension, saying, "Ah, ah."

I took off the trench coat and said, "So you see how it's done? That's what it's all about."

They smiled and bowed, and I tossed the trench coat on a table, which I saw was covered with model-making paraphernalia. I went over to have a closer look. Someone had been building model airplane kits and had left a reference book lying on the desk. I thought it was a history of First World War aircraft, because the cover painting showed biplanes wheeling in a cloudy sky. When I picked up the book and flipped through it, I found that it was about boring postwar machines, so I laid it back down in disappointment.

Everything—our allegedly dire circumstances, my childhood, the Asian men's dependence on me, my Grade-Z imitation of a Gestapo agent in spike heels, and the aircraft reference book—was a cheap fraud.

MAY 31, 1996

Sometimes the expanse of ground I walked was a beautiful sandy beach, and at other times it was the grassy border of a park. I pointed out various sights to myself—relics and artifacts that protruded from the sand or grass.

"That's a nice urn," I'd say. "Ooh, look at that old column!"

Up ahead, Tim led a group of tourists. He wore a uniform of dark blue pants and a light blue shirt. Either a park ranger or a police officer, he told the crowd what the artifacts on the ground meant. I caught up with them just as Tim described something that looked to me like a rusty, corroded flintlock pistol.

"Aw, there now, y'see?" he drawled. "Thay-it's just whut Ah'm a-talkin' about."

The tourists and I gazed at this thing in fascination. As I examined it, however, I realized that it was actually carved from wood and nowhere near as valuable as I'd thought. We turned away from it and moved on until we came to a wooden carving of a human skull about fifteen feet tall. It had been almost totally consumed by fire. There weren't any visible flames, but one whole side had been reduced to glowing, red embers that flared up in the breeze. Either lightning or an arsonist had struck. I looked around for someone to help me put it out.

Across a nearby highway, a fire engine pulled into a concrete rest stop. I went through a passageway under the road and approached the firefighters. They crawled all over their vehicle and looked to be fit and competent. I immediately felt that my little pile of embers was nowhere near serious enough to bother them. Also, Tim had gone off to summon his own firefighters, and soon two separate units would be converging on a fire that didn't need even one. My actions were wrong and unnecessary, but I couldn't stop.

When I approached the firefighters, I found myself tongue-tied and confused, unable to explain what I wanted. They crowded around me expectantly, and I gestured back over my shoulder to the burning skull, saying, "See? See what I mean?"

I couldn't make them understand. One by one they wandered off, until the only firefighter left was a thin man with curly, blond hair. He gazed at me with twinkling, amorous eyes, his David Crosby mustache hiding his smile. I realized with a sinking feeling that he was hitting on me.

"Well, where *is* this big fire of yours anyway, hmm?" he purred, standing with his arms folded and his hips thrust forward.

Looking back over the highway, I saw that a fire engine had arrived, the crew hosing down the wooden skull. I'd completely failed in my mission, and now this guy was attracted to me, the very last thing I wanted or needed.

JUNE 1, 1996

I carried several large paper shopping bags, the twisted handles looped over my forearms, and I was in a breathless rush. The mall was as cavernous as an airplane hanger, decorated in pink, beige, and pale orange. After racing around and not finding what I wanted, I went into a store that had almost no merchandise. There were only two shelves and one clothes rack. Three male employees sat behind the counter, talking animatedly.

They seemed very familiar, reminding me of a group of gay Christian alcoholics I'd met in Paris when I was seventeen. They'd barricaded me in the kitchen and made me eat raw bean sprouts until 3:00 a.m., telling me that the vegetables would clean me right out. These men had the same campy, ironic quality that only partially concealed their viciousness. One was a blond guy who looked like a biker but cuddly and vapid. Another had a red crew cut, a mustache, and mirrored sunglasses. The third was a Middle Eastern party-boy, with curly, black, disco hair; rolling eyes; a hooked nose; and tight polyester pants. All three gazed languidly into space, sighing, "Oh. Oh. Oh. Oh."

Feeling nervous and ridiculous, I went over and asked them if they could show me something new and fashionable. All three got up and led me to the single clothes rack, where they pointed out a cotton skirt, blouse, vest, and tights in mauve. The blouse had a wide, elasticized band in the middle designed to cling tightly to a well-toned midriff. It was a vaguely Indian ensemble, the type of outfit granola girls wore when I was in college. All that was missing were leather sandals.

I was horrified and asked if the clothes were made for men or women.

"Oh, men. For sure!" someone answered. "You'd look great in it!"

They grabbed me by the ankles and flipped me onto my back. All three stood over me, laughing.

"Try it on!" one said.

They yanked off my pants, and I saw that I wore white cotton briefs, the type of underwear I'd had as a child. I still clutched my paper bags, and my legs kicked in a spastic, froglike manner. Now my feet sported red high-heeled shoes, and my spindly, pale, thrashing legs—like those of a middle-aged German comedian doing an elaborate pratfall—revolted me. Though I laughed as loudly as the clerks, I was ashamed and terrified.

JUNE 14, 1996

My parents hired me to work on the house they'd bought for my great-aunt. It was located on property that resembled a ride at Disneyland, with small ponds everywhere and an outhouse that was suspended off the ground on two mechanical bird legs. Crowds toured the site, gathering around the outhouse, which raised and lowered itself over a pond. It swayed and danced whenever someone used it. The people surrounding it sang a cloying little tune, like something from a children's TV show.

> *Doot-doot-doot,*
> *Doo, doot doo-doot,*
> *Doot-doot-DOOT!*
> *Doo, doot DOO-doot!*

Then they'd laugh as though they'd never seen anything funnier.

There was a mechanical raccoon in the water next to the outhouse. It made me feel cheated, as though it were the only phony item in a world of genuine magic. I knew everything else was fake too, but I was still indignant. It operated on some sort of clockwork or animatronic principal, moving its head around, feebly snapping its jaws, falling over on its side, and righting itself. It seemed designed to represent an animal dying from some horrible disease, like glanders.

My father put me to work scraping paint off a brick wall that had some kind of turbine set into it. I had to climb a ladder and use a device that was a combination chisel and heating element. Dad tried to explain what I should do, but all the people running around the property distracted him. He mumbled and scratched his rear. I finally gave up trying to understand him.

The area I had to scrape was as wide as a barn. Looking at it depressed me because I knew it would take forever to get it done. While I was up on the ladder, a young white guy in green overalls came over. He had long, blond hair and a heavy, ragged mustache. Above his mirrored sunglasses, he wore a thick headband made from a twisted rag.

"Can I buy the front door of your house, man?" he asked. "It's an antique."

My mother appeared. "Just imagine," she said. "He wants to take our door away from us!"

"And I *do* too," the man said, nodding his head.

"Where would we get another like it?" Mom asked. "We'd be all alone in the house with no door to keep out the strangers!"

When I came down off the ladder, my father sidled up to me.

"He's gonna take the door anyway," Dad whispered. "He doesn't care what happens to us. He's just the type who'd do that."

It was incredibly frustrating that my parents couldn't or wouldn't just tell the guy that the door wasn't for sale. The three of them went around to the front of the house, and a few minutes later I saw the man in green coveralls walk off with the door tucked under his arm. Selling the door would lead to trouble for all of us, I knew. Since I'd expected my parents to do it, all I felt was weary sadness that my fears had once again been confirmed.

I suddenly found myself at a gas station. It stretched for miles in all directions, the pump islands hundreds of yards apart. I walked back to my car from the gas station office, looking for something. Several young black women came toward me, carrying long, orange electric extension cords all tangled together. They shouted happily to each other, and I knew that they had what I needed. As they passed me, I stooped and grabbed one of the cords, giving it such a powerful jerk that it flew out of the woman's hands. I unplugged the cord from the socket connecting it to another, tossing that cord back to her and keeping the one I had.

The women stopped. *"Hey!"* one screamed. *"Watchoo doin'?"*

They seemed quite capable of killing me. I knew I'd really screwed up, but I shrugged and said nothing, fixing them with a steely look as I dragged the extension cord back to my car. They glared in silence as I tried to get the long cord inside my car before they made up their minds to attack.

Then I was outside a metal airplane hanger. It housed the record company that represented the band Kiss. I wanted to crow about the success of my Gene Simmons interview, so I went through the chain-link gates and approached an elderly security guard standing next to a small hut.

"I'd like to go in," I said. "I'm the guy who wrote the article about Gene Simmons."

The guard put his arms over his head, pressed his legs together, and began doing a slow, ecstatic dance, writhing sinuously and snapping his fingers like a belly dancer.

"I know, I know," he cooed. "Everyone here is so happy. It's just *wonderful.*"

Another man appeared, carrying a soccer ball. The three of us began kicking it against the side of the hanger. Each time it hit the metal, it made a loud clang. I was afraid we were too noisy, so I kicked very gently. The other two laid into the ball as hard as they could, and just as I realized that everything was fine, that this was how they passed their lunch hour every day and nobody cared, one of them kicked the ball on to the roof and it disappeared. I was extremely disappointed because the next time the ball came to me, I would've really let loose.

Since the game was over, I went into the building and found myself in a lunchroom. It was beige and totally anonymous, with a few chairs, tables, and vending machines. I sat at one of the tables and saw that pages from porn magazines were taped all over the walls. The photos were of young women having sex standing, their faces contorted in happy grimaces as they bit their lips. I was aroused and embarrassed. The images were everywhere, many of them photocopied.

People came in to greet me as the author of the Simmons piece. I couldn't appreciate their praise because the pornography on the walls distracted me. My fans noticed how I kept glancing around me. They began producing dirty magazines from their briefcases.

"I've got this type," one young woman said, showing me a German publication with faded colors and repulsive models.

"This is what I read," said a white-shirted man, holding up a magazine in which the models were all blonde; wore corsets; and had enormous, saggy breasts.

Everyone around me had his or her specific taste, and they were eager to share. I felt more and more uncomfortable and tried to think how I could get them to stop, but suddenly I was naked and couldn't stand up without them seeing. To my right was a group sitting at a table; it included a guy who was in the ninth and tenth grades with me in the Netherlands. He was still fifteen, with greasy, curly brown hair and an Errol Flynn mustache. In class he'd once taken a paper and pencil and shared his detailed mathematical formula for calculating the size of a girl's anus. My discomfort made him taunt me for a full year.

As I sat there naked, he watched me with amusement. His eyes flicked down my body, and he made swift, sardonic gestures with his hands, chopping the air and tapping his nose and lips. It was as though he sent me messages in a secret code we shared, but I knew it was just an obscure way for him to make fun of me.

His mouth twitching, he enjoyed my humiliation, the way he had in high school when he bragged about his foul sex life. Exactly as I'd done back then, I sat in silent wretchedness and prayed for deliverance.

JULY 29, 1996

My girlfriend was Jennifer Aniston. I knew she was a famous actress, so I was ridiculously flattered. We sat in my college dorm room, chatting for hours, and then we went to bed. She undressed and I lay on top of her, fondling her breasts as she gasped and cooed in my ear. I slid down her body and saw that she had no pubic hair. It made me feel that what we did was tainted and utterly wrong. I was on the rebound, since Noreen had just ended our horrible, deranged relationship.

Even though Jennifer didn't arouse me, I told myself that I was passionately in love with her, and we had to have sex because that was what people in love did. My emotions were a stew of tenderness, protectiveness, aloofness, and extreme guilt. She also made me feel dirty; being with her was an act of criminal depravity.

Then it was morning, and I was supposed to take a business trip. Jennifer saw me to my car. As I put my suitcase in the trunk and admired Jennifer's beauty, her face went an awful shade of orange. She looked as though her skin had suddenly become deeply frostbitten. Her expression became regretful, and an enervating wave of misery washed over me. I knew she'd changed her mind about us. I didn't love her, but my heart was broken.

"What's the matter?" I asked, fully aware of what the answer would be.

"Oh, well...I don't think this is such a good idea," she mumbled, gazing over my head.

I was horribly upset, thinking, *I knew it was too good to be true. The sex and what I felt last night were just too spectacular. I knew this would happen, just like it always does.*

These were childish lies. Still, it was vital for me to maintain the fiction that I loved Jennifer. Admitting the truth—even to myself—would make everything worse.

CHAPTER EIGHT
THE FOURTH NIGHTMARE CLUSTER

The trigger for this cluster was my interview with Gene Simmons of Kiss. It took us a couple of weeks to set up a meeting, during which time he and his publicist made me feel as though I were a supremely irritating oaf with no idea what I was doing. Only years later did I recognize the compliment they paid me—or paid *Bass Player,* at least—by acceding to my demand for a face-to-face interview.

As I wrote in both *In Cold Sweat* and *Ghosts and Ballyhoo,* spending two hours with Gene Simmons was incredibly stressful, not because of him but because I was terrified of screwing up. And—to be frank—Gene initially wasn't helpful in putting me at ease. I can't blame him, since he had no idea if my plan was to write a serious, respectful piece about him or skewer him to make my bones by taking down a legend. He showed a lot of courage when he agreed to the leap of faith I proposed. Still, he tested me for at least half an hour before he trusted me. Those thirty minutes were beyond grueling. The voice in my head kept up a constant chant of *Why don't you just quit, Tom? Why don't you just quit, Tom? Why don't you just quit, Tom?*

I spent two weeks transcribing the interview and then another week writing the article. The entire time, I had to fight off the conviction that I'd utterly botched it and come up empty. Then, during the long waiting period between submission and publication, all I could think of was what I should've asked, should've said, and should've written.

This was my most important interview to date. I knew that a lot rode on it. As soon as I saw the layout of the July 1996 issue of *Bass Player,* the nightmares stopped.

* * *

JANUARY 29, 1996

It was a small, brightly lit house or inn decorated in a style that combined western and Japanese influences. Each room had its own shoji sliding door and low bed. There were sunken dining or visiting areas surrounded by light wooden railings, everything plush, clean, and inviting.

I was in bed with Carmen. My unease—almost revulsion—was familiar, but I'd never associated it with her. For years I'd thought only of our time together. Though I'd wanted so badly to feel her skin against mine again, I now knew that this was a catastrophically bad decision. Taking it any further would destroy me. As much as I missed her, she was poison.

She lay next to or underneath me, staring vacantly at the ceiling. Even without being able to see her features clearly, I knew her expression was blank and absolutely unresponsive. In her right hand, she held a small container full of a whitish, puddinglike substance made of human breast milk. She tried to force it on me in a gentle yet relentless, implacable way. I kept turning my head away as she tipped the container toward my lips; her actions made me re-experience all the despair, sadness, rage, and loneliness of the final year with her. I knew that if I stayed in bed with her, it would result in something awful, but I wanted so badly to be back with her that I ignored the alarm bells ringing in my head.

Carmen was naked, her long white legs spread and her thick mound of pubic hair scratching against my lower body. I felt luxurious nostalgia tinged with the squeamishness all other women except for her had engendered in me. Suddenly, she managed to get a mouthful of the breast-milk pudding past my lips. It was ghastly, a sweet, salty, intimate flavor, what I imagined it would be like to lick the inside of a person's chest cavity. She'd made me eat the pudding totally against my will, not caring a bit about my sensibilities. It filled me with such sorrow that I scrambled out of the warm, cloying bedclothes to get away from her. I spit out the pudding, and it slopped down the front of my shirt.

The gamey taste in my mouth made me drool in a steady flow like a faucet. Unable to speak, I stared at Carmen peering at the ceiling in complete indifference. Beside me, Stuart—the drummer from my band in Tokyo—appeared. As he looked from me to Carmen and back again, he winced as though embarrassed. I pushed past him and went out into the hallway, overcome with anger at myself for returning right back to where I was two years earlier.

I went down into one of the sunken living or dining areas and saw a shoji slide open. Stuart sat up in the low bed next to the doorway, his sheets and blankets tangled around him.

He stretched and stood. "All that effort for nothing," he said.

It was a lie. He wanted me to think he meant his attempts to fall asleep, which had come to nothing because it was dawn, but I knew he was talking about something else. It was a bizarre show put on for my benefit, an attempt to fool me. I rejected it completely, even though I knew he just wanted to spare me pain.

FEBRUARY 14, 1996

When I decided to return to Japan to find Carmen, everyone told me that I'd be making the biggest mistake of my life. I knew it too, but I went ahead and threw away everything for which I'd worked so hard: my embryonic writing career, my understanding of my dysfunctions, the progress I'd made in addressing them, and the changes I'd brought about in my relationships with my parents and siblings. They'd all go down the drain. Though flat broke, I spent three thousand dollars on a round-trip, first-class airline ticket. I had to find Carmen and patch things up, even though I knew I'd fail, and the attempt would end in disaster.

Then I was in Tokyo, standing on a street corner waiting for Carmen to pick me up. I had no luggage and my pants were far too long. They completely covered my shoes and dragged ridiculously, the cuffs already trod into rags. I had no memory of the flight or getting from the airport to the corner where I stood. As I waited I was flooded with anxiety because Carmen had a new life now. I'd have to turn right around and head for home, but the thought of facing my disapproving family—having wasted three thousand dollars on an airline ticket—kept me from leaving.

Tim's car pulled up with Carmen at the wheel. She leaned over and opened the passenger door, avoiding looking directly at me. Her smug smile confirmed it: I was an absolute joke. Since I knew she performed for an unseen audience that watched us raptly, I tried to brazen it out. We drove back to her house in silence as Carmen changed to a fat, blonde woman. She was married to a doctor and had two children.

When we arrived at her house, she took me inside and pointed to a wicker dog bed in the corner of the living room.

"That's where you'll be staying," she said.

I was numb. It was obvious that she did this only to torture me. Now I had to decide which was worse: the humiliation of returning to California after less than a day in Japan, or the humiliation of sleeping in a dog bed in Carmen's house. I went out the front door to go back to the airport and catch the next flight.

Once I'd left her home, I realized that I'd miss her too much. The only solution was for me to live in her tiny front yard, where I had a curtained shower installed. I showered constantly, for days at a time, while Carmen and her family came and went. In between showers, I just sat on the ground, doing nothing.

After one shower I knocked on the front door and whipped off the towel. My physique was disgusting. I was diamond shaped, with a huge spare tire and mammoth, wobbly buttocks. Carmen opened the door, twirling, her arms out and her violet bathrobe and blonde hair flared into wide cones. She looked like some kind of crackpot flying machine from the Industrial Revolution. The house was full of men, her suitors. I went inside and she spun by, ignoring me, her face locked in a rigid smile. Naked and absurd, I stood in the foyer until a man noticed me.

"At least now you know what she's all about," he said. "Why don't you put on your clothes?"

"She's only doing what I'd do in the same situation," I replied. "And I'm fine the way I am, thank you very much."

I tried to wither him with my austere, uncaring dignity, but he broke into jolly sputters as he backed away. Standing there with my hands at my sides, I felt worse than I ever had about myself.

FEBRUARY 28, 1996

My father decided that the entire family would commit suicide. We were at a motel in a foreign country, probably Germany. Both Dad and Mom were very young again, in their early thirties. I couldn't see my siblings, but I felt their presences in the enormous rooms, which were decorated in a grotesquely gaudy style, with crystal chandeliers, vases, faux Greek statues, and red-velvet furniture.

The plan was that we'd asphyxiate ourselves in the green-tiled bathroom using my airbrush compressor, which I'd converted to a gasoline-powered donkey engine. It spewed thick, blue smoke. Dad took the compressor into the bathroom and started it.

"When I'm dead," he told us, "it's the next person's turn." He closed the door.

I wandered around the suites, impatient and nervous as I waited to die. Though I knew that what we were doing was absolutely obscene and deranged, I wanted to get on with it. Every few minutes I checked on my father. I'd open the bathroom door and look at the cloud of blue smoke. My father would be seated on the floor against the wall, his legs drawn up and his forearms resting on his knees, or he'd be pacing back and forth, his hands behind his back.

"Not yet," he'd snarl. "I'm not dead yet."

After several visits to the bathroom, I suddenly got suspicious. I went to the master bedroom where my brother Pat had shot himself and lay under the covers crosswise on one of the beds. When I pulled back the bedspread, he had a big smile on his face.

He opened his eyes. "I didn't really do it!" he said.

The pistol he was supposed to have used was in its holster on the nightstand. I pulled out the gun and sniffed it, determining that it hadn't been fired. This made me very angry. I ran back to the bathroom, where my mother crouched like a Bedouin beside the door. Her expression was familiar, a mixture of defiance, indifference, contempt, fear, and playacting. I recognized it immediately as the mask Carmen always wore when we fought during our last year together.

It was clear that Mom had no intention of gassing herself, and then I realized that nobody else did either. They were all part of an elaborate hoax designed to make my father kill himself. I was shocked, horrified, and completely disinterested. Opening the bathroom door, I marched into the thick, choking blue clouds to find my father. When I became dizzy and faint, I knew I was about to die. I didn't care.

Then I was outside, next to a concrete-lined ditch or trough set into the ground. A small crowd surrounded me, babbling in a foreign language and urging me to do something. I rolled up the left sleeve of my sweater in preparation for dipping my arm into the trough, which was full of mineral spirits or thinner. My goal was to try and find a switch, faucet handle, or valve set into the side of the trough. The liquid was dark and gave off a powerful solvent stink. I didn't want to put my arm into it but knew that others had tried before me and failed; I'd show them how to do it the right way, even though I didn't really know what I was supposed to do.

Kneeling next to the trough, I bent over and put my head on the grass. I slowly dipped my arm into the thinner, making sure to keep my sweater sleeve dry. As I felt around on the slimy sides and bottom of the trough, I muttered a stream-of-consciousness torrent of meaningless words.

"When I was in Japan those apples were really something else for chopping up albums on the tables left behind when the forest whackers who never really understood what it was like to sleep with Carmen over the moon and far away but without processed foreign matter couldn't have shipped axles because it wouldn't have been anywhere near the salary I was paid for simply washing cots from local hostels that didn't excite the mobile resources of slow-moving restaurateurs on the beachcombers' flattened locale—"

Suddenly, I pulled out a cheap plastic bowling ball, a battered, hollow sphere with several sets of finger holes in it. I held it up.

"*See? See?*" I shouted and roared with laughter. "*Get it?*" I was utterly clueless about what I meant.

There was no response from the faceless, shapeless forms around me. I'd made an utter ass of myself. Though I knew that my demented performance had been absolutely incomprehensible, I was still enraged that nobody laughed, applauded, or did anything to lessen my embarrassment. I dropped the ball and put my arm back into the liquid.

Once I'd completely searched the trough dozens of times, I got up and let one of my brothers take over. I couldn't tell which brother it was, either Pat or Paul. Swinging my arm to dry it off, I joined the onlookers and started up another raving monologue.

"Luckily the fish police absented themselves to Carmen's able-bodied masterpiece off the edges of the carpet factory in the right-handed whale notion that we'd last seen capturing energy waves blasted forward once the total price of those wandering minstrel sock artists had amply encapsulated each of the warrants proffered in positron accolades that we'd easily run into before the rain came and placed all of us on extended mattress colonies due to the crisis-management team not fully expecting safeguards and flotilla crews to completely overextend their—"

"We found your watch!" my unidentified brother called.

I went over and saw that the watch he held up looked just like mine, which was still on my wrist. This was the watch that I'd dropped into the trough nine years ago. It was still running; looking at it I felt incredible guilt, pain, and loss over my childhood, my young adulthood, my current life—everything. The sum total of my experience was just one pathetic missed opportunity. I longed for Carmen, for all the friends I'd once had, for whatever peace and security I'd ever been able to garner.

It was imperative that I deny the watch was mine. When I tried to explain to my brother and the staring crowd—whose faces I could now see clearly—that the watch had nothing to do with me, I couldn't speak. All that came out of my mouth was repulsive, high-speed bursts of stuttering, like machine-gun fire.

Ah-guh-guh-gug. Dih-geh-geg. Uh-guh-guh-gih-guh-gek. Dee-goo-goo-geg.

My brother held the watch toward me and shook his head.

"Oh, it's yours, all right," he said. "It's yours."

MARCH 1, 1996

The orphanage seemed to be constructed entirely of tile and chrome rails for handicapped people. Like a public swimming pool, it smelled of chlorine and echoed with children's shouts.

I was small again; where I lived, malignant older boys or adults pursued me. The chase was a ritual that always ended the same way, in my capture. I could never see my pursuers clearly. Their rounded, shorn heads were faceless and menacing as they stooped over me. When I was in their grip, they caused me incredible pain. I tried everything: holding myself completely still, squirming, flailing my legs, raising myself up as high as I could like a star perched on the top of a Christmas tree. Nothing eased the stabs of agony that shot deep into my bowels. Although the pain was excruciating—severe enough to drive me insane if it continued unabated—it was also familiar. I'd experienced it many, many times. The only thing I could do was grit my teeth and wait for the pursuers to finish and leave, as they always did.

This time the pursuers crammed mud, pieces of metal, and other rubbish up inside me. When they let me go, I had trouble walking. Bits of foreign matter dropped out of me, but it didn't relieve the packed-full, distended sensation. Now that the painful part of the ritual was over, the other little boys and I were led into an office where two naked young women sat on a large desk. They leaned back with their spread legs lifted into the air, supporting themselves on their elbows and smiling seductively. Their expressions promised naughty fun, not pain.

Their vaginas began to clap, the pink-and-vermilion flesh glistening. The orphanage staff switched on music—a funky, bass-heavy tune—and the women closed their eyes in ecstasy, synching their genitals to the beat. We were told that to clean ourselves out, we had to become aroused. That would override what had been done to us. I realized that as perverted as the situation was, I had no other hope, so I let it happen. Slowly, the debris packed inside me fell out. The relief was indescribable, like being freed from a dungeon.

More naked women joined us, along with sweaty, thuggish-looking, corpulent young men. Pumping their fists, the men did a mocking parody of black booty dancing. One of them—a horrible, beefy, shirtless moron with bulging eyes—suddenly developed his own flapping vagina that grew and grew, traveling up his torso as if he were being split in half. It sickened and terrified me. This was much worse than the women's crazed, animalistic display.

A black man dressed in a sheik's robes flew through the air behind another thug, entered the back of his skull, and exploded from his mouth. The lout's head turned inside out. It became a pink-and-purple nozzle covered with teeth, white ligaments, and yellow-gray brain tissue like gobbets of Brie, the long tongue hanging. Then the head snapped back into its correct shape. The sheik dropped to the floor in a victorious stance, his fists on his hips and his chest thrown out. Everyone cheered and high fived each other, a response that made me feel utterly alone and doomed. I'd never seen such evil and corruption.

Then I was an adult again, driving my car down a busy Los Angeles street as wide as Santa Monica Boulevard. To my left, two cars were involved in an altercation. One was a dark red, anonymous sedan of the type favored by TV detectives in the seventies. The other was a squat hot rod, converted from a forties' passenger car. It was also dark red, with a folded-down convertible top, an exposed engine, chrome exhaust pipes, wide tires, and chrome Guide headlights. The driver had a heavy, raggedy blond mustache and wore a bandana on his head, mirrored sunglasses, and a sleeveless chambray work shirt. His passengers—two men and a wild-haired woman—were also dressed like bikers.

The two cars weaved in and out of traffic. As they arrived at the intersection, the sedan sped into a left-turn lane bordered by a cement island. The driver of the hot rod slammed on his brakes and backed up until he was about two yards in front of the sedan, which was blocked in by cars ahead and behind. Standing in his seat, the hot rod driver produced a large automatic pistol and fired into the sedan windshield, his shoulders and forearms bouncing with the recoil of each shot. He looked as though he were doing some menial chore, his mind on something else. The three hot rod passengers covered their ears, their expressions a mixture of excitement and resigned embarrassment. They seemed to expect this kind of behavior from their driver.

I realized that this was actually happening, that I was actually seeing a person being murdered right in front of me. The hot rod driver finished shooting into the sedan, threw his car into gear, and took off, the tires screeching. I followed to get the license plate number. The hot rod shimmied all over the road, the passengers laughing. I felt such rage that I wished them all dead.

At that exact moment, the hot rod became airborne, the front end shooting straight up at an angle of ninety degrees. I'd seen the same thing happen to Formula racing cars. It stood vertically for a moment and then fell backward and landed on the passenger compartment at seventy or eighty miles per hour. There was no roll bar, so the passengers were ground down to chest level as if by a giant power sander. The top of the woman's head detached and slid like a hockey puck behind the car, the long tresses of hair trailing. After scraping down the street for several hundred feet, the hot rod mounted the curb and crashed into a thrift store where several nonchalant black people stood around. None of them reacted.

The four occupants of the hot rod were now just a tangle of viscera, blood, and shredded clothing.

I punched the air. *"All right!"* I screamed. *"There* is *a God after all!"*

Singing Duran Duran's "Girls on Film," I drove over a few hills and saw that every store I passed was being looted. The pleasure I took in the violent deaths of the hot-rodders turned to shame. I was no different than the looters. We were noxious fiends, human detritus. Then the stores were gone, leaving a gravel road with slag heaps on both sides. Not sure why I did it, I made a U-turn in the deserted road and drove back to the scene of the accident.

By the time I arrived, the bodies had been removed, and the car was on the back of a flatbed truck that had also been converted into a hot rod. The truck driver secured the crashed car with straps, whistling cheerfully as he worked. He had a big, blond mustache and mirrored sunglasses. I knew he was a friend or relative of the dead hot rod driver; his casual attitude filled me with despair because such people were capable of anything. They were too dangerous to engage on any level, but my life was full of them.

My mother's car was parked half a block up from the flatbed truck. She sat in the driver's seat, doing something that I couldn't make out. I stopped, got out, and knocked on the front passenger window. Mom smiled, so I opened the door and hopped in beside her. When I told her about the events I'd just witnessed, she stared at me blankly, not responding.

"Why won't you listen to me?" I asked. "Don't you understand that I just saw someone being murdered, and then four people were killed, and I'm just as bad as they are?"

Nothing. She didn't even blink.

The flatbed hot-rod truck pulled up next to us, and the driver get out, so I locked my mother's doors and waited for whatever would happen to us.

MARCH 16, 1996

My family and I were in a refugee camp in Iraq, Somalia, or some other desert hellhole. It was also the muddy, red highlands of Vietnam or Cambodia. I lay under a sunshade that consisted of a large tarpaulin held up at its four corners by long poles, forming a tent without walls. Though I experienced everything from a first-person viewpoint, I also saw myself from a distance, being simultaneously actor and audience. The audience-me noted that I was vaguely Asian in appearance, extremely thin, chinless, and had black hair and no teeth.

The people I thought of as my family were strangers of no specific ethnicity, generic archetypes of hopelessness and poverty. We were all confused, afraid, and apathetic, certain that we should leave but unable to muster the energy. Suddenly, I realized that the enemy had descended without us noticing, and we were all about to die in unspeakably horrible ways. The audience-me was detached, clinically aware of gruesome atrocity stories from the Middle East, Southeast Asia, and Latin America, while the participant-me was petrified, swooning at the prospect of experiencing it first hand. My fear was divided into utter panic and a murky, muted anxiety, a sort of dopy nervousness. The refugee-me knew that the other me had read of this and seen it on TV. I deeply resented the safety of the audience-me, the white American man. His life was as real and accessible as my memories of being a Third Worlder.

Even though we were all doomed, I still couldn't rouse myself into action. The enemies were tall, muscular men in black T-shirts, ski masks, and camouflaged pants. They were armed with automatic rifles, grenades, and machetes. Some walked, some rode motorbikes, and some carried cans of red enamel spray paint to daub political slogans on our dead bodies. They smiled under their masks, nodding and chuckling to each other as they unslung their weapons. Many swung clustered, cylindrical hand grenades, tied together and fused to explode in concert. Either Irish terrorists or South American irregulars, they were proficient at slaughtering unarmed civilians like us.

They spread out among the laconic, aimless refugees, who still took no notice of them. I snapped out of my trance and was electrified with terror and anguish. It was actually happening. When they killed me, it would hurt, and there was no escape. My sister held my sixteen-month-old nephew Hunter, and as I contemplated what he'd endure at the hands of these monsters, I began crying helplessly.

In front of me, one of the hooded motorcyclists hurled a smoking, fizzing cluster of grenades into the tent of a family we knew. The tent was partially flooded by a small stream; it exploded in a shower of green water and torn, bloody flesh that rained down on me. Men screamed but women covered their mouths with their hands, shushing the men and warning them to make no noise because that would just drive the terrorists to higher levels of savagery. This was a ritual, both parties vastly experienced in it. The refugees would die passively in the hopes that they'd be granted a swift and relatively merciful death.

"Oh shit! Oh shit!" I wailed over and over as the terrorists hacked, shot, and blew up everything in their path. It was only a matter of time before they turned their attention to us. I stood there crying and screaming and saw a cluster of grenades land in a puddle outside the tent. A thin refugee jumped on top of it, as though he were about to do pushups. When the grenades detonated, he was blown in half.

I wondered why I hadn't thought of that. It was fast and total, and he obviously didn't suffer. I looked around for the next bundle of grenades to lie down on, as the terrorists closed in from all directions.

MARCH 24, 1996

I didn't recognize the room. As I lay in bed, I dreamed that I lay on my stomach under the trunk of a car, trying to coax a black-and-white cat over to me. The cat crouched beneath the engine. I kept leaving and returning over a period of several days, though I couldn't remember what I did during the time I was away. It seemed to be a symbolic, representational absence, as though I were reading a book or being told a story. When I was offstage, what happened didn't matter.

In the dream I eventually gained the cat's trust, and it slowly crawled over to me. I felt very protective toward it. It was a really beautiful cat, big and healthy looking, with bright, wary eyes and an appealingly diffident manner. I wanted very much to stroke its fur.

As the cat approached, someone firmly grasped me by the ankles, preparing to drag me out from under the car. Another person stood by, ready to do me terrible harm. I couldn't see them, but I knew that they were both older men. They were blank and robotic; what they'd do to me would lack any emotional component whatsoever. Though I knew they'd hurt me badly, I concentrated on the cat. It was necessary for me to save it, to show it that there was someone in the world who'd never mistreat it.

The cat finally reached me and flopped down on its stomach, allowing me to stroke its back. I felt intensely grateful toward it. As soon as I made peace with the cat, the person holding my ankles pulled me out from under the car. He tucked my legs into his armpits, clamping them between his biceps and the sides of his chest and shifting his hands to grip me around my knees. His body was soft and revoltingly warm. The other man began probing me. The stabs of severe pain I felt deep inside me were familiar, but I experienced none of the fear and helplessness that had always accompanied these assaults. For some reason I felt much stronger and more able to defend myself.

"*No!*" I shouted. "*That's enough!*"

As soon as I spoke, I woke up in the unfamiliar bedroom, realizing that I'd made things much worse for myself. A hulking black mass crouched over me, radiating a strange, impersonal hostility. It was totally indifferent yet driven to inflict pain on me. A purveyor of misery and doom, the presence was as removed as a stone carving.

I knew that this time would be the worst ever. With no escape, I tried to hide in the bedclothes.

APRIL 7, 1996

I was part of a large crowd inside an auditorium painted light blue and full of metal railings and rows of padded seats. My sister Carrie was there with her baby son Hunter. Some of my other siblings were also present, but I couldn't see their faces.

Some sort of crisis had made everyone rush for the exits. People were tightly packed in the aisles, immobile. Ahead of me someone carried Hunter so that he could see back over the person's shoulder. He screamed and held out his arms toward me, so I shoved through the crush of bodies to reach him.

When I got to him, I was utterly shocked to hear myself say, "Sorry. You're on your own. Good luck!" Then I turned away.

Filled with grief and self-hatred, I pushed my way through the masses and emerged from the auditorium, at a loss for why I'd done such a terrible thing to Hunter. Beneath an overcast sky, the ground was muddy and bare, with large puddles of stagnant water everywhere and the deeply rutted tracks of wagon wheels. An Airedale terrier ran around in front of me, barking joyously. It had a stubby, wagging tail and a square head, its eyes partially obscured by hanging locks of fur. The dog sprinted ahead and disappeared, to my great relief. Its presence was so painful it nearly made me cry.

After walking for a very long time, wondering where I was going, I came across the Airedale lying on its side in the mud. Its head submerged in a murky, green puddle, it breathed in the water. The surface of the puddle was roiled with bubbles and foam. I stopped and watched, overwhelmed by a sense of unendurable tragedy.

The dog lifted its head out of the puddle and looked around. Blinking slowly, it seemed confused and lost. After a few seconds, it lowered its head into the puddle and sent up bubbles again, as if it wore an aqualung.

It saddened me almost to the point of insanity because I knew that what I saw was depraved, a mockery of nature.

APRIL 13, 1996

As I looked for the party, a crowd of strangers swirled around me in the dark, not letting me see their faces. I was deeply uneasy in their company. We walked the snowy streets of the unknown city, the night not cold but close and suffocating instead, as though we were in the tropics. The houses were Swedish Modern, with steeply angled gables and bland concrete balconies on the second floors. Some of them were on such steep hills that the driveways looked like cement slides or chutes.

Flea—bassist of the Red Hot Chili Peppers—was part of the crowd. Sometimes he was nude and at other times he was dressed in a buffalo skin and a multicolored, wooden Native American ceremonial mask with feathers, pop eyes, white lips, and straw for hair. I found him horribly unsettling and powerfully erotic. Though I knew I wasn't gay, I wanted to have sex with him. This disturbed me because he cavorted as if he were completely out of his gourd, screeching, dancing, and spinning like a dervish. In one of his nude moments, he flopped down on his belly in a ridiculously steep driveway, his arms stretched out in front of him like those of a high diver.

"Don't you want to get up and stop messing around?" I asked.

He looked at me and shook his head.

"No. No I *don't!*" he said with such petulant, childish emphasis that I turned and left him lying there. I wanted desperately to get to the party.

After I'd walked a few yards, Flea appeared beside me in his wooden mask. He slipped his arm around my waist and cuddled his head into the space between my neck and shoulder, cooing and giggling. I was extremely embarrassed but aroused again.

When we caught up to the rest of the crowd outside of a brightly lit club, I didn't know how to explain to them my relationship with Flea, since I myself didn't understand it. The outside of the club was painted peach above shoulder height and a bright, vivid light blue below. It was a beautiful combination. The building had no windows, and a bouncer manned the roped-off single entrance.

Suddenly, I realized that I was about to attend a theme party to honor the Tate-LaBianca murders. Some people were dressed like Charles Manson or his followers, some like Sharon Tate, and some like generic sixties freaks. I wanted nothing to do with them or their party. It was an obscenity.

I found the man whose idea it was to throw the party. "Nope. Nothing doing," I said. "I'm outta here. 'Bye."

Even though I was genuinely angry, I didn't know why I spoke in such a contrived way. I reached out to the party planner, intending to give him a firm, dismissive, insulting handshake, the equivalent of a "How dare you, sir!" glove-slap.

The planner looked like a thin David Crosby, with a heavy, blond mustache and frizzy hair. He hesitated and then grabbed my hand with both of his.

"Why, man?" he asked, flabbergasted and deeply hurt.

"*Because I knew some of the people who were there,*" I roared, "*and it would be an insult to their memory to attend something like this!*"

I meant the victims of the Oklahoma City bombing, not the Tate-LaBianca murders. In both cases I was a liar. My histrionics were a cynical attempt to draw attention to myself. It was inexplicable that I'd exploit such atrocities for self-aggrandizement. Why did I warp my justifiable fury over terrorism and mass murder into a sleazy performance concocted to garner the admiration of people I despised? The fact that there was no answer filled me with shame.

Knowing that I'd made no sense, I left. My car was parked two blocks away, but I walked past it as though I didn't see it. I wondered why. Maybe I wanted to find a restaurant. It was very dark now, and I realized that three young Asian men followed me on the sidewalk. One ate a sticky bun, and the other two spoke to each other in thickly accented English. The bun eater came up close behind me, and the other two fanned out on either side, laughing and blathering. I thought they might be gangbangers up to no good, so I stepped into the street to let them pass. They smoothly moved with me, as though the four of us were a school of fish.

They were about to rob and kill me. When I saw that one held a knife, I felt swooning horror and despair. It was entirely real, not a dream. I was about to be murdered. With no hope, I spun and kicked at the man directly behind me. He jumped back, and the one with the knife lunged at me. I grabbed his wrist and twisted the knife out of his hand. Now *I* was the one with a weapon; the three gangbangers were at my mercy. I slashed at them, and they ran, piling into a car parked down the street.

Stunned at how I'd turned the tables on my assailants, I hurried into a nearby greengrocer's. A young Asian man in a white apron approached.

"Excuse me," he said, "but that's my brother's switchblade. You have to give it back."

When he tried to take it from me, we struggled violently, our hands inter-twined. The car with the other three Asian men was now outside the store, so I jerked the knife away from the greengrocer and turned to face the street. The car peeled off.

I looked down at the knife. "This isn't a switchblade," I said. "It's a buck knife!"

Then I went back out onto the increasingly snowy, increasingly dark streets, looking for my car. I knew it was in the opposite direction, but I couldn't figure out how to turn around. My brain seemed to not work anymore.

I saw several Norwegian-style electric buses with the cable attachments on the roofs, and I thought I should probably board one so I could go back and look for my car. After walking for what seemed like hours, I understood that I was totally lost and would never find my car. The thought panicked me.

As I rounded the next corner, another band of Asian males appeared, this time seven or eight adolescents and small children. I knew that these were even more savage than the ones I'd escaped. As I tried to run, I found that I could move only at a strolling pace. The children sang and spoke loudly in Chinese; one flitted in front of me to cut me off. He was trained to get between my feet, tangling them together so I'd fall. I felt a flash of admiration for their complete ruthlessness and professionalism, even though I knew that this time I really would die. My life would end horribly in seconds.

As the child zoomed toward me, I held up my buck knife, but I was too slow. I could barely move now, and my hand felt weak and flabby. The child pulled out his own knife, and I knew that he'd cut me using a special technique designed to cause the maximum amount of damage with the fewest strokes. It would produce a lattice of slashes in my flesh, a series of marks resembling a tic-tac-toe game. I was doomed.

The child sang a hip-hop tune in Chinese, making popping and scratching sounds like a DJ. He sliced my right forearm, the blade cutting so deeply into my flesh that it hit the bone. It was indescribably unpleasant, though not exactly painful, an amazingly intimate, internal sensation. The blade moved as fast as the needle of an electric sewing machine. Each time it bit into my arm, another tendon or ligament was severed, until my fingers lost all strength and straightened out uselessly. Then he started on my left arm. He'd slice up my entire body, and I'd be unable to stop him or run away.

CHAPTER NINE
(NOT SO) RANDOM WEIRDNESS

These are dreams that weren't nightmares, exactly, but they also weren't very enjoyable. I gave them their own chapter rather than include them in the clusters. None involve bloodshed or overt predation. Some of the symbolism is obvious, and some is meaningful only to me. I understand all of these dreams.

A couple of notes: On December 28, 1995, Tim and I were almost murdered by a gunman at our bookstore. I dreaded going to sleep that night, because I was sure I'd have the mother of all nightmares. To some people what I dreamed about *is* the mother of all nightmares. Skip to December 28 if you want to see for yourself.

Secondly, I reconnected with Carmen in early 2010 when I joined Facebook under a pseudonym. We'd had no contact for eight years. It seemed pointless for me to continue avoiding her. The pain of losing her hadn't abated in the slightest, and I'd lost just about everything else I'd ever loved. Our time together now seemed to have been nothing more than a supernatural dream, as Stephen Crane put it.[3] Though we e-mailed each other for a while, I ended our correspondence after I sent her a link to a video. It was Art of Noise

---

3 "Intrigue," Verse VIII. See Thomas Wictor, *Ghosts and Ballyhoo: Memoirs of a Failed L.A. Music Journalist* (Atglen, Pennsylvania: Schiffer, 2013), page 209.

playing "Close to the Edit" live during the Concert for the Prince's Trust at Wembley Arena in London, 2004.

"Close to the Edit" had been Carmen's favorite song. She introduced me to it, and it became my favorite song too. We tried to play the diabolically difficult bass line ourselves but figured that no human could ever master it, since Art of Noise had used a sequencer. Well, Trevor Horn did it magnificently on an electric bass, so I sent the link to Carmen, thinking she'd flip.

Instead, she wrote back that she didn't even remember the song.

I simply could not accept what I read in her E-mail; we'd tried to play "Close to the Edit" on our basses countless times. We'd talked about the disturbing video with the little punk girl making her chopping motions, directing the men to destroy the musical instruments. After much rumination I decided that saying she didn't remember the song was Carmen's diplomatic way of telling me that I'd crossed a line by reminding her of our life together. It broke my heart all over again, but I did what I thought she wanted and stopped writing.

That's the backstory to the last dream in this chapter.

*   *   *

JULY 6, 1986

I carried a tennis racket and wore gray tennis shorts as I walked through a high school cafeteria. Gleaming chrome was everywhere, and the harsh fluorescent lighting made the students appear older than they were. All were between sixteen and eighteen. I was the tennis coach, a sham because I didn't know how to play. My wooden racket was a mendacious prop.

The cafeteria was filled with round, high-standing cocktail tables; the students ate and drank on their feet. As I passed a group of kids, a very tall girl gave me a blatant once-over. She resembled a more attractive Chris Everett-Lloyd and was dressed in trendy, brightly colored sweats. Her long body was slim and angular, with narrow, boyish hips, wide shoulders, and small breasts high on her chest. Unnerved, I didn't look directly at her, but I sensed that her smile was relaxed and self-assured.

I told myself I had an appointment, which was a lie. There was no reason for me to be in the school. Then the tall girl cut in front of me and flounced along, swinging her round bottom in an aggressive, attention-getting arc. Embarrassed, I stopped. The girl glanced over her shoulder and came back. She looked rapacious, like a thirty-year-old businesswoman on the prowl.

"Hey!" she said, standing face to face with me, no more than six inches away. "We're exactly the same height!" Her voice was deep and musical. I felt myself blush.

"Yeah," I said, "and you're exactly half my age." That wasn't true; I was twenty-four.

I walked around her and headed toward the lower dining hall. She followed, joined by a silent friend with short hair and heavy makeup slathered over her small, young-old face.

"Nice shorts!" the tall girl said from behind and caressed my buttocks.

I turned and grabbed her wrist. Her expression was so funny—a kind of teasing mock horror—that I laughed even though I was mortified.

"Stop that!" I ordered, but she just smiled.

When I moved off, she followed, not speaking but stroking my hips and trying to force her hand down the front of my zippered shorts.

"Cut it out! Stop it! Knock it off!" I yelled, in shock yet immensely excited. I wanted to punch her for violating me and making me like it. Instead of pummeling her, I shoved her away and hurried down the stairs toward the lower dining hall.

"Dangerous," I muttered.

"I'll bet you *are*," another attractive girl-woman coming up the stairs said with an arch look. It was so disconcerting that I nearly broke into a run.

I hurried into a circular service area where students took their trays of food into a dining area. Unlike the cafeteria upstairs, this one looked like a military mess hall, with long tables that had benches attached. The tall girl snuggled up tightly against my back. She wormed her hand past my belt into my shorts, cupped my genitals, and gave me a playful squeeze.

"Coming through!" she called. "Coming through with valuable cargo!"

All those fresh-faced striplings turned and looked, and I felt old, depraved, despicable, and humiliated, even though I was also aroused almost to the point of detonation. I pulled the girl's hand out of my shorts and whirled to face her.

"Look!" I shouted. "I don't even know you! Will you just leave me alone?"

She pursed her lips and blew me a kiss, laughing at me.

I laughed too, in frustrated amazement and to keep from losing my mind. The tall girl's heavily made-up friend appeared; when the two fell into conversation, I stepped behind a nearby counter and crouched to eavesdrop, wanting to know what this was really all about. No one had ever come on to me so aggressively. I didn't believe for a second that she was sincere, but if she was, I had to decide whether or not to respond. If I *did* let her seduce me, I was without question a pervert.

As I peeked out from behind the counter, I saw the tall girl shake her head.

"No, Mary," she said. "It's not what you think."

That convinced me that someone had put her up to it. Her interest in me wasn't real.

Older people who may have been teachers walked by and smiled down at me. I realized how creepy I looked squatting there, so I stood. My friend Burt sat at a table by herself, smoking and reading a book on her lap. There was a plate with the remains of a meal in front of her. I flopped down across from her, and she looked up, startled.

"Hey, Burt!" I shouted. "There's some girl after me! It's like she wants to rape me!"

Burt cocked her head. "I told her all about you, Tom. I thought I'd do you a favor because you're having so many problems."

I was aghast and flattered. "Jesus, Burt! That's exactly what I *don't* need! She's too young. Tell her I'm married."

"She knows," Burt said, smiling. "She doesn't care."

"Okay. Then I'll tell her myself." I wasn't married, as Burt knew. We both lied to each other about my marital status. That upset me greatly.

I got up and walked around the dining room, all the high schoolers watching me carefully and looking away when I made eye contact. The tall girl sat alone next to a window. She'd changed into a knee-length purple dress with shoulder pads. It made her even more attractive. Though I felt extremely awkward and dirty, I approached her.

"Hi," I said.

She looked at me coldly.

"What's up?" I asked. Now she seemed to hate me.

"I just lost my job because of you," she snapped. "You'd better be damn grateful that I set you up with a sure thing: Me!"

She smiled gloriously, all her hostility gone. I felt a rush of love, and I knew that I was about to make the worst decision of my life.

SEPTEMBER 2, 1993

It was night in California. I stood in Tim's back garden, scanning the sky. Dozens of strangers surrounded me; others perched on nearby car roofs or houses. I didn't see any of my family except for my brother Eric. The crowd murmured expectantly as we waited for an event that had been foretold. I didn't know what, but I was excited and apprehensive.

The night sky was incredibly clear, with more stars visible than I'd ever seen. It seemed that the stars glowed much more brightly than usual. Something of profound importance was about to happen.

"There it goes!" a man shouted.

All the stars in the sky began moving toward a central point directly over Tim's house. They slowly coalesced into a bright blob that resolved into a triangle, the three corners blunted and the center an empty space. It looked as if it were made of thick neon tubing millions of miles long. I felt incredible exhilaration and panic, knowing that everything would now change. The world would be so different that it would bear no relation to how it was before this happened.

The giant shape in the sky became more defined and then slowly began to rotate counterclockwise. Every star visible had merged into the triangle, which now spun with such speed that it appeared to be a brilliantly lit circle. The crowds cheered wildly, and though I was amazed and breathless with awe, I couldn't shake a feeling of terrible foreboding.

Then it was the next day, and the entire earth's population was involved in a test designed to see who the previous night's events had affected. Lines of people went into public buildings everywhere. We'd prepared for this, hugely intricate logistics having been devised to quiz all of humanity on the same day. There was a terrible sense of urgency, as if we had only a short time to do this before something happened. Suddenly, I realized that it was a weeding-out process. I already knew that I'd be one of those not changed by the star-triangle, and I dreaded what would happen to me.

The line I joined went into a gymnasium. I made my way to a table where about twenty people sat. A harried, middle-aged woman directed me to a seat and gave me a piece of paper covered with lines of hieroglyphs—squiggles, circles, and strange lettering. The woman stood over me.

"Well?" she barked after a few seconds. "Can you read it or not?"

Failure would doom me.

"I can't," I said.

She snatched away the page and yelled, "Get out!"

As I stood, I saw Eric at another table holding his own sheet of paper. He read the writing aloud.

"Epscapella prescatolo prandabpacolo abscadala."

The *R*'s were rolled and the vowels sounded Spanish. Several administrators rushed over to listen. They were flushed and bursting with pride. Eric was nonchalant, as though he'd expected this. When he finished reading, the administrators slapped him on the back and led him out of the gym, showering him with accolades.

"Congratulations!"

"You're one of them, all right!"

"That's fantastic! Good for you!"

Glad that Eric had passed, I also envied him because I knew that he'd survive whatever purge was about to take place. In the hall outside the gym, a large window showed a brick courtyard. I went over to it and saw a crowd of children. When Eric emerged with a wide smile, they enthusiastically welcomed him. He and the children formed a circle, joined hands, and began dancing a clockwise hora, singing and shrieking with joy.

The future belonged to these new people; I was obsolete. It was outrageously unfair and cruel.

AUGUST 31, 1995

Dressed in a long, dark trench coat, I explained the value of building scale models to a class of middle schoolers. Part of the of the lesson plan required that I walk them to a nearby hobby store that was also a dwelling. It had been partially demolished; we picked our way through the debris, looking for model kits.

One section of the wooden floor had dropped down about two feet. Scattered across it were toy German soldiers that I recognized from my childhood. They were molded in hard, gray styrene and could be painted. The possibilities for conversion and use in dioramas were endless. I made sure no one was looking and then stuffed the soldiers into the pockets of my trench coat. As I did so, they transformed from Second World War Nazis to First World War storm troopers, complete with long-handled shovels, puttees, and grenade sacks. I was elated because they were extremely rare. In fact, I knew that no company manufactured them. They were unique, the only set in existence. Since I could never afford such treasures, I had to steal them.

With my pockets full, I rounded up the children and took them back to the school. I removed my trench coat and laid it over the back of a chair, suddenly uneasy at how strange the classroom was. It was like the open front of a bombed-out building, mostly empty space, the floors and tables somehow suspended in mid-air.

Stealing the plastic storm troopers made me so happy that I couldn't concentrate on my teaching duties. I just wanted the class to end so I could get to work on my dioramas.

My mother entered the classroom in a 1940s Black Dahlia-type suit with hat, veil, white gloves, and tiny ornamental handbag. She looked to be about thirty years old. Without a word she made a beeline for my trench coat and rummaged through the pockets. Since she was about to deprive me of my storm troopers, I dismissed the class and tried to rationalize my theft.

"Look," I said, "They were just lying around in a pile of junk. A real collector who knows their value should have them. They shouldn't just sit there and rot."

"Now, you know better than that," she said, completely expressionless. "I thought we were through with this kind of thing. I thought we'd decided you wouldn't do this anymore."

As she spoke, she waved a handful of soldiers at me. Then she put them into her little handbag and walked away. I followed her up a flight stairs.

"Nobody will even know," I whined. "It's all right! Really!"

She ignored me. I stopped and watched her sashay away, her hips swinging in her stylish skirt.

Now I have to hide everything from her, I thought. *Nothing's safe anymore.*

I went back down to my classroom, heartbroken because I'd never get my hands on such fine German storm troopers again.

SEPTEMBER 1, 1995

Robin Wright rode along with me in a two-door Lincoln convertible from the late seventies. She was pretty but squat and stumpy, with short limbs and no neck. I was both an observer of the scene and a participant, flying alongside the car and steering it.

I look like John Savage, I thought as I drove and watched.

It was night, and Robin kissed, hugged, and caressed me. Despite her passion, she had a distant, preoccupied look that changed to a grimace every now and then, as if she sat on a sharp object or needed to rearrange her underwear.

She took off her dress and rubbed her naked body all over me, thrusting her crotch into my thigh, climbing on me, her movements becoming increasingly frantic as her face remained impassive. Everything was wrong; she was a deviant, a complete wacko. At that moment the car shot off a cliff and exploded on the jagged rocks below.

Robin had gotten out before the car went over and now wore khaki pants and a baggy, long-sleeved shirt. A burlap sack with eyeholes cut into it covered her head. She looked like a terrorist or kidnapping victim. Feeling ruthless, I confronted her.

"I know what you're going to do," I said. "You won't get away with it."

Though I'd already been killed in the car crash, I behaved as though my death were a premonition instead of something that had already happened. Robin gulped and fidgeted under her sack, and I glowed with satisfaction at having her in my power. She was now under my control.

Then I was on the lower landing of the Tokyo Tower, a large enclosure about four hundred feet off the ground, comprised of soaring glass windows. I was with a group of people I didn't trust. They made me afraid and contemptuous, but I wanted to be one of them. As Julian Sands gave us a lecture on the tower, I glanced down and saw that I sat on a small, wooden vehicle shaped like a pillbox hat turned upside down. It had four little wheels on two steel axles.

"I'll make a bet with you," I said loudly.

Sands stopped and examined me with a kind of puzzled, condescending amusement, the way he might regard a flea circus.

"I'll bet you three thousand dollars," I said, "that you can't sit on this thing and scoot backwards toward the windows, looking up in the air, without stopping."

"Why on earth would I want to do that?" he asked, smiling and glancing around at the room. They all chuckled, and I wanted to murder the smug bastards.

"Because you'd be too *afraid* to," I sneered in a lisping, Betty Boop voice. My answer made no sense. He'd want to do it because he was too afraid? I tried to brazen it out, painfully aware that I came across as a moronic weirdo. Though I knew what I wanted them to understand, I simply couldn't explain it. I was challenging Sands to play a game of chicken with me, to test his courage and to experience the disorientation and fear one has when walking along the edge of a precipice. Scooting backward toward the windows would be scary.

To my surprise Sands agreed to the wager, so I stood and rolled the tiny car over to him. He sat down and pushed himself backwards along the floor with his feet, head tilted up toward the ceiling. His expression was rapt.

"*Whoa, whoa, whoa!*" he shouted as he got closer to the windows, and I knew that I'd won the bet.

Suddenly, I was back in the convertible with Robin Wright, speeding along the dark road at night. She was naked, rubbing herself all over me. Now she was skeletal, with swollen joints, spindly arms and legs, high cheekbones, and a razor-sharp jaw line. I was about to go over the cliff again, but I didn't care.

"Ah don't cay-yer," I drawled to her.

She silently continued her busy, flapping, standoffish exploration of me.

SEPTEMBER 13, 1995

I crept through the dimly lit corridors of a sunken submarine at the bottom of the ocean. The weak incandescent bulbs on the ceiling were encased in metal wire baskets, and the walls were painted a dingy cream. Everything looked rundown and rusty.

Opening a door, I went into a room and saw a man sitting behind a desk. He wore a dark blue naval dress uniform with three gold stripes on each sleeve. Though the part of the room where I stood was dry, the man was underwater.

He appeared to be encased in a block of transparent gelatin; the wall of water in front of me pulsated gently.

This was the sub captain. He resembled Jojo the Dog-Faced Boy, but instead of fur, he was covered in thick, green seaweed. It grew out of his scalp, forehead, cheeks, and the backs of his hands; tendrils also came out of his mouth. Slumped in his chair, he eyed me with a sly, evasive expression that made me hate him.

He spoke, but no sound came from his weed-choked mouth. The water was full of junk from his desk: in- and out-trays, glass beakers, mementos, pens, papers, notebooks, and manila folders. Everything floated and swirled like graceful, slow-motion acrobats, as though caught in faint currents.

All I could think of was escape.

DECEMBER 8, 1995

Tim and I sat side by side in a pair of folding aluminum lawn chairs in the left-turn lane of a busy intersection. We were engaged in conversation with two people across the street who sat in their own lawn chairs. The roar of the traffic was so loud that we had to shout, waving our arms and gesturing. I couldn't understand what we said, although we seemed to be giving the others instructions. Surveyor tools and equipment surrounded us.

A car entered the lane, slowly rolling closer and closer as though it were about to run us over. We yelled at the driver, a tiny, middle-aged white woman with ridiculous Harpo Marx hair and a double chin that made her look like an elephant seal. She gave us a big, blank smile. At the last second, Tim and I leaped up and pulled our chairs out of the way. As the woman coasted through the intersection, I saw that her ancient car was made of aluminum, like our chairs. When it was beside me, I gave it a violent shove with one hand. It seemed to weigh about ten pounds. Flipping onto its side, it ground around in a circle, the wheels spinning, until the engine stopped.

The woman climbed out through the front passenger window.

"Well, you stupid cunt!" I screamed. *"What do you think you're doing, eh?"*

My words sounded scripted and ridiculous. I overdid my rage to try and impress Tim. It was a silly, pointless performance that I knew would only make him embarrassed for me, but I couldn't stop.

"I just thought I'd teach you boys what it was like to have your way blocked," the woman said with a broad smile. "I thought I'd show you what it means to be inconvenienced."

"We were *not* in your way, you stupid, ugly, fat, miserable bitch," I said.

My voice was sonorous and majestically false, like that of a televangelist. A crowd had gathered, and everybody stared at me as though they couldn't believe what an imbecile I was.

The woman didn't seem bothered by my insults. Even though she was crazy and dangerous, I realized that Tim and I were to blame for what she'd done. Sitting in the left-turn lane of an intersection was incredibly dumb. Still, I felt we were justified in sitting there. We'd been irresponsible and gone too far, but we had every right to do so.

DECEMBER 28, 1995

The bustling hallway was a din of kitchenware, silverware, and shouts, some sort of preparation. G. Gordon Liddy and I sat at a table, facing each other a few feet apart. I interviewed him about Watergate, his time in prison, and his candle trick. As we spoke, he simpered, giggled, gave me coy glances, and smiled with a warmth and affection that I found deeply flattering.

I kept thinking he was the bassist Tony Levin, one of my music idols; I'd forcefully remind myself that no, he was G. Gordon Liddy, someone who represented so much that I hate. I made myself ask tougher and tougher questions.

"Why did you tell people to shoot federal agents in the head? In that article about your time in prison, weren't you embarrassed when you talked about lying awake with a club, waiting to be attacked? Don't you get sick of trying to be so macho? Isn't having a high pain threshold just a genetic luck of the draw?"

Though he spoke so softly that he was unintelligible, I found myself liking him more and more.

"Why, you're not at all the bugaboo you're made out to be in the news!" I finally blurted.

I felt a wave of love for him, despite my stinging awareness that he'd seduced me with lies and transparently phony bonhomie. Ashamed and afraid, I was also indifferent. None of it mattered. Seeing that I'd come around, he lowered his gaze to the table in a cloying display of cuteness, turning his head and batting his lashes like a young girl on her first date. He even blushed.

There was no question: I was a complete joke as a journalist, an interviewer, and a man. And yet it was decisively, categorically unimportant. Nobody would ever know or care.

MARCH 9, 1996

The office building was somewhere in the Midwest. My entire family and I were on the roof, several stories above the city. My father was in his thirties again, wearing his black horn-rims and a checkered, short-sleeved, button-up shirt. All of my siblings and I were small children. I couldn't see any of their faces, and there were a lot more of us than just the five I knew there should be.

The ancient building was abandoned. Glass-fronted refrigerated cases— the kind that hold frozen foods in supermarkets—were lined up along the edges of the tarpaper roof. The cases were empty and filthy, with smeared, filmy glass and puddles of dirty water inside.

My father pointed to the cases. "See those, kids? Remember what they used to be in Venezuela? Remember when we used to visit them?"

We walked around, examining the cases, and I felt nostalgia mixed with dread. I *did* remember them, but they were something else when we used to visit them. They were a zoo or a hobby shop back then, not refrigerated glass cases. I knew something had changed, but I couldn't figure out what. It made me sad to see how deteriorated the cases had become.

Even though I knew I wasn't yet an adult, I retained all my present-day memories. I'd gone back in time to become a child again while remaining the grownup I was today. It was hideous to imagine everything I'd have to go through all over again, only now I'd be old enough to understand it.

APRIL 15, 1996

Tim and I decided to burglarize the neighbors' house in search of something I knew I'd recognize once I saw it, even though I didn't know what it was or why I wanted it. Since the neighbors weren't home, we opened the gate in the fence that separated our yards and went onto their property. Though the side entrance to their mansion was locked, we somehow broke down the door without damaging it.

Inside, we headed for the basement, which was as big and well stocked as a public library. I'd never seen most of the titles and wanted badly to steal them. As I thumbed through book after book, still unsure why we were there, I noticed a carton and several loose packs of Marlboro cigarettes on one of the shelves.

That was what we were after.

I turned to tell Tim that we'd found what we wanted, but before I could speak, I heard the rumble of a vehicle pulling up to the house. From the basement I could see through the living room floor because I suddenly had X-ray vision. An earth-moving dump truck twenty feet tall rolled into the driveway; I didn't recognize the elderly woman at the wheel but thought she was probably one of my ancestors from the nineteenth century. Our neighbors' children sat in the cab with her. The truck parked and the kids spilled out, preparing to open the front door of the house. We were trapped.

"Come on!" I yelled at Tim. "We have to get out of here!"

We raced up the basement stairs into the living room just as the children came inside. There was no way we could close the side door of the house and lock it behind us to conceal our attempted burglary, so we just took off. I hoped that the kids—who stood within arms' reach—simply wouldn't notice us.

As we ran across the yard toward the gate in the chain-link fence, I fell forward and loped like a wolf on all fours. We charged through the gate and slammed it. I was terrified that if the kids had seen us, we'd get into the worst trouble of our lives.

APRIL 28, 1996

The large room had wooden plank floors, slat walls, and heavy oaken beams across the ceiling. It was rustic and somehow Catholic, simultaneously suffocating and comfortably familiar. Someone sat nearby, radiating an impersonal, synthetic kindness, like a statue of Abraham Lincoln. He wore a robe or winding-cloth, and his big, rubbery lips were set in an expression of pious compassion.

A long, heavy wooden table filled much of the room. Some sort of game had been set up on its top. The object of the game was to use your thumb to shoot steel ball bearings into complicated tunnels made of paper and cardboard. After rolling around for several minutes, the ball bearings would emerge from the tunnels, and a player would be declared the winner. The rules of the game were utterly incomprehensible to me. Someone had explained them to me several times, but it was like calculating moles in chemistry class. My mind just seized up and quit.

I crouched next to the table and flicked a few ball bearings with my index finger, sending them into the tunnels where they petered out or got lost. None of my ball bearings came out. I couldn't do it the right way and felt bored and anxious, incapable of understanding the point of the stupid game or why I played it.

After several of my bungled attempts, the man in the robe approached. With chortling, indulgent patience, he showed me how to shoot a ball bearing with his thumb. It careened through the maze of tunnels with such speed that it popped out of the other end, flew off the table, hit the wall, bounced back to me, and stopped at my feet. I realized that his way of playing was much more efficient and competent than my own. This excited me because now I could excel instead of fail, but I was immediately distrustful of the man. There was something sinister in his attention, something unseemly about a grownup taking such an interest in the games of a little boy. I then understood with total despair that I was no longer an adult but a child again.

MAY 1, 1996

It was evening, and I was on the second floor of a restaurant or nightclub. One of my brothers—Tim or Paul—was with me, but I couldn't tell which. He was a teenager, while I was my present age of thirty-four. The place was dark and crowded; the music, babble of raised voices, and endless clinking of glasses were deafening.

My brother and I sat next to a window overlooking a large, cement-lined pond lit with several ground-level floodlights. Rough-edged stones bordered the pond, which seemed to be very deep, the transparent water around the edges transitioning to a murky green in the center, where the bottom was no longer visible. Every time I looked at the water and floodlights, I felt terribly uneasy. They reminded me of something I knew I should remember but couldn't.

The restaurant was decorated in a Spanish or Mexican style. "Astrid"— wife of my friend "Charles"—sat in the booth opposite my brother and me. As she chatted with him, she was suddenly naked. She slid down the padded bench until she was horizontal, her head propped against the bench back. I could see her clearly, as if the wooden table were made of glass. The lighting changed to a cool blackish green, making her skin look iridescent and unbearably sexy. Her body was toned to a spectacular degree, her small breasts pointing toward the ceiling and tipped with erect nipples the size of my thumbs, her stomach flat and smooth, and her thick mound of pubic hair gleaming in the strange light. I wanted to run my hands all over her, to bury my face between her legs. The urge to have sex with her was almost irresistible, even though I now knew that she wasn't Astrid but someone else.

As she talked, I had to look away from her to contain myself. She was so beautiful and alluring in her nakedness that I wanted her to stay there all night, despite the havoc she wreaked on my psyche. I glanced out the window and saw that a group of men in suits and ties had gathered around the cement pond. They took turns running at the water as fast as they could, diving in and skipping like flat stones along the surface. Some of them went several yards before sinking. They seemed drunk, crazy, or retarded, whooping and shrieking. What they did made me very uncomfortable. I wanted them to stop, for their own safety and mine.

Astrid now sat outside the window in a chair attached to the building. I snaked my arm through the window and held her hand. She smiled, a flirty, pouty, cutesy, fey expression that I completely distrusted, but I ignored it, still wanting badly to sleep with her. We silently watched the men skip across the pond, and when I next glanced at her, I saw with peevish disappointment that she was fully dressed in a baggy, black jacket and oversized jeans, like a gangbanger. She gave me that mock-bashful, flirty-pouty look again, and I realized that she was actually Carmen, not Astrid. I was furious and disgusted that she'd tricked me that way.

Then I was in a vast, underground parking garage. The ceiling was held up with fluted concrete columns, and there were no cars anywhere. Dozens of signs warned of electrical equipment and their dangers. The signs had jagged cartoon lightning bolts printed on them in yellow, with smoke and bright red lettering. I tried to find a way out before it was too late.

A stairwell seemed promising, but I didn't want to enter it. After I dithered for a few minutes, a rushing, shouting, clattering sound came from the darkness, steadily growing louder. I passively waited for the thing in the stairway to appear. The thought of trying to escape didn't even occur to me.

To my utter shock, it was George C. Scott. He ran up the stairs with super-human speed, his white hair flying. The left side of his face was a smooth, bright pink burn scar that looked freshly healed, his left eye completely covered over with skin. He was outfitted as a mountaineer, with a heavy jacket, backpack, breeches, woolen knee socks, boots, ice cleats, and an Alpenstock. His arms and legs pumped in a jerky, mechanical way; as he passed, his remaining eye rolled at me, and he howled out an incoherent greeting. Flushed and happy, he sprinted up the stairs and vanished.

I was flabbergasted, having just read in the *Enquirer* that he was near death from heart disease and phlebitis. He seemed healthier than I was. Though relieved that he was okay, I felt that he was tempting fate. I waited a few minutes and then went up the stairs, looking for a way out.

After trudging up several flights, I left the stairwell and entered a thickly carpeted, luxurious foyer that resembled a department store display window. An elevator waited for me, so I got in, not knowing where I wanted to go or why.

MAY 29, 1996

I'd purchased a pair of birds to cheer myself up. They looked like crows but were as small as sparrows. Their wings had been clipped, so they were flightless. I brought them into my house and set them on the curved back of a cane chair at my dining room table. The birds perched there and cheeped to each other. I felt guilty for having them, but I was also glad.

My sister's late dog Sam was there. His coat was a mottled black, tan, and gray instead of the white-and-biscuit Samoyed-color he wore when he was alive. He sat on the floor next to the chair and made snapping, whining lunges at the birds, his jaws closing with the familiar wet, clopping sound he produced when he played mock-biting games.

"No, Sam!" I scolded, even though I felt guilty about that too, since he was dead, and he'd had such a horrible life. I just didn't want him to hurt my birds.

Somehow it occurred to me that the birds were sterile. I therefore went out and bought them two fledglings no bigger than wasps and capable of flying. I put them on the table next to the two adult birds, worried that the babies would get away. The birds raced around and hopped into the air, having fun together. It was great that they liked each other; the problem was that the fledglings got smaller and smaller until they were the size of houseflies. If they fell off the table, I couldn't pick them up without crushing them.

I squatted next to the table, which had turned into a miniature amphitheater with arched openings lining the sides. Toy cars scooted along the tabletop at eye level. From my viewpoint it looked like a full-sized amphitheater or movie set. The cars were the sort of cheap, blow-molded plastic toys bought in supermarkets, but they produced authentic engine noises, their tires squealing. The birds attacked the cars and banged against their sides. They focused on a lemon-yellow vehicle in particular. This car grew bigger and more solid as it kept returning to the archway through which I peered. It would almost drive through the arch but then swerve away at the last second to bounce off the far wall of the amphitheater.

The baby birds became as small as gnats, too fragile for me to even touch. I now stood on the tabletop with the cars, which were real. They veered, spun out, and careened in all directions. I saw clearly that none had drivers. A gray Aston Martin appeared; unlike the other autos, it was still a toy. I'd owned one as a child, and I remembered that it had a tiny, ejectable plastic passenger figure that would fly through the roof if you pressed the right button. As it came closer, it transformed into an actual car. It flew past and crashed into one of the amphitheater walls, the rear underside bursting into flames.

The car doors opened; Sean Connery and a beautiful, blonde model got out. Connery was young and very handsome. He wore a white tuxedo shirt and black bowtie, a complicated red-and-blue bulletproof vest, and black tux pants and dress shoes. Armed with a flamethrower or laser gun, he looked dirty and exhausted. The blonde model beamed and waved to a crowd that had materialized around us. She was like a living photo from a 1966 *Redbook*.

"You're James Bond!" I said to Connery.

"Yesh," he answered in his distinctive voice, giving me a tired glance.

The two gnat-sized baby birds circled his head, and he tried to shoo them away. They were so small and insubstantial that I was afraid he'd smash them, but I didn't say anything.

Then everybody winked out. Hundreds of people had surrounded Connery, the blonde, and me. In the next second, I was alone. There was a large, ragged hole in the concrete where the Aston Martin had been, so I went over and looked down into it. The hole showed a floor beneath me, and I saw myself lying in rubble, as if I'd fallen through from above. At that instant I began seeing from the viewpoint of the me who lay in the rubble; I now looked up through the ragged hole in the ceiling.

Though I expected to see myself looking down at me, the me on the floor above had become a redheaded dandy in a beige suit, with a beige trench coat draped over his shoulders and a green Tyrolean hat tipped forward to cover one eye. He had a thick, filterless French cigarette—a Gauloise or Gitane—in an onyx holder a foot long.

Standing like Jack Benny, clasping the elbow of the hand with the cigarette, he lisped, "Well, we'll thee about *that*, won't we, Mithter Bond?" He raised an eyebrow, tapped his cigarette ashes on me, and stepped back from the edge of the hole.

Suddenly, I was driving through a small Norwegian town, on my way to a monument that was once a church and had been preserved as the oldest surviving example of medieval architecture in the country. I arrived at the structure, which consisted of two bell towers connected by the sort of glass display I'd seen in the Paris Metro or London Underground. The building looked cheap and mass produced, like a Taco Bell. A woman sat beside me, narrating our progress aloud, but I didn't turn my head to look at her.

I stopped the car, got out, and walked over to the monument. It was now a glass cylinder, upright like a column and filled with mannequins dressed to portray various periods in the town's history. I was deeply impressed. The scenes were complex and well executed, with an amazing amount of detail and realism crammed into such small areas.

"Wow," I said. "These are just like the drawings in the textbooks we had when we were kids!"

I was glad I'd stopped, but when I looked closely, I saw that the mannequins wore only red-and-black thrift-store clothes and had wigs made from carpeting. They showed no part of the town's history and were there only for entertainment. Feeling cheated and foolish, I got back in my car and drove out of town. My passenger had vanished.

The road snaked across a wide paved lot beside a gray suspension bridge that served no purpose. There was no body of water anywhere in sight. A roadblock ahead had created a miles-long traffic jam; I knew I couldn't waste any more time, so I pulled off the road onto the lot, gazing at the beautiful autumn colors of the scenery around me. I was in Pennsylvania. The thought was gratifying and unnerving, since I didn't know what to expect from a place I'd never been.

As I crossed the lot, it became an open field, rutted and hard to traverse. One of the police cars from the roadblock detached itself and sped down a dirt track running perpendicularly to the direction I headed. He was going to cut me off because I'd committed a criminal act. When I came to the edge of the field, I found a deep ditch full of sludgy water and drainage pipes. I was trapped.

The police car pulled up in front of me, the officer inside wearing a railroad engineer's denim coveralls, striped hat, heavy gloves, and red bandana. When he got out of the car, his clothing had changed into a standard highway patrolman's uniform of dark green pants, pale green shirt with short sleeves, and Smokey the Bear hat. He had bright orange hair; thick rimless glasses; a double chin; and blubbery, protruding lips. Closing his door, he said something unintelligible to me in what I knew was the local dialect.

"What?" I demanded in an exaggerated, bitchy high schooler's tone. "What did you say?" I knew this would get me into worse trouble, but I couldn't stop.

"Papers," he replied. "Got a license?"

He stood next to me in the field. My car had disappeared, and I was left with just my thick wallet, which I began pawing through.

A man joined us. He wore a red-and-black checked hunting jacket, a red cap, and red pants. His black, scraggly beard framed a mouth full of yellowed snaggleteeth, and he smoked a home-rolled cigarette.

The cop said something to him in dialect: *"Ihm goam bim doom foobadoo boamadoam!"*

"A-hee-hee-hee-hee!" the man squealed, infuriating me.

I handed the cop my business card, and he began jiving and undulating, like a black street thug from the seventies.

"Right on, mah bruvvah," he said. "Check it *out! Ooo-eee! Shee*-yit!"

That pushed me into anger so intense it was like a psychotic break.

"All right!" I screamed. *"What's your name? What's your badge number?"*

He ostentatiously displayed his badge, jutting his chest at me like Marilyn Monroe, still bopping and dancing. I took out a pad and pencil to jot down his name—Ueltz—and his number, which was A835Y1. As I tried to write, I became so tired that I could barely keep my eyes open.

"That's right," the cop said, tapping the pad. "Schudemoen Ueltz. *Uh*-huh. *Mmm*-hmm. That's me!"

The pencil slipped out of my fingers, and my eyelids were now so heavy that I couldn't see. I dozed for a few seconds and awoke with a jerk. Patrolman Ueltz watched me, his fists clenched in a running attitude, and his legs bent at the knees.

"Ch!" he hissed. "Ch! Ch! Ch!" Each time he made the sound, he moved one fist forward and pulled back the other. I realized that he was playing choo-choo train, like a child. He began going faster and faster, *ch-ch-ch-ch-ch-ch-ch-ch, chchchchchchchch,* his arms pumping furiously and spittle flying from his huge lips. This demented display horrified me, but I was also so tired that I just shut my eyes again and let my head droop down onto my chest.

JULY 22, 1996

The video rental store was brightly lit. I was there with my girlfriend, either Carmen or Noreen—I couldn't tell which because I couldn't see her face. We discussed films and settled first on a Leni Riefenstahl documentary about sports, though it wasn't *Olympia*. After that we couldn't decide what else to get. We talked about it for what seemed like hours, until I was ready to scream.

"Do you like the Three Stooges?" I asked in exasperation.

She shrugged. "Well, I can take them or leave them."

Though I still couldn't make out her features, I knew that she gave me a sad half-smile.

"You've gotta see them," I said. "They're totally German."

She agreed, and I picked up the box to take it over to the clerk. At that moment I noticed that Joanne Woodward had entered the store, along with her daughter Lisa McCree, a local news anchor. Woodward looked like Juditha Brown, the mother of Nicole Brown Simpson. She had the same long, dyed hair; big Hollywood sunglasses; and tanned, leathery, wrinkled skin. McCree seemed depressed. She stared at the floor as she followed her mother.

I now knew that my girlfriend was Noreen, but I decided to think of her as Carmen. She'd told me that she was a good friend of Paul Newman and Woodward. I wasn't sure if I knew them myself. When Woodward walked by, she nodded at me.

"Joanne?" I called.

She turned and raised her eyebrows.

Leading Noreen-Carmen by the hand, I approached Woodward, having decided to be completely open about my new relationship. There would be no more secrets. I positioned Noreen-Carmen in front of Woodward, stood behind her, and put my right arm over her shoulder so that it rested on her upper chest. Noreen-Carmen was much taller than I'd realized, about six feet, and I was able to press my cheek against hers. She radiated intense heat, like a campfire.

"Have you met my girlfriend Carmen?" I asked Woodward.

"Why *no!*" she said, smiling at us in an openly patronizing way. "But I've heard so much *about* her."

After I introduced them, they chatted for a few minutes. It felt good to be honest about Noreen-Carmen. I knew she'd lied to me about knowing Woodward and Newman, but I didn't care, just as I didn't care that Woodward thought we were bozos.

After we said goodbye to Woodward, we went back to the table where we'd left the two videos. Lisa McCree stood there, rubbing her eyes with the heels of her hands and sighing loudly. I picked up the two videocassettes and showed them to her.

"What's the matter?" I asked. "Don't you like sports?"

"Oh, I don't know. I guess I don't," she said.

I was embarrassed to have shown her the videos, so I told Noreen-Carmen that we had to leave.

SEPTEMBER 12, 1996

Tim took my Blazer for a ride. He drove it across our yard, through his garden, and over our neighbor Nellie's driveway. When he reached Nellie's front lawn, the car began bouncing twenty feet into the air. I knew Tim would be badly hurt, so I could barely watch.

The Blazer bounced several times and stopped. Tim got out, his hair puffed into a ball three feet in diameter. He looked totally absurd.

"Man," he said in a dazed voice, shaking his head. "That was bad. *Real* bad."

I tried not to laugh. Though I felt sorry for him, I knew he'd gotten what he deserved for driving my car without asking.

JULY 11, 2009

My father had erected an elaborate, Michelangelesque scaffolding in front of his house so that he could paint the underside of the eaves. He'd used planks and steel pipes, the structure enclosing the large bushes in front of my mother's bedroom window.

As I stood there marveling at this latest piece of madness, my father came out of his house and ambled over to me. He was about twenty-five, wearing a gray 1940s double-breasted suit.

"Why'd you put up this scaffolding?" I asked. "Is it even safe? Why didn't you just use a ladder?"

"Of course it's safe," he said. "You don't think I know what I'm doing? I can't stand on a ladder all day. This way I can sit and take my time. What I'll do is start on this end and work my way up to the top of the eaves and then go down to the other end. I bought paint and primer all in one. It'll take a few weeks, but I'd rather take the time to do it right than hire someone who'll screw it up."

His tone was friendly and completely impersonal, as though he couldn't have possibly cared less about either the project or me. He was humoring me, the way he would a silly child.

"But what's the point of enclosing the bushes?" I asked.

"'But what's the point of enclosing the bushes?'" he mimicked, giving my words a careful, overly concerned earnestness.

When I glared at him, he smiled and shrugged, his hands stuffed into the pockets of his trousers.

I tried again. "Isn't this way too much work?"

"'Isn't this way too much work?'" he answered.

For a second I wanted to punch him in the face, but then I understood that he didn't know any better. All he could do was approximate human behavior. His mimicking was a putdown, harmless goofing around, and a serious attempt to figure out what I meant.

He wore a disposable, paper forage cap, like a fry-cook's hat. Written on the side in jaunty, red calligraphy, it said, "Fetus With A Really Big Head."

APRIL 17, 2010

Carmen and I arranged to meet at a restaurant. It would be the first time I'd seen her since 1994. I was terribly nervous but happy that we'd finally been able to put the past behind us.

She was already at our booth when I arrived. I didn't recognize her at first because she had a pageboy hairstyle.

"Hi there!" she chirped with a wide, artificial smile. I sat down across from her, feeling as though I'd never known her. She was a complete stranger, no different from the first person I'd see on the sidewalk if I walked out of the restaurant.

"How've you been?" I asked.

"Great! I can't tell you how fantastic everything is! You should've been there!"

I wanted to remind her that I hadn't been there because she'd driven me away, but there was no point in bringing it up. It didn't matter anymore.

"There is one thing I wanted to tell you," she said.

"What?"

"I've changed my name. My new name is Viqueline. Everybody calls me Vicky."

It was the stupidest thing I'd ever heard in my life, and it depressed me almost to tears. I could never call her Vicky. She was as much a Vicky as I was a Biff. As she chatted about tennis and wine, I realized that there was nothing left of the person I'd loved so much.

Then I remembered that Vicky was one of the sixteen personalities inhabiting Sybil Dorsett, the pseudonym for Shirley Ardell Mason. Vicky was a precocious, confident little French girl, the only personality who knew about all the others and could explain to the psychiatrist what was going on in Sybil's head.

My knowledge of Sybil had led to the online relationship I had with "Ariel," the second-craziest person I'd ever encountered. For six months she chased me all over the Internet, spilling my secrets, taunting, mocking, slashing and burning, afflicting me without letup and confessing to crimes in my name to try and get me arrested.

Meeting with Carmen was a disastrous mistake. She'd hated me as much as Ariel and Noreen. How could I be sure that the hate wasn't still inside her, ready to spring, like a tiger hiding in the bushes at night?

The hate would never end because I'd never stop seeking it out.

CHAPTER TEN
THE FIFTH NIGHTMARE CLUSTER

In May of 1996, I became involved with Noreen, the Ghost in Los Angeles. It was one of the most harrowing, brutal, inhuman episodes of my adulthood. I've never met a more cruel person. A trained therapist, she encouraged me to unburden myself to her, and then she used this information against me. She showed her true colors only after I called Carmen in June to tie up a final loose end. When I heard Carmen's voice for the first time in almost three years, I instantly fell out of love with Noreen. Carmen burst into tears, laughing with stunned, unbelieving happiness. That call snuffed out something in me. It was incontrovertible proof that Carmen knew as well as I did that we were supposed to be together, but we'd blown our chance forever.

Since Noreen is blessed with exceptional powers of intellect and perception, she sensed what the call had done. She began attacking my career, my relationships with my family, my emotional problems, my manhood, and my sanity. It was an all-out attempt to destroy me, yet it was impersonal, just a game. There's a very famous actress who does the same thing for the same reasons, according to Joe Eszterhas. These implacable destroyers are scientists. They want to see how much damage they'll be allowed to do.

At the time I was defenseless against such assaults. If it happened again today, I'd just laugh. It's not that I'm stronger; the reason is that what I have left are things that nobody can ever take from me unless they give me a lobotomy or decapitate me. I'm now immune to the sort of pain that Noreen inflicted on me. All of her criticisms were accurate, even though she didn't make them to try and help me. Also, when a person is as removed from normal human interaction as I am, what weapon can you use against him? As Geezer Butler said about Black Sabbath, I'm so far out of the mainstream that most conventions and standards have no relevance to my life.

Finally, what Noreen did can't even begin to compare with what other people have done. Noreen is like Marlon Brando in *The Wild One*. He was terrifying to audiences in 1953, but his character of Johnny Strabler is a witty, likable gentleman in comparison to the real-life monstrosities we hear about or run across today.

Beginning in June of 1996, I had the longest nightmare cluster ever. It finally ended in May of 1997. There were other nightmare clusters after that, but in 1998 I stopped keeping the dream diary for reasons I stated in the introduction to this book. The nightmares got so bad in August of 1996 that I lost the will to record them. They were exclusively about violence, madness, and being completely alone. Carmen was in all of them, always abandoning me, laughing at me, dying, or presenting me with something hideous. I wrote down only two.

For a solid month, every night was like those two dreams. I woke up bathed in sweat, my heart clobbering me like a drop forge and my body aching as though I'd been in an eight-hour barroom brawl with John Wayne. When I couldn't sleep anymore, I wrote to Carmen to apologize for the terrible things I'd said to her the last time I'd seen her. I thought this might end the nightmares. It didn't, but Carmen accepted my apology and offered her own. We wrote on and off until 2002, the year I finally recognized that I was a failure as a music journalist and cut off contact with almost everybody I knew.

The really bad nightmares didn't stop until 2011, when Meniere's disease allowed me to purge myself of my chronic rage. I still have unpleasant, frightening dreams, but they're not about me. My nightmares are now garden-variety expressions of the worry I feel for others. They're manageable.

Looking back on my relationship with Noreen, it's easy to see that her goal was to find out if she had the power to make someone so miserable that he'd take his own life. Until I was forty-five years old, I often thought of suicide. It was my ace in the hole, a way to escape pain and awareness. The only reason I didn't do it was because there was no guarantee that taking my own life *would* end my pain and awareness.

Today, killing myself is inconceivable. Although I have an incurable illness and live virtually cloistered, I look forward to each day, because each day I improve a little more. Each day I learn a little more, understand a little more, and advance a little more. Each day I create a little more art. I believe—and plenty of people think I'm insane for saying this—that I'm given signs of being on the right track.

If I'm insane, who cares? I don't and neither should you. My insanity allowed me to achieve clarity, and it helped me see my father through his indescribably horrible death, an experience I could never do justice even by hiring actors to recreate it. What Dad put himself and the rest of us through is simply beyond your comprehension.

Noreen was a sweet, playful little kitten pouncing on my ankle in comparison to my father's demise. And there are other things too, that far outshine Noreen's efforts to obliterate me. However, they're not for public consumption. They define me, are the source my rage, and keep me apart from the rest of you. I allude to them only as explanation. I've learned the very, *very* hard way that recounting them serves no purpose. It robs me of my dignity, the way it robbed me of Carmen and other attempted relationships. The experiences robbed me of my life, but my silence is how I've defeated them. I've robbed *them* of their stature. They were important only to me. Now they're important to nobody.

What's important is that I'm still here, and as my friend Scott Thunes reminded me, I haven't just survived. I'm a *success,* because I'm happy.

*　*　*

JUNE 11, 1996

I was part of a group performing some kind of investigation inside an old mansion or hotel. We may have been doing a seismic retrofit to bring the building up to code. There were about ten of us in the crumbling structure, which had thirty-foot ceilings and walls made of yellow-brown bricks that looked as if they'd been taken from an ancient Middle Eastern archeological site. The place was like a Hollywood set depicting the interior of an Egyptian pyramid.

As we walked along a hallway next to a stately flight of wooden stairs, a severe earthquake shook the building. We flattened ourselves against the wall.

"There's going to be flooding!" a man shouted. *"Hold on!"*

I hugged the wall, trying to cram my face into it. On my left more of our team staggered in, dazed and covered in dust. One of them—a young black man—joined me and copied my stance, his face twisted with fear. A river of green water poured through the doorway, filling the room up to our knees. My ear against the wall, I heard rustling and squeaking from inside. The black man and I turned and faced the bricks; he was on the verge of hysteria, his mouth trembling violently.

The wall had changed from brick to crumbling plaster, which bulged and rippled as something right under the surface pushed at it. Whatever it was also chirped and produced strange, echoing barks. I realized that it was a nest of rabid vampire bats.

To the left of the black man, the plaster slowly swelled out almost two feet. The bulge ripped open, and a cloud of flies spewed out like black smoke.

"Run! Everybody out!" somebody screamed.

We scattered, knowing that the bats would soon follow. I ran as fast as I could up the nearest flight of stars and yanked open door after door; behind each was a brick wall. A second flight of stairs brought me to the glass lantern room of a lighthouse. The lamp was missing, but I could see where it had been bolted to the floor.

Outside the sliding glass door was a metal screen door. I opened the glass door, and as I reached for the handle of the screen door, I saw that the hand-rails of the gallery surrounding the lantern room were covered with giant bats. They hung by their feet, their membranous, fleshy wings folded around their bodies and making them look like a row of vaginas five feet tall. One of them took flight and headed right for me. I slammed the screen door and grabbed the handle of the glass door, hesitating. The bat effortlessly chewed through the metal screen as if it had been a spider web. Its teeth were razor sharp and harder than steel.

Mesmerized, I waited until the bat had cut its way completely through the screen before I closed the glass door. Since the entire building was surrounded by thousands of hungry bats and they were inside all the walls, there was no escape. I ambled back down the stairs, rapidly losing interest in my fate.

JUNE 15, 1996

The house seemed to be in Norway and was decorated in a horrendously ugly Japanese and college-dorm motif. It combined the features of every home in which I'd ever lived. I sat by myself on a long, low sofa, feeling cranky and Teutonic. It was night, and I was an unpleasant, petulant person.

Across my spacious back yard in the house behind mine, my neighbors fought on the concrete sidewalk near their back door. I could see them through the big picture window of my living room. A youngish couple, they'd just returned home.

"Awright, awright already! Shaddap! Are you outta yer mind?" they shouted at each other.

I couldn't discern anything about the man, but the woman wore a ridiculous, cartoon French maid's outfit in black. The rear of her skirt had been replaced with a transparent material, displaying her naked buttocks. It scandalized and excited me.

That is one damn sexy, independently minded broad to go around dressed like that, I thought.

My 1950s wording and leering repulsed me. They were so different from my personality that I wondered if someone were beaming his own thoughts into my head. I got up off the sofa and went to a sliding glass door that separated the living room from the back porch, which had another glass door that led to my back yard. When I opened the second door, I saw that my yard was filled with men. There were about a dozen of them, homeless bums with sleeping bags at their feet. They all peered over the fence, watching my neighbors squabble and search for their house keys.

Seeing these men in their dirty, disheveled clothing filled me with rage. One was bald and chinless. He turned to me and displayed broken-off fangs protruding from his closed mouth.

I pointed to the sky and screeched, *"I want all you fuckin' drunks off my property immediately! Do you know what I'm going to do if you don't get the hell out? I'm going to call the police!* Voy a llamar la policía. *Do you understand?"*

As I yelled, I floated about ten feet above the scene, looking down at myself. I looked absurd and ineffectual, like a meek, sweatered pharmacist. Nobody would ever take me seriously, and I knew they shouldn't, since it was just a cheesy performance for unseen watchers I wanted to impress. I also realized that I endangered myself for no reason. Why did I go out among them and make rude, blustering threats that would only provoke them?

The men stared at me, their faces blank and robotic. A balding guy with a red-and-black flannel shirt and a fringe of shoulder-length, blond hair gazed at me with smug, calculating hostility, nodding his head slightly and poking his tongue into his cheek. He looked dangerous and totally disreputable, a corrupted lumberjack. Though Nordic in appearance, I knew he was Puerto Rican.

Slowly the rest of the men became more animated, mumbling ominously and moving toward me. The flannel-shirted guy gazed at me in ever-increasing good humor, his hand on his hip. I saw that the neighbors had stopped looking for their keys and watched us over the fence, expressionless. Some of the men began questioning me in Spanish.

"*¿Qué vas a hacer? ¿Por qué vas a llamar a la policía? ¿Qué te da el derecho de hablar con nosotros de esa manera?*"

I slid shut the outer door, blocking out their voices. Now I was furious. I went back into my living room, closed the inner door, and stamped around aimlessly, wringing my hands. The whole thing had to be some kind of setup, an elaborate hoax. I looked out the window and saw that what I'd taken for grass in my yard was actually sawdust dyed bile green. This was proof that it was all phony, so I slid open the door to the porch to go out and tell all the homeless men that I was on to them. They were all fakers.

As I reached for the porch door, it opened and the homeless men crowded inside, led by the Nordic Puerto Rican lumberjack. He smiled at me with warmth and compassion, producing a large knife from behind his back. His expression set off such an explosion of terror in me that I nearly passed out.

A butcher *knife,* I thought. *He's going to* butcher *me like a hog.*

Holding out the knife, he advanced slowly and said either, "Do you think I can get close enough to you with this?" or "Do you think it's long enough for you?"

I couldn't decide which sentence he'd actually crooned, since I heard both. He was about to murder me, and it would be unbearably painful and horrifying. I turned to my left and raced down the hallway that led out of the sunken living room. As I ran I tried to pick up weapons I passed, including a baseball bat, a sword, and a metal rod. Each either crumbled into dust or disappeared as soon as I touched it.

I could barely move, my legs rubbery and useless. My arms lacked all strength, as though the muscles had been replaced with fat. Ahead of me I saw a door. After what seemed like minutes of thought, I recognized it as the porch door, through which the bums had crashed into the house. Either I'd turned around and run back to it, or it had somehow moved in front of me.

My thinking was incredibly slow; I felt each thought move up the base of my neck and into my brain, like a ball of gas or vomit. After an eternity of running, I realized that the Puerto Rican lumberjack with the knife was about to pop out of the door and cut off my escape. He'd really kill me. I'd actually die, right there in my house, at that precise moment. It would be ghastly beyond belief.

Just as I decided that I'd better not try to run past the door in my slow, clumsy, addled state, the lumberjack charged out of the darkness with the knife raised over his head, his mouth wide open in a silent bellow of triumph and lust.

JUNE 22, 1996

I'd arrived at the old apartment unexpectedly. The middle-aged man and woman who owned the place were very angry at me. I knew I was either in France or Argentina, but I had no idea why I was there. After I put down my suitcase inside the front door, I walked past the fuming woman. She was dressed in the Edwardian style, in a high-collared, puffy-shouldered shirt-waist, her hair piled in a two-stage Gibson Girl updo.

The rooms were full of empty cardboard boxes and piles of dirty clothes. I barreled through them, looking for the couple's child. I may've been a student on an exchange program, but everything about my circumstances was confused and sinister. My brain simply couldn't function. All I knew was that I had to find the child. As upset as she was, the woman didn't tell me to leave or make me stop snooping.

In a bedroom the woman and I discovered a small corpse in a heap of clothing. It was impossible for me to tell if it was a dead human or an animal. Looking at it I felt the chill of great and immediate danger. The woman crouched next to the body and gave me a watery look of recrimination. She was such a cipher, such a gutless, weak-kneed nonentity, that her opinion of me shouldn't have mattered, but she made me feel insanely defensive. I tried to explain that this had nothing to do with me, that it wasn't in any way my fault, but I'd forgotten how to speak and could only make sputtering noises: *plip-plip-plip-plip-plip-plip-plip.*

Her husband came in. He looked unmistakably French, with a pencil mustache; large, dark-circled eyes; and a greasy, black comb-over. His checkered turn-of-the-century suit had a high detachable collar. Without speaking, he somehow accused her of being responsible for the death of the child or animal. He tore his sparse hair, gestured, and emoted as effectively as a mime. The woman continued to squat despondently next to the dead thing. She supported herself with her fingertips on the floor as though she were about to start hopping like a frog. Her husband remonstrated in perfect silence for several minutes and left the room.

I followed in my new nonverbal state, unable to explain that neither the woman nor I were to blame. Though only six feet behind the man, I lost sight of him. As I hurried from cluttered room to cluttered room, a terrible sense of foreboding built inside me. I came to a foyer next to a majestic stairway and found the man lying on the floor, worming his way into a black, plastic garbage bag. Only his struggling legs were visible. Embarrassed and disgusted, I tried to make him stop.

"*Oh man, come on!*" I shouted, the only words I could manage.

Throwing himself in the trash was an overreaction and would just make things worse for everybody. His head appeared through an opening at the top of the bag; he stared at me with complete disinterest, and I saw that his wife was in there with him, lying by his side. She looked dead, and I understood that I'd indeed killed their child and would now go to hell. An avalanche of panic smashed through me because it was actually going to happen. It wasn't a dream.

The floor on which the man and woman lay opened up in a swirling spiral, like a nebula. It was the gateway to hell. Before I could run, a woman clamped onto my back, her soft arms around my throat. I could tell from the rounded contours of the warm face pressed against my right cheek that she wore an ear-to-ear grin. Unable to resist, I was drawn toward the nebula, feeling as weightless as a soap bubble. My head buzzed and vibrated as if shocked by a powerful electric current. The couple in the garbage bag disappeared into the hole and I followed.

I floated down through the floor into a large room hung with displays on the walls. The centerpiece was a doll that was either Cyndi Lauper or Courtney Love. I couldn't tell which, even though I knew it was one of them. A life-sized head on a dwarf's body, it was in an attitude of cruci-fixion on a bundle of large sticks. As I floated past, it gave me a look of perverse, self-pitying defiance, as if begging *and* daring me to feel sorry for it. I realized that it wasn't a doll but the actual singer, and whoever she was, she deserved her place in hell because she refused to change or admit to her sins. I didn't know if *I* deserved to be here. Though I'd killed the child, I was deeply repentant.

As the woman on my back and I floated down sloping, bile green hallways and through crowded rooms, I heard a sonic wallpaper of murmurs, whis-pers, and declamations. Unseen people babbled, some narrating my progress downward.

"And now he passes by another room and continues descending, confused and terrified, wishing desperately he'd done things differently in his life..."

The woman clinging to me became gelatinous entrails. Her arms were suddenly loops of intestine that I dislodged. They came apart and fell to the floor in globs, sections slipping through my fingers. I came to an expansive barroom filled with people, some of them celebrities. One of the walls was entirely covered with a mirror, and I noted my reflection. Although I still had my ponytail and beard, I was now bony and sharp featured, my face a gently smiling mask. When I skimmed over to the bar to get a drink, I became aware that I was covered in fecal matter. From head to toe, I was uniformly spattered with tiny, greenish blobs of shit that sprayed off me, as if I were generating them myself like a sprinkler. They formed a fine cloud around me, a shit mist. I was truly in the Christian hell.

Above my head Charlie Sheen appeared on a balcony, surveying the crowd. I wasn't surprised to see him in hell, but as I came to grips with my situation, I wondered how these people could be so casual about spending eternity in this ugly, filthy, soulless place. A party was underway, and the denizens of this netherworld were jaunty about their fate. Despite the gentle smile I still felt plastered on my face, I was in an agony of horror and guilt, finally accepting that I deserved to be here but thinking it was still unfair.

At that moment I found myself in my bed, struggling with a black shape in the darkness. I lay on my right side, pinning the arms of this thing against the wall. It was flabby and insubstantial, as if it were made of loosely rolled-up newspaper. Even so, if I let go, it would attack me. It writhed feebly, and I felt something else push up through the mattress against my chest. The trip to hell was only a dream; these two things in bed with me were the *real* danger. There was nothing I could do except hold on and try to keep them from getting loose and exterminating me.

JUNE 24, 1996

Noreen and I were on the metro in Germany. At first it was just normal subway cars with benchlike seats and overhead hand straps, but then it became enormous children's wagons connected with rope. The tracks were under about a foot of murky, greenish yellow water, and the conductors wore civilian clothes and carried flashlights. They were young, cocky, and irreverent, like the ubiquitous Euro-protestors of the 1980s. As the wagons careened and swayed, they called to each other, laughing and whooping.

The trip took forever. Noreen and I sat in silence, not looking at each other. After what seemed like years, we pulled into a station. I got out of my seat and made my way forward to the exit, an absurd action on my part because there were no doors. The open wagon had only low walls; I could've stepped out anywhere, but it was necessary to stand in that specific place. When we stopped at the platform, I got off, leaving Noreen behind. I trotted urgently through the chaotic station until I came to Carmen's apartment. It was built into the wall, between a newspaper kiosk and an information booth. I pulled open the door and entered without knocking or ringing the doorbell.

Inside, it was sloppy and warm, clothes piled everywhere on the floors and hanging off the furniture. The rooms were suffused with a dark blue light that was warm and sensual. I felt uncomfortable yet emphatically at home, as if I'd returned to the womb. Though the apartment gave me a sense of safety, it was cloying and false, an obvious illusion. I went through two or three doorways until I found Carmen's bedroom. She lay naked on her disheveled bed, waiting for me, her arms and legs open and a terrifying, deranged smile of welcome on her face. I plopped down beside her on the bed, inserting my hand between her legs. Her body was exactly as I remembered it. I was so glad to be back, and I recognized that this was a fatal mistake. Noreen was so much better for me, so much more real, sentiments I knew to be as fraudulent as the refuge the apartment offered.

Carmen's hips thrust against my hand, and she laughed.

"This is so *bad!* I knew you'd be back. Bet she doesn't know what we're doing, huh? You just couldn't stay away, could you? I've never known such a weak little shit as you. I could do anything to you, and you'd still want me, wouldn't you?"

I looked at her face and saw that she was "Nakamura," the woman I'd been with before Carmen. She whipped her head in circles and rolled up her eyes until only the whites showed. It made me unbearably aroused. She was totally corrupt and lacked all boundaries. I knew that she'd let me do anything I wanted to her, that I could debase and exploit her in whatever way I could image, and she'd comply.

She laughed throatily, a promise that we were about to have an absolute blast. As I took off my clothes, she squished her breasts together with her hands, making them point straight up, her erect nipples more than an inch long. She was precisely what I wanted, and as I got on top of her, I felt relaxed and sadder than I'd ever been in my life. I knew I'd thrown away everything I'd built with Noreen, which was all phony too. Nothing was real—nothing except filth.

Then I was on a hill, looking down on a series of apartments that resembled my college dormitory. Clotheslines were strung everywhere, and dilapidated cars were parked under and around the wooden stairways and fire escapes.

I'll never get away, I thought.

JULY 9, 1996

I lay in my bed, trying to sleep. Suddenly, two men began breaking the window, only inches from my head. They smashed the wood and glass with their bare hands, berserk as feeding sharks. I was utterly paralyzed with terror. Noreen's disembodied voice encouraged them.

"Don't worry about him," she said with the sexy, husky laugh she used when she wanted to be especially contemptuous. "He can't do anything. *Get him!*"

Shocked that she'd egg them on, I also knew that *of course* she'd egg them on. I'd discovered right at the beginning that she was evil, yet I'd stayed with her for a whole month. Her betrayal was what I deserved.

The two men burst through the window and tumbled onto the floor in a shower of glass. All I could see of them in the dark were shaven heads and black hoodies. When they windmilled up toward me, I finally threw myself out of my bed and lunged for the door, wondering why I bothered. It was too late.

The hall that led to the kitchen was now a hundred yards long. As I ran, the men crashed into the walls. Their footsteps pounded the wooden floorboards so violently that I bounced. Though they sounded as if they were demolishing my entire house, they were mute, as silent as gravestones.

A small area on the back of my neck began tickling. That was where the men would plunge the ice pick. They fell on me and brought me down, gripping me with hard, male hands as wide as the length of my forearm. I was lifted into the air and bashed against every flat surface, as if the hallway spun end over end.

JULY 14, 1996

It was either a luxury hotel suite or a mansion, and I was trapped. The party had been going on for days. Empty beer cans, spilled food, snack wrappers, and clothes were scattered everywhere. The rooms were full of men, some of whom I recognized from high school. One in particular looked utterly degenerate. His face was lined and yellow skinned, his hair was long and greasy, and he cackled like a cartoon witch.

I floated around the rooms, hovering near the ceilings and gazing down on the mess below. The host of the party lay stretched out on a low bed among tangled sheets and blankets. He stared up at me, his ankles crossed and his hands clasped behind his head. I hated and feared him. In his white slacks and tennis sweater—his dark hair slicked back over his perfect head—he was smug and arrogant, a languid, wealthy college student from the 1930s. He reminded me of Leopold and Loeb.

Sickened, I floated out of the room and drifted over to a sofa where two younger men sprawled; they looked less reprobate. I descended to the floor in a crouching posture.

"You must do what you're told or you'll never be allowed to leave," I told them. My pompous tone was absurd; I sounded like the worst Shakespearean actor ever. "Listen to me! I beg of you! It is a matter of life and death!"

Embarrassed, I then tried for sardonic and world-weary.

"So whatta you guys think about these bastards? Are they creeps or *what?*"

Since I was naked except for white jockey shorts, I knew that nothing I said or did would sway them. I was now a child about seven years old. Floating right above the floor, I held myself in a push-up position on my fingertips. As I spoke I'd lever myself into a vertical attitude and flutter my fingers at the two young men. Then I'd sink down prone again. I didn't understand why I waved at them, since they scared me nearly out of my mind.

All of the men in the entire suite or mansion crowded into the room. They gathered around and took turns stabbing me with pocketknives, penknives, bayonets, stilettos, and steak knives. I was in two positions at the same time: standing and bent double, and lying with my shoulders on the floor and my feet behind my head in the Yoga "plow pose" or *halasana*. Sweating and roaring with laughter, drunken men loomed over me. Their faces became featureless, yet somehow their silhouetted heads and rounded shoulders projected feral, unrestrained relish.

I tried grasping the men's wrists as they stabbed me, but they were much too strong. My hand—feebly clutching at the rock-hard, corded wrists—looked to be no larger than that of a baby. The knife blades gouged their way deep inside me, the intense pain mundanely familiar. I'd experienced it many times before and would continue to do so in the future. Though torture, it was nothing new. The assault didn't shock me, because I'd expected it. This was very well-trod ground.

The only difference was that these men had a special malevolence. Their stabbing was much more vicious and painful than usual. When each blade was withdrawn, I was blessed with indescribable relief. But as soon as the agony subsided, another knife was shoved inside me, sometimes forcing me up on my toes. I gritted my teeth and waited out each bolt of pain.

After stabbing me thirty or forty times, the men seemed to lose interest. I lurched to the door, ran into the hallway, and then just stopped. Soon I'd have to face it all over again. There was no escape, no matter what I did. To try and change the inevitable was pointless.

JULY 19, 1996

The supermarket was in San Francisco. I watched a guy on roller blades try to pull off a monumentally incompetent act of shoplifting. He was a blond man in his fifties, dressed in a gas station attendant's long-sleeved, blue work shirt with a white oval stitched to the left breast. I couldn't make out the name written in red thread. He had a young hipster's trendy, asymmetrical haircut and black Gen X pants, but he looked totally worn out and pathetic, with a puffy, lined face and magnificent bags under his eyes.

Over and over he'd stuff things into his pockets and try to sneak past the checkout clerk with his stolen goods hanging from his shirt and pants. Every time he got to the front of the line at the register, a uniformed security guard would try to grab him. The skater would then either spin around the guard and get back in line, or he'd put a brown paper bag over his own head and skate away. This made the guard lose track of him and stop the chase. The guard would return to his place next to the automatic sliding doors, spot the shoplifting rollerblader in the line again, chase him, and then lose him again.

I watched this in an agony of frustration. The stupid security guard was taken in by tricks that wouldn't fool a three-year-old. I knew I shouldn't get involved, but I couldn't help myself. For the seventh or eighth time, the skater donned his paper bag and lost the security guard, who ran out the front doors in utter confusion. I walked over and grabbed the skater, wrestling him to the floor and restraining him by wrapping my arms and legs around him. I lay on my back, and he was on top of me facing away, as if I rode pillion on a motorcycle behind him.

"Come on, buddy," I said. "Just settle down. I've got you."

I'd never called anyone "buddy" in my life. Even in such dangerous, stressful circumstances, I had to put on a show and try to be someone I wasn't. My pathological need to perform was reprehensible.

The rollerblader struggled in a playful, flirty way, as if he didn't take any of it seriously. As he writhed against me, his head turned to the side and I saw that he was trying not to smile. Suddenly, I was terrified. I knew I'd made a very bad decision.

"Aw, c'mon man!" he said. "You don't even work here! You're no cop!"

"No, I'm not, but you just pretend I am, fella, and everything'll be all right."

More schmaltzy, abnormal unreality. I couldn't control it.

At that moment a tall, middle-aged Asian man with glasses walked in. He carried an M-16 assault rifle in his left hand, the barrel pointed at the ceiling. Skinny and repulsive, he was a caricature of milquetoast ineffectuality. His balsa-colored, polyester suit and side-parted hair made me think of a computer programmer or an accountant, someone who had no contact with the outside world. He smirked proudly, and when I saw that he wore earmuffs, I knew what was about to happen.

"All right, everybody," he called in a reedy, nasal voice. "What I'm going to do is kill you all with this rifle. You won't know if I'll shoot you in the head or in the body, from the front or from behind. You won't be able to prepare yourselves."

He looked around, his right hand on his hip, and I knew he wasn't kidding. We were all about to be murdered. I stopped struggling with the skating shoplifter and just lay there on the floor. Though I didn't want to die, I lost all volition and decided to just wait for it. If my unquenchable thirst for attention hadn't compelled me to apprehend the ridiculous shoplifter, I wouldn't be facing death at the hands of a disgusting, inadequate maniac.

JULY 23, 1996

The room was in the basement of a strange house. Bare bulbs hanging from the ceiling were so bright and harsh that I couldn't see anything outside the cones of light they cast. I carried a stuffed Winnie the Pooh doll that my baby nephew Hunter liked. The doll was kept in a wooden toy chest at my parents' house, and Hunter would play with it when my sister brought him over for a visit.

As my eyes adjusted to the light, I found that I stood over a toilet attached to one of the walls. Though I didn't know why, I had to get rid of the bear. I put it in the toilet and flushed, watching the doll go down the pipe feet first. When it had almost completely disappeared, it got stuck, only the top of its head and one ear visible.

I'd done a horrible thing; Hunter would miss his bear, and it would clog the pipe and cause the toilet to overflow.

A long, polished wooden stick lay on the floor. I picked it up and poked it into the toilet to dislodge the bear. Dry-heaves wracked my body, but I kept trying to hook the doll and draw it out. Finally, I threw the stick across the room—so nauseated I was about to keel over—and reached into the toilet, plunging my hand into the icy, skin-crawling water. With my eyes closed, I pulled out the doll by its ear and held it over the toilet as the water drained from the cloth in a stream that sounded like urine.

When the noise tapered off, I opened my eyes. The bear was sodden and much heavier now. It dangled from my fist like a dead child. I felt panic and unmitigated self-loathing at ruining one of my nephew's favorite toys for no reason. When the rest of my family found out, they'd treat me with the contempt I'd so richly earned.

JULY 27, 1996

My brother Paul and I sat in the front room of my house. He delivered a leaden, droning soliloquy on his plan to kill me. His speech was infuriatingly slow, deliberate, and condescending; he gestured pedantically as he leaned forward and described how he'd shoot me in the left eye with a pistol that was in his car.

"The bullet will penetrate your cornea, pass through the vitreous humor, out the sclera, and through the sphenoid bone and into your cranium. Let me finish. From there it'll destroy the left frontal lobe, the temporal lobe, and the brain stem. I estimate your death will occur virtually instantaneously, no more than one-eighth of a second after I pull the trigger."

I listened with enthusiasm, nodding vigorously and saying, "Yeah-yeah-yeah-yeah-yeah" like a weasely sidekick in an old Tex Avery cartoon.

Paul said in plain English that he was there to kill me, but I thought he meant someone else, possibly our father. In a detached corner of my mind, I knew he was going to murder *me,* not Dad. Though nervous about the prospect of being shot to death, I also welcomed it.

Paul stood.

"I'll be back in a minute to do it," he said and went out the front door into the night.

I pointed my left index finger in the air. "I'll be here!"

As soon as the door closed, I snapped out of my dopey, trancelike state and realized that he was actually about to murder me in my own house. It wasn't a joke or a game. I scooped up a toy I'd been playing with—either a plastic army tank or a stuffed teddy bear—and flew through the house toward one of the back doors. If I could get out the side gate before Paul came back, I'd escape.

My toy under my right arm, I threw open the back door, ran into the garden, and hurled myself off the ground. I executed a flawless ballet jump, the grand jeté. Maybe tonight would be different, and I'd make it to the gate.

Paul roared out of the darkness on my right, precisely when I expected. He threw his left arm around my shoulders and yanked me against his chest in a smothering embrace. I felt rather than saw his pleased little smile.

His breath blowing across my cheek was part of the routine, a reminder of all the other times this had been done to me. He pulled my head down by the hair and shoved a pistol into my left eye, the metal digging deep into the socket. My eyeball and its closed lids were forced into the muzzle. I braced myself for the pain of the bullet entering me.

Paul's overpowering presence sucked away my will to defend myself. I didn't bother to struggle, because I was doomed. Right at the moment I knew he would, he fired, sending a blinding flash of white light deep into my head.

AUGUST 3, 1996

As Carmen and I stood on the tarpaper-and-gravel roof of a building, sirens began going off all across the city. Screams and the sounds of car horns, screeching tires, and multiple collisions floated up from the streets. We looked over the edge; white-helmeted police officers fired into churning hordes. Store windows shattered. Molotov cocktails arced, creating blossoms of flame that zigzagged, fell, and lay still.

"What's going on?" Carmen asked.

"It's war," I said. "They announced on the radio that we're about to be bombed."

She burst into tears and hugged me. "What do we do?" she sobbed.

I didn't have the heart to tell her that there was nothing we could do. San Francisco would be a major target. We had only minutes to live.

There was a flash in the distance, followed by a black-and-orange mushroom cloud rising skyward.

"Oh no! Oh no! Oh no!" Carmen wailed.

We were engulfed in a deafening wave of sound, a deep, electronic humming like the noise of a cataclysmic ground fault. Carmen let go of me and covered her ears. Sheet white, she squeezed shut her eyes. I kept mine open; this would be the last time I ever saw her.

The sky became watermelon red, with yellow clouds like mustard gas. I could still hear hundreds of car horns honking and people screaming. As a powerful wind blew, I looked up and saw a Russian Tupolev Tu-95 Bear, a strategic bomber with swept-back wings and four turboprop engines. It was Tim's favorite aircraft. Silver and beautiful, it slowly passed overhead, only about a thousand feet up. When it was a few hundred yards down the street, it dropped a stubby, metal cylinder that looked like a depth charge. I watched the bomb fall for what seemed like hours. It was a thermonuclear device that would level the entire city.

When the bomb reached the level of our rooftop, it exploded. The shock wave made me see stars. Beside me, Carmen disintegrated. All the flesh on the front of her body shredded and flew off behind her in a spray of what looked like raw hamburger. Her face was instantly stripped to the bone, only her bulging eyes remaining as she shrieked through her exposed teeth. She did a back flip and flew off the building, her scream trailing after her.

Watching her die was so painful that I searched the roof for something sharp to gouge the image of her flailing, defenseless hands from my brain. I couldn't understand why I hadn't been killed. It wasn't fair to Carmen. She'd wanted so badly to live, while I didn't care what happened to me. Now she and everyone I knew were dead, and I was left alone in a demolished, radioactive city.

The building started to collapse, a tremendous relief. I'd die after all. As I plunged downward, steel beams and chunks of cement smashed and hacked at me. To my bitter rage, they didn't hurt in the slightest.

AUGUST 5, 1995

Back at our apartment in San Francisco, I approached Carmen in the kitchen. She stood with her back to me as she prepared dinner. Ecstatic to be with her again, I slipped my arms around her waist and bent down to bury my face in her hair. My hands sank into what felt like warm gelatin.

I pulled away and saw that my hands were covered with blood.

"What's happening?" I screamed at her. *"What did you do to yourself?"*

She turned around and held up a carving knife in her right hand and what I knew to be her uterus in her left. A gash ran from her crotch to the center of her chest. The edges were folded back, like rolled slices of roast beef, and I could see her liver, spine, and stomach.

When she smiled, blood dribbled out of her mouth and down her chin. It was all over her teeth, as though she'd been eating a freshly killed animal.

"I did it for you," she said in a froggy, bubbling voice. "Now we can get married."

SEPTEMBER 15, 1996

I was in a seedy motel room, waiting for Carmen. We had to get back together because I was dying without her, but I also knew that when we did reunite, I'd lose something forever. I didn't care. The arrangement was for her to spend the weekend with me, seventy-two hours of sex and reconciliation. I was afraid, aroused, and ashamed.

Suddenly, she breezed into the room. She was much taller than I remembered, and she was blonde. I looked down at my body and felt loathsome as a toad. She rushed me the way she used to and kissed me, her tongue snaking around inside my mouth. Even though I was almost comatose with happiness to be with her, I noticed that she seemed preoccupied, not really paying attention. I also knew that she was seeing someone else. It didn't matter; the important thing was that she was with me. I hugged her, and she pulled back.

"If we're going to do any fucking," she said, "we'd better start now!"

I was shocked. She'd never spoken like that before. Then we were both naked in bed. She squatted on top of me and guided me into her with her hand. I thought I might die from the sensation. She bucked violently, panting and moaning, her eyes closed.

"You're fucking me! You're fucking me!" she screamed.

What was wrong with her? She was like a mental patient. I was utterly panicked. She howled like a siren and then it was over. I didn't climax.

"If I were seeing someone else," I said, "what I'd do now would be to go to him and get some from him too. That way I could do two guys on the same day."

"Yeah, I guess you're right. That's what you'd do, all right." She nodded in a mock-rueful way, fluttering her eyelids.

"You're not going to spend the weekend with me after all, are you?" I said.

She shook her head. "No, I'm not," she said with grotesquely fake, apologetic smile. "I'm really, *really* sorry!"

I watched her get dressed and leave, and in a few minutes, I put on my own clothes and went outside into what looked like a renaissance fair. There were large pots of food sitting on long tables. I loaded up a plate with stew, cornbread, and vegetables while everyone around me stopped what they were doing and silently stared. They all knew what had just happened in the motel room. I looked up and saw Carmen approach; she'd donned a dark trench coat and carried a briefcase. Stopping next to me, she filled her own plate with food and faced the silent crowd.

She held up the plate. "This is my boyfriend," she said. "My *real* boy-friend." Then

she looked at me with a phony wince of alarm, pretending to be horrified at what she'd

just said.

"All right. If that's the way you want it," I said. I threw my own plate to the ground and marched away from her, literally, swinging my arms and pumping my legs like a mechanical toy soldier while imitating a military snare drum: *dt-d-dt, dt-d-dt, drrrrrt-d-d-d-d-d-dt, d-dt.*

It was a pathetic, demented performance, but I couldn't stop. People turned away in disgust; I marched, made snare drum sounds, and began physically shrinking in size. The further I got from Carmen, the smaller I became. My buttocks expanded and my hair became a cap of tightly permed white curls. In seconds I was transformed into a fat, middle-aged, German *Hausfrau* in polyester stretch pants and a sleeveless blouse. I couldn't bear to see Carmen's reaction, so I kept marching until I was less than an inch tall.

SEPTEMBER 22, 1996

The wide plain was somewhere in the Midwest, all gently rolling hills and grasslands. It was tornado season, and I nervously watched the sky as I helped a man plant rice shoots in a paddy. He was big and middle aged, wearing jeans and a red-and-white checked flannel shirt. Stooped over, he blathered nonstop, his folksy monologue a kind of sonic backdrop.

"So what Ah said to 'im was, 'Don't you ever, *ever* think you can get away with nothin' like that when *Ah'm* runnin' the show, buddy. You mess with me, you gonna wish you ain't *never* come outta y'momma's cooch.' An' he looked at me like his ass was on sideways an' he had ta shit. Someone tries ta fuck witcha, y'kick 'im in the nuts straight away, or he's gonna *double*-fuck ya. That's what mah daddy tol' me back when I was no bigger'n a corn nubbin."

He splashed in and out of the water with the sort of melodramatic, overly businesslike determination that told me he was a fraud with no idea what he was doing. Though the paddy was hot and slimy—like a lake of vomit—I wanted to submerge myself in it up to my neck.

The rice farmer was famous for refurbishing German First World War aircraft, including a Fokker triplane and a Halberstadt CL.IV ground-attack fighter. The Halberstadt continually flew over our heads as we worked. I'd glance up at it, admiring the workmanship of the restoration. On one of its sorties, I saw a funnel cloud forming directly above us. I thought about diving down underwater and lying there so that I'd get sucked up into the sky, figuring it would be an amazing experience. Since it would also kill me, I decided I'd better take cover instead. The Halberstadt buzzed us again, but now it was a Japanese super-deformed caricature, all squashed, bulbous, and cute. I felt terrible that such a valuable, imposing aircraft had been turned into a cretinous joke. Overhead, the tornado grew, dipping down out of white clouds shaped like cubes, dodecahedrons, and prisms.

Then I was inside an airplane hanger that was also an office-supply store. Everything was neat and painfully sanitary, with stark fluorescent lighting and cardboard boxes stacked against the walls. The double doors swung open, and a tiny, one-man helicopter flew in, a foot or so above the floor. It looked like a Bell H-13—the M.A.S.H. chopper with the tail made up of steel tubes— but the cockpit was a passenger car instead of a big, acrylic bubble. It flew right up next to me and turned onto its side.

I was terrified that the rotors would hit the cement floor and shatter, sending razor-sharp metal fragments in all directions. However, the rotors were very short, only about two feet long. The helicopter was designed to land on its side, an idea so ridiculous it was insane. I hurried out of the store before a salesman could tell me about it. The helicopter was a perversion, and I was afraid someone would either try to sell it to me or get my approval.

Outside, I found myself on my college campus, which was up on a mountain overlooking Portland. The city seemed much closer than I remembered, but then I realized that I now had the eyesight of an eagle. I could make out the faces and clothing of individual people strolling around, getting on electric trolleys, and crossing streets. It was as if I peered through a powerful telescope.

Suddenly, eight or ten white contrails appeared over the city and lengthened rapidly. They were ICBMs, fired from military bases that the enemy had commandeered. The contrails swooped in toward the city, and the missiles smashed into their targets. Orange-and-black mushroom clouds, smoke, and flying debris obscured the view of the surviving buildings. When the dust settled, armed men swarmed the downtown area, shooting everyone the missiles hadn't killed. With my eagle eyesight, I saw that they were dark-skinned Middle Easterners. They shot news crews that covered the attack, and I knew that soon they'd notice the campus and stream up here to murder us.

The whole thing had a foretold, inevitable quality, as if it had already happened years ago. I was numb with fear and totally unmoved, having expected this all my life. A few open-mouthed students stood around me.

"Terrorists!" I screamed. *"They'll be here any second! Get away from the dorms! Go hide in the woods!"*

They fled and I turned back toward the city. The terrorists were on their way up the road to the college. Carrying assault rifles, rocket launchers, heavy machine guns, and other weapons, they'd arrive in a few minutes. I turned and ran into my dorm to warn the residents, but once inside the building I knew it would take too long. If I were going to survive, I had to get out and hide as quickly as I could. I raced outside and ran toward the barbed wire fence that separated the campus from the surrounding forest. Even though the fence was eight feet high, I vaulted it with ease, as if the earth's gravity had been turned down. I landed in the woods and hid behind a bush only a yard from the fence. It was too close to the college; my instincts shrieked at me to go deeper into the trees. I stayed behind the bush anyway.

Gunfire broke out all over the campus. People screamed and scattered, while right in front of me on the other side of the fence, a young man and woman tossed a red, rubber kickball back and forth. I lay on my side, my legs drawn up. My shirt and pants were gone, and now I wore only white jockey shorts. Armed men ran past without seeing me, despite the fact that I was in plain sight. The college was both in Portland and on the property of my house in Texas; this confused me into paralysis. Completely exposed and feeling amazingly stupid for remaining where I was, I couldn't force myself up to find a better hiding place.

A middle-aged black man joined me. He was thickset, with an Errol Flynn mustache. I knew he was somebody famous—an actor or TV personality—but I couldn't place him. He knelt next to me in a white T-shirt and khaki work pants.

"We'll be okay if we keep our heads," he muttered. "Just hang on."

I trusted him completely. He'd get me out of this jam.

The sounds of gunshots and explosions increased as the terrorist attack spread. From my right, a group of women arrived, somehow at the behest of the man with me. They were the counter-terrorists, Asians wearing white blouses, navy blue skirts, and traditional wide-brimmed Korean hats. They gathered in front of me and stripped down to their underwear. Their bodies were smooth and muscular, with gorgeous buttocks. Despite my fear and torpor, they aroused me to near-delirium. As they knelt to pull combat fatigues, assault rifles, and hand grenades out of duffel bags, they giggled in my direction and covered their mouths. Then they dressed and strapped on their gear, complaining to each other in Japanese that they all had to wear the same clothes. Once fully outfitted in helmets and flak vests, they were coldly professional. There was no doubt that they'd clean the terrorists' clocks. They cocked their weapons and moved off.

Since the man with the Errol Flynn mustache had vanished, I got up and ran along the fence toward a granite fountain that sat in front of a plaza, the heart of the campus. Somebody—either one of my brothers or Carmen—was with me. I couldn't tell which because I couldn't see the person clearly. When we reached the fountain, we lay behind it on the grass and waited. There was an explosion on the stone stairway between two buildings in front of us; the Japanese counter-terrorists had begun their work. Glass and hunks of cement flew everywhere, and an Asian man was blown along the ground toward us. He hit the base of the fountain and sprawled on his stomach. I knew he was a North Korean infiltrator, so I ran around the fountain to try and kill him. As he moaned and kicked his feet, I snatched up his pump-action shotgun by the barrel, swung it like an ax, and smashed him on the back of the neck. He stopped writhing and lay still.

I grabbed one of his legs and dragged him back to where my companion lay. Behind the fountain, I inspected the shotgun. Such a weapon would be extremely useful. This one looked too small and toylike to be effective, the spare shells looped to the wooden stock only half an inch long. Suddenly, I regretted hitting the Korean. Whatever he was, he didn't deserve what I'd done. I wiped his bloody neck and hoped I hadn't broken it.

Face down, the Korean shook his head, mumbling and laughing into the ground. He seemed sweet and docile. I gently took off his jacket, folded it up to make a pillow for him, and turned him on his side. When he looked comfortable, I leaned down and pushed him through the grass by the soles of his boots. We moved away from the fountain and down the sloping hill toward a quiet rose garden with concrete benches. Sunken like an amphitheater, the garden was a peaceful hideaway invisible from everywhere else on the campus. We'd be safe there.

Now the Korean lay on a blanket, and I pulled him along a paved walkway with a downward slope that became alarmingly steeper the closer we got to the garden. I worried that the Korean would fall out and hit his head on the flag-stones. The path ended on the top of the circular brick wall that surrounded the garden. About ten feet below me, Emma Thompson sat on a bench dressed as a nineteenth century British nanny. Next to her was a toddler riding a wooden rocking horse. The little boy wore an ankle-length, long-sleeved gown, the type seen in Victorian photos. My concern for the Korean evaporated, and I abandoned him on the path. It was as though he no longer existed.

I took the stairway down into the garden; Thompson and the toddler attracted and utterly repelled me. Squatting beside them, I peered at the fair-skinned little boy. He had shoulder-length blond hair, a freckled nose, and full lips. Up close he looked like a corpse. His eyes were blank and filmed over, and his mouth hung open. He was as devoid of life as a specimen preserved in alcohol. Thompson turned away in apparent shame. Though I was outraged at the child's condition, I also found him revolting. I stood and left the garden because there was nothing I could do for the boy. He was already a goner.

OCTOBER 9, 1996

Wearing scuba gear, I worked in black water at the base of a pier. It was night, and I collected silver Roman coins from the mire. There were thousands of them. I had a flashlight that illuminated a circle about two feet wide on the mucky bottom. When I shone the light around me, the beam went less than a yard. The water was like ink.

A monstrous shark circled me in the darkness. Though it was invisible, I could tell that sometimes it stopped and hovered, watching me. When I tried to see it with my nearly useless flashlight, it flexed its body and whipped away. Its sudden movements generated pressure waves that made me sway, and clouds of greenish brown silt momentarily reduced my vision to inches.

As I put the coins in a bag, I knew that at some point a mouth four feet wide would rush out of the blackness, right at my face, but I couldn't stop. It was inordinately stupid of me to have gone into the ocean at night. No amount of money was worth being torn to shreds by giant teeth. I was terrified, panting into my regulator, my wetsuit full of sweat. Yet there was nothing I could do now. If I stayed, the shark would kill me. If I swam to the surface, the shark would kill me. If I backed past the pilings of the pier toward the shore, facing the open water, the shark would kill me. It was too late. There was no way I'd survive this. Coming down here in the first place had doomed me.

I sensed onrushing bulk and raised my flashlight; what looked like a concrete wall flew past as the shark turned at the last second. It was as big as a city bus. In the silty water, my flashlight may as well have been a birthday candle.

Soon it would all be over. I numbly picked up more gleaming coins, waiting for the shark to finish playing with me and end my life.

OCTOBER 15, 1996

The ancient, well-kept castle was in Vienna. In a master bedroom, I prepared for a tryst with Jennifer—the Second Ghost—a girl I'd loved in high school. I was completely relaxed and contented. Though I hadn't seen Jennifer in fifteen years, I'd pursued her the entire time so that I could have sex with her. Now it would finally happen.

Our room was superbly decorated in dark-stained oak and bearskin rugs, with a king-sized bed that looked so comfortable it made me want to cry. This would be the best sexual experience of my life. My anticipation made me almost delirious, yet I was also preternaturally calm. Jennifer was my soul mate. She'd make everything perfect.

When she appeared, I was surprised that she was still a teenager. I knew she was thirty, but she looked no more than sixteen. Her warm smile banished my uneasiness. We'd spend days in this opulent bed; it didn't matter how she looked. I approached her and took her hand, guiding her into the room. She moved gracefully, like a gazelle, and I became very excited thinking about what would begin in just a few moments. I led her to the bed and threw back the blankets, taking off my clothes in the same motion. Jennifer got in bed, still smiling as though she loved me with all her heart.

"Have you been happy since the last time we saw each other?" I asked.

"Everything's been great!" she said. "I'm working for Exxon and I have the nicest house you've ever seen. I couldn't be happier!"

We were both completely at ease. I took off her shirt and gently squeezed her small breasts, the sensation of her warm flesh against my palms almost making me explode. Moving down her body, I kissed her stomach and the insides of her thighs, the familiar tangy, female smell making my head spin. She arched her back as I peeled off her panties, and I saw that she wore a flesh-colored, plastic dildo secured by a strap around her waist. Two testicles made of blue, fuzzy knitted yarn were attached to the base of her fake penis. The whole apparatus looked cheap and homemade, like something she'd bought from a street vender for a dollar.

I sat up, my desire immediately extinguished. Jennifer smiled shyly; I knew she'd done this to make me more comfortable. Though shocked and insulted, I understood her motivation. I wondered if I should take off the cruddy plastic phallus and try to get back in the mood. My mother would have the answer.

Then I was outside the castle, talking to my mother as she harvested turnips or potatoes in a field. She was about twenty-five years old and devastatingly beautiful, wearing an off-the-shoulder peasant blouse, a long skirt, and a headscarf.

"Is it all right if I have sex with Jennifer even if she's wearing a plastic penis and looks like she's only sixteen?" I asked.

Part of me felt filthy and subhuman, but another part was sure that it was perfectly natural for an adult son to discuss his sex life with his much-younger mother in such graphic terms.

Her eyes flashed. "Get back in that bed and take off that penis!" she said.

Everything would be fine. I left my mother tilling the field and made my way back up to the bedroom. Jennifer was still there under the covers, so I got in beside her and gently removed the dildo and furry blue testicles. Since she had a mature woman's vagina under the fake male genitalia, I assured myself that she wasn't a teenager.

This would make up for all my missed opportunities. It was the supreme moment of my life, an utter travesty.

NOVEMBER 2, 1996

I answered the door, and it was Noreen.

"You wanna come over to my place tonight?" she asked.

"Sure," I said.

"Okay. Be there at seven. 'Bye."

Though she was crazy and evil, I couldn't get enough of her small, muscular body and musky scent. Her utter lack of inhibitions and easy availability made her the ultimate fantasy object, a living sex doll. If I resumed our relationship, it would be unforgivably stupid. It was also deeply embarrassing that the rest of my family—with whom I lived—saw how much I still wanted to be with Noreen. Everybody knew that if I went to her condo, we'd screw each other's brains out. Having my private life exposed like that made me feel sheepish, the emotion that always swamped me when I had sex with anybody but Carmen.

I put on a strapless, red cocktail dress from the 1950s and packed an overnight bag. While hurrying through the TV room to get my red, high-heeled pumps, I noticed a purse on the sofa. It didn't belong to anyone in my family. Each time I went from my room to other parts of the house to gather more clothing, earrings, and jewelry, I saw the purse and got more agitated. Finally, I opened it to see what was inside. It contained makeup and a set of house and car keys. I knew immediately that the purse was Noreen's. Since she'd left, how could she drive to her condo and get in without her keys?

My thought processes were very slow. Pondering the question made me increasingly panicked. After several minutes of staring into the purse, I peered behind the sofa and saw three small suitcases. I unzipped them and found several changes of women's clothing. Noreen hadn't left after all. She'd been living upstairs in the attic, spending the days in hiding and coming out at night to roam our house undetected. The thought of these nocturnal intrusions enraged me. It was my fault that this insane, dangerous person was here among us. I was responsible for bringing her in. If she hurt my family, I'd be to blame.

I had to warn everybody, but I was so choked with shame that I lost the ability to speak. As I went into the kitchen, the door to the second-floor stairway opened. Noreen shambled out in a raggedy, black, Flintstones cave-dress. Her fabulous breasts were exposed, and her skin was gray and pasty. Hunched over, she gazed up at me with the whites showing under her irises. My skin prickled from the storm inside her, the whirlwind of blazing rage that she barely held in check. She shuffled past, looked back over her shoulder, and smiled, the corner of her mouth stretching up to her ear and exposing a row of pointed teeth. It was the grin of a rabid wolf. She'd been hiding upstairs for months and was now ready to play.

When I tried to say something, my voice wouldn't rise above a whisper. To achieve even that, I had to scream as loudly as I could.

"You have no right to do this," I whisper-screamed.

Noreen went into the TV room. She plopped down on the couch next to her suitcases and raised her eyebrows, the wolf-grin replaced with a smirk. Her cave-dress had changed into a miniskirted business suit and stiletto-heeled boots, all in black. Perfect circles of rouge like decals decorated her cheekbones, chin, and forehead. Her animalistic quality—the impression she gave of being on the very edge of control—scared and infuriated me. This was some elaborate revenge plot she'd launched to punish me for telling her to get lost. Though I ached to beat the crap out of her, she was so terrifying that I wanted to run from the room.

"What...are...you...doing?" I asked, forcing the words through my con-stricted throat, my neck and vocal cords straining in agony.

Noreen said nothing. She just smiled, crossed her legs, and jiggled her booted foot up and down. I went into the kitchen, where Tim bustled around with a perforated spatula as big as a snow shovel. About thirty pounds of bacon fried in an industrial-sized mega pan on the stove. A crystal punchbowl overflowed with the contents of several packages he'd already cooked. There was enough bacon to fill a steamer trunk, the greasy smoke and stench of hot fat almost making me throw up.

I cornered Tim and tried to explain Noreen's presence and apologize for bringing her back into our lives, but now it was impossible to speak. All

I could manage was a clenched-jawed, grunting whistle, incomprehensible even to me. As I tried to force out the words, Tim's face crumpled and he started bawling like a two-year-old. I felt terrible, even though I knew it was fake. He never cried; this melodramatic display was supposed to make me feel guilty.

It *did* make me feel guilty, because I'd put everyone in danger. Still, I wanted desperately to have sex with Noreen. While part of me recoiled at what I'd wrought, another part tried to figure out the quickest, least-complicated way of getting Noreen into bed. The guilt and the lust couldn't be separated.

NOVEMBER 19, 1996

In my living room at night, I tried to record a TV program on the VCR. I was extremely confused, as if I were stoned or half-asleep. Several minutes went by as I just stared at the TV and the remote control in my hand, trying to figure out how everything worked. The nonfunctional state of my mind scared me. I felt as vulnerable as a child, ripe for exploitation.

The program I tried to record was a late-night talk show that would feature a pop singer I liked. I couldn't remember her name. The show had a satellite hookup to London, where Elizabeth Hurley—the interviewer—waited alone on an empty stage. She and the audience were completely motionless and silent. When the pop star finally appeared, she was horrendously ugly, an ashen, cadaverous, somehow mangled version of Madonna. She was so hideous that I tried to yell for Tim to come see her, knowing that he'd find her hilariously repulsive. I couldn't form words; all I could do was bark like a dog.

On the TV Hurley assumed a ham actor's dramatic poses as she asked her questions. She also added portentous pauses and emphases to her words.

"So when did you...*start singing?*" she asked, pointing accusingly as the camera zoomed in on her and the house band played a brassy fanfare. The contrived weirdness upset me because it was what idiots substituted for wit. I felt bad for the singer, whose moment in the limelight was being sabotaged.

Why wasn't Hurley booed and yanked offstage with a sheep hook? Everyone in the audience was a moron.

Tim and our sister Carrie came into the living room. I couldn't make the remote work to play what I'd recorded from the interview. Besides, I'd captured only one-second segments. My own actions were as demented as Hurley's. When I tried to explain just how bizarre and unsettling the show was, how the singer looked horrible and Hurley behaved like a lunatic, I was utterly tongue-tied.

All that came out of my mouth was, "Um...Um...Um...Um...Um...Um..."

Carrie sighed and walked away, shaking her head. In the kitchen doorway, she turned and seemed about to say something, but then she just sneered and disappeared. Tim silently took the remote from my hand and fast-forwarded through what I'd recorded, which was utterly worthless. He showed me how to set the TV on channel three and press "Record." After handing back the remote, he went out to the back porch to smoke. He hadn't said a single word, as if I were a nitwit he was used to setting straight.

I knew something was wrong with my brain, but I couldn't even begin to comprehend what. Tim and Carrie had humiliated me so badly that I just went back to watching the awful interview. Now all the lights were off in the living room, the TV casting its blue glow over me as I sat cross-legged on the rug less than one foot from the screen. A towel had appeared on my head; I wore it burnoose style.

Outside, I heard loud music and the babble of young voices from another of the neighbor's all-night *ranchera* parties. After a while several gunshots rang out, each about five seconds apart. They sent me into near-catatonia. I fumbled with the remote, trying to turn off the TV and VCR. Invisible bandages encased my hands, I couldn't control my fingers, I couldn't think, and I had to use a penlight in the increasing darkness. Once everything was switched off, I went outside into the garden and saw Tim standing under the eaves, smoking.

"Who's shooting?" I asked.

He ignored me.

The noises from the party grew more frantic; it now sounded like an orgy in which the participants were beaten and killed. I felt as if I were about to lose my mind from agitation. The black sky looked painted—no stars, clouds, or moon. A sickly orange light played over the garden, making everything seem diseased and off-kilter. Crashes and stealthy scuttling sounds came from my Great-aunt Marion's house next door.

There were five or six cats in the garden with us, two adults and three or four kittens. They ran in and out of a small cave they'd excavated at the base of a tree. The kittens all had human heads resembling those of old men or the moai statues on Easter Island. They glared at me as they raced around. I'd seen them before, living in piles of sand under Marion's house. They made me afraid and nauseous. I couldn't stand them.

Tim opened the gate of our slat fence and gently tried to shoo out the cats. As he leaned down, I saw that the trees in Marion's yard were full of gypsies plucking oranges and lemons and dropping them into bags. It made me want to die. How could people be so depraved that they'd deliberately target the defenseless?

"They're ransacking the place," I said to Tim.

He didn't respond.

"*Look!*" I screamed as loudly as I could. "*They're ransacking the place!*"

Tim shone a flashlight on one of the trees, illuminating an elderly woman perched on a branch. In her veiled pillbox hat, pearls, and housedress, she looked like O.J. Simpson's mother. Tim glanced at her disinterestedly for a second and then went back to trying to get the cats out of the garden. His indifference was an unbelievably disrespectful affront. When I tried to explain to him why criminal gypsies were important, I couldn't speak. All I could do was stutter. Every few syllables, my mouth locked open and I had to close it by pushing up my chin with my hands.

The gypsies began taking things from the rear porch of my parents' house. They wheeled away a bright green bicycle, filled their arms with my niece and nephews' toys, and carted off furniture. Their brazenness made my seething indignation boil over. I was so angry that I wanted to burn them up with a flame-thrower. Abandoning my efforts to reach Tim, I walked down Marion's newly poured concrete driveway toward the street. I now wore a small backpack so stuffed with clothing that it felt like a basketball strapped between my shoulders.

On the street dozens of gypsies stole everything in sight, hauling away plants, lumber, tools, and lawn decorations. I'd never wanted so badly to kill someone. It was a specific craving; murdering them would save me and bring me peace. Though the sky was still totally black, the scene was illuminated starkly as if from spotlights on police helicopters. It looked like black-and-white documentary footage of Nazi atrocities.

I took a deep breath. *"I'm going to call the police!"* I shouted. *"¡Voy a llamar la policia!"*

As soon as I said it, I knew what a stupid thing I'd done. Overwhelmed with a sense of endangerment and exposure, I frantically looked up and down the street for a cop car. A Volvo or Saab was parked in front of our house, surrounded by several young men. One glanced around, put his hand in the pocket of his gray hoodie, and strolled casually in my direction. He was coming to kill me.

When I turned and tried to run, I seemed to be neck deep in molasses. My arms and legs barely moved. I tore off the ridiculous, hampering backpack and looked for the gate in our fence, but my eyesight was now affected along with my motor skills, my thought processes, and my speech. A screen of leafy plants obscured my vision; in order to see, I had to turn my head to the side, nearly upside down.

Four or five planks in the fence were broken, the tops snapped off, so I knew that the gypsies had gone into our garden. Running in slow motion, bent sideways with my head upside down, I hopped clumsily over the fence to look for Tim. I had to try and help him because it was my fault that the gypsies were after us. If I'd kept my mouth shut, everything would've been fine. Part of me wanted to flee and leave Tim to fend for himself, but I knew there was nowhere to go anyway.

Behind me the young man in the gray hoodie stepped over the torn planks into the garden. He carried either a pistol or an axe handle, and he advanced with such businesslike determination that I lost all will to resist. Stopping in my tracks, I waited for him to free me from the pain that never ended.

MARCH 24, 1997

My family and I walked around a lake in Europe. The path was wide and tree shrouded, and my parents and siblings surrounded me. I couldn't see their faces. We piled into a red Volkswagen bus and drove to a cathedral with a long flight of stone steps leading up to it, like the Capitol Building in Washington, D.C.

When I got out of the vehicle, I found that I had a white, longhaired cat in my arms. I called her "Luva," after Carmen's cat. She was stretched out on her back, like a nude model in a provocative pose, and she had tiny handcuffs on her rear paws. Mortified, I knew that people would think I had a secret fetish and the need to expose it in public.

On the steps of the cathedral, a woman reporter approached.

"*Ooh,*" she said, looking at the cat. "That's pretty *wild,* those handcuffs!"

She leered and winked. I felt horrible because the handcuffs *did* involve some depraved game I played with the cat. Nobody would accept that I genuinely loved her. The handcuffs would prejudice everyone against me. As much as I deserved it, I still thought it was unjust.

I left the cathedral and was instantly back on the path around the lake. As I passed a darkened house in the woods, the cat began speaking to me in a small, feminine voice.

"He's in there," she said. "Please don't let him get me."

As the cat spoke, a light turned on inside the house, and concentrated rays of demonic lust poured out at us. I was flooded with numbing terror. Some inhuman predator had taken notice of the cat, and it was my fault. The guilt was overwhelming. Even so, I thought it was unfair to saddle me with the responsibility for what would happen. I loved the cat, but my love was sick and twisted. Everybody let me know it in a million ways, just about every day. Since the world judged me unfit, I put the cat on the ground.

"Go away," I said. "I can't save you. I'm sorry."

The cat looked terrified as she clumsily scampered off, the handcuffs on her back paws forcing her to hop like a rabbit. I knew I'd just murdered her. Whatever lurked in the house would stalk and devour her. Other cats—mangy strays—appeared out of nowhere. They raced into the woods after my cat. I had an image of my cat lying dead and decomposing behind a building. That beautiful, sweet little animal would be a discarded pile of bones and gray, rotted flesh because of me. I had to immediately commit suicide to atone for what I'd done, even though I'd had no choice. Keeping the cat would've been just as bad as letting it go.

I continued along the path until I found the Volkswagen bus parked in a gravel lot. My family sat inside, only my father missing. Though everybody's faces were still indistinct, they were all much younger than I was. My siblings were preteens again, and my mother looked to be about twenty-five. She sat in the front passenger's seat, staring out the windshield with a tranquil smile. Someone came up right behind me and stood there, breathing on the back of my neck. Without turning, I knew it was my father. I climbed into the bus to get away from him.

Instead of sitting down, I crouched on the floor next to the first row of seats, cleared my throat, and held up my hands.

"Can I have your attention?" I called, feeling like a buffoon. "I just want to tell everybody that because of me, Luva is dead. I left her behind, and now she's lost."

Nobody reacted. I was thankful and furious. There was no reason for me to try and tell these people anything, but I couldn't stop. Part of me felt that as long as I kept my mouth shut about the cat, I'd be all right. By talking about her, I made myself even more of a pathetic clown; worse, I revealed my fundamental immorality. Despite what it would do to me, I had to try and explain.

I told them about the handcuffs, the house with the demon, and the mangy cats that had killed Luva. The words spilled out of my mouth in an incoherent torrent. I couldn't understand them myself. As I babbled hysterically, my mother shook her head at me, her eyes closed and her mouth set in a smile of deliberate obliviousness. The faster I spoke, the faster she shook her head. Right as I was about to scream at her or smash her face, the cat popped her head through the open doorway of the bus. She glanced at me, winked, and retreated. The relief I felt was indescribable, a kind of rebirth. I was so grateful that I nearly wept, but I maintained my composure to keep my family from laughing.

After a few seconds, the cat jumped into the bus and meowed at me. She no longer had the handcuffs on her back paws. I picked her up and hugged her, thanking God that I hadn't murdered her after all. Even though I was a sick, ugly, dangerous pervert, at least I hadn't hurt this defenseless, innocent creature. As I held her, I tried to ignore my family, who watched with sniggering disgust.

MAY 24, 1997

Tim drove me along a desolate stretch of freeway that looked like the Canadian province of Alberta. After several miles, we stopped on the shoulder. Tim opened his door and leaned forward to fiddle with something on the floor. When I heard a vehicle pull up behind us, I looked back over my shoulder. A dark brown UPS truck had stopped only a couple of inches away. The driver vaulted out of his seat and raced over to Tim's door.

"*Floor it!*" I screamed at Tim. "*Let's get out of here!*"

Tim moved very slowly, as if he were drugged. He turned his head and gazed at the UPS man, who pointed a pistol right at Tim's face. The longhaired driver was dressed in jeans and a trendy button-up shirt. Holding the semiautomatic pistol sideways in the gangbanger grip, he was impossibly handsome, like Dan Cortese.

He shouted incoherently through his clenched, beautiful, white teeth. Even though he didn't even know us, he hated us. Tim still hadn't reacted. I flattened myself against the door on my side, knowing that the gunman was about to open fire.

First I felt a strange, tingling pre-impact of the bullet right in the middle of my forehead; then there was an awful draining sensation, as if my life force were being sucked out. It bled into the air around me, suffusing it with the vitality that would soon leave my body. The empty space surrounding me became human and alive, full of emotions, while I turned into an insensate block of wood. I half closed my eyes and tried to make myself as small as possible.

When the UPS man fired at Tim, some of the shots would pass through him and hit me, miss him and hit me, or both. However it happened, I was about to be murdered, and I was completely helpless to save either my brother or myself.

The gunman ranted and Tim sat in frozen incomprehension. I hated them both. A whining scream built in my throat, and as it turned into a roar of raging despair, the pistol exploded in deafening, flaming muzzle blasts. Bullets hit me in the forehead, teeth, and right eye, sledgehammer blows that made everything go black.

CHAPTER ELEVEN
GHOSTS AND BALLYHOO

After I was diagnosed with Meniere's disease on October 7, 2011, the last of my chronic rage departed. It wasn't voluntary; instead, it was more of a road-to-Damascus moment in which the crusty scales fell from my eyes. I'd been on a slow, upward trajectory for about three years. Incurable illness was the final motivator, the catalyst for a full worldview makeover. As far as I can tell, it's permanent. Though I still have problems with anger and depression, they don't rule my life. I interviewed some of the biggest names in music, built incredibly beautiful scale models, and published four books while crippled by a sense of near-total worthlessness and illegitimacy. Now that I've shed that conviction, maybe the sky's the limit. Or maybe a meteorite will kill me tomorrow. What will be will be.

On March 23, 2012, I began posting as Arthritic_Tom on Talkbass.com. My plan was to share a few stories about what it was like to be a failed music journalist, and then I'd see if I could publish novels. As always, nothing went the way I thought it would. My posts resulted in a book deal for *Ghosts and Ballyhoo,* an opportunity I'd not only *not* even considered but then vehemently refused when it was initially offered.

Things seemed to be going so well that I contacted Carmen and told her that she'd gifted me with something that I would never have experienced without her: three years of complete happiness. For that I'd always love her. She accepted my message and gave me permission to write about her in my memoir. The terrible sadness that I felt for nearly twenty years was banished. It happened instantly, the evening she sent me photos of what she looks like today. A message accompanied them.

I HATE any photo of me (with or without a hat), but since you already know me... why try to hide.

Beginning in late April of 2012, I finally began having dreams about Carmen that weren't nightmares.

All the dreams in this book that postdate 1998 are drawn from memory. It was easy, because my dreams stay with me. Tim is amazed at my ability to remember conversations, interviews, and dialog from movies. That inborn skill served me well when I was a music journalist—especially when the tape recorder cratered and I had to recreate the entire exchange; I'm talking about *you,* Stephen Jay—but it's also been a major burden. There are plenty of memories and nightmares that I wish I could purge from my consciousness.

On the other hand, good memories and nice dreams help sustain me. So my near-perfect recollection is just one of the two-edged swords we all carry.

Ghosts and Ballyhoo was officially published in July of 2013. As I expected, I had some failure-illegitimacy dreams about it, but they're so funny that they don't really count. They're more like parodies of my previous failure-illegitimacy dreams.

One note.

My father died early on the morning of February 23, 2013. When I finally went to sleep at about 6:00 a.m., I had the dream you can read below.

*   *   *

MAY 8, 2012

I drove Carmen in a convertible on the Pacific Coast Highway. Her long hair blew all around her. She wore sunglasses and sat against the door, facing me with a gentle smile. We were both our present ages.

"You used to get carsick," I said. "Don't you still?"

"No. Not when people drive carefully."

Though her deep, creamy voice was exactly as I remembered it, she was a different person. Now she was calm and relaxed, the way she'd been from 1989 to 1992. It wasn't that she'd changed, I realized, but that she'd recovered.

"I can't believe you've been gone for twenty years," I said. "I was positive we were going to spend our lives together."

"We have," she said.

It was a relief to learn that the past two decades hadn't been wasted.

No longer in a car, we skimmed along above the surface of the road, lying horizontally and gazing forward, like two fighter planes. To keep moving at seventy or eighty miles per hour, all we had to do was reach down and push off the asphalt with our fingertips. I felt airy and clean, like a cloud.

"For twenty years I've wanted to take you to Hearst's Castle," I said. "I always knew it would make you laugh like crazy, and I've missed your laugh."

She seemed embarrassed. "I've forgotten how to laugh. I'm really sorry."

"Don't be sorry. It's not important," I told her.

As I spoke the words, I thought I lied to make her feel better. But it was true: I didn't care that she couldn't laugh anymore.

MAY 14, 2012

Carmen met me for lunch at a sidewalk café. She gave me the goofy smile that utterly transformed her face, the magic trick that she told me she'd stopped doing in 1994. We ordered salads and tall glasses of peach nectar on ice.

"I'm going to ask you something that'll upset you," I said, "but I have to know. Remember that Blue Explorer-shaped Aria Pro II bass I had?"

She ate a bite of salad. "Yeah. It was gorgeous."

"Well, when Tim and I got home from San Francisco after I moved out of our apartment, I could never find the bass. It had a black case with red writing on it. I promise I won't be angry, and it won't change how I feel about you, but did you steal the bass? You loved it, so I always wondered if you just kept it."

"If I'd kept it, I would've remembered it," she said. "It was a great bass. I'm sure I didn't steal it."

I was sad that she wouldn't admit to taking it, but I understood why she lied.

Then we were on the beach, walking barefoot on the hard-packed sand close to the water. The sky was cloudy, and the air was cold and damp.

"Mom still has the polished stones you gave her in 1991," I said. "Since Dad died and Mom got sick, she's been asking tons of questions about why you drove me away. She still really likes you."

Carmen smiled. "I don't mind if she asks. That was a long time ago. It's a lot easier to talk about now, isn't it?"

"Yes, but only because we're never going to get back together. It took me twenty years to accept that."

"It's too bad you accepted it," she said.

"No it's not. I *had* to accept it."

"But how come you didn't ask me if *I* accepted it?"

I didn't know what she expected of me, since she'd gotten everything she ever wanted. She'd even said the last time I saw her that one reason she drove me away was because I didn't make enough money. Our breakup was entirely her doing. Yet *I* was somehow to blame for not coming back for her? Did she think we could be happy together now, cloistered in my one-bedroom hovel as I self-published books and endured rotational vertigo attacks for the rest of my life?

With no idea what to say, I walked on in silence until I saw the tiny inlet where we went for our sea glass and polished stones. There were thousands of brown, green, blue, and white fragments scattered across the sand, along with glossy little rocks that gleamed as though they'd been varnished. It was the most sea glass and polished stones we'd ever found.

"Wow!" Carmen said. "We should've brought buckets."

It hurt that whatever she picked up, she'd take home to another man, but there was nothing I could do about it. Besides, we were on our beach again, collecting sea glass and polished stones again. I had no reason to be upset. Looking at her in her jeans, sweater, and baseball cap, I loved her as much as I did the moment I met her. Everything was all right because nothing had changed.

AUGUST 18, 2012

I walked alone through a destroyed urban landscape that looked like Germany at the end of World War II. There was rubble everywhere, and half-demolished, windowless brick or concrete walls lined the streets. It was a movie set, and then it was the inside of a bombed-out cathedral that stretched from horizon to horizon. I was afraid and so lonely that I thought I'd go insane.

Suddenly, a Catholic saint with a full-moon halo shot up out of the debris, like a telephone pole propelled by compressed air. Dust, bits of brick, and junk flew in all directions. The saint held both hands out at his sides, palms facing upward at the level of his shoulders. It was a classic, medieval gesture of abject supplication. His head faced forward, but his eyes gazed skyward and his mouth was open. He looked like a satire of a pious, preening, self-aggrandizing showoff. Physically much larger than I was, he was a flesh-and-blood human, a statue, and a representation in a stained-glass window all at the same time.

Accompanying his eruption from the earth was a smarmy, triumphant note sung by a choir: *Ahhhhhhhhhhh!*

Startled and angry that religion would be injected into this catastrophe, I shouted, *"You can't be serious!"*

Yet I found it incredibly funny too. Every fifteen or twenty feet, another saint popped up, always with the same prayerful posture and note from the choir: *Ahhhhhhhhhh!*

After it had happened a dozen times, I was laughing so hard that I had to sit on a broken pew to keep from falling down. The saints made the endless destruction bearable.

NOVEMBER 21, 2012

My friend Joe Cady built an army tank. He and I were part of a club, like paint-ballers, and we drove around getting into mock battles with other people who had fake German tanks. The men in the German tanks didn't take things as seriously as Joe and I did. We had full World War II-style uniforms, while the "Germans" just had coalscuttle steel helmets or field caps. Joe did everything in the tank while I rode along as a passenger. He steered the thing, loaded the gun, aimed it, and fired; I just sat there and hoped for the best.

When we encountered enemy tanks, Joe opened fire. There was no way to judge who won these battles because everybody used blank shells and there were no sensors on the tanks. We blasted away at each other, but since the shells didn't produce any damage and nobody wanted to admit defeat, nothing was resolved.

One of our battles led us into a hospital the size of a mall. As Joe and I drove around in the corridors, we argued over a map.

"This can't be right," I said. "We shouldn't be having a tank battle in a *hospital!*"

"You're wrong," was all Joe said.

We happened upon some guys in a German tank who were in the middle of their own argument. Three of them smoked cigarettes, and the fourth one told the others that the German tank manual allowed smoke breaks only from 9:58 a.m. to 10:00 a.m.

"Minus two. Case closed," he kept saying.

Finally, they got back into their tank and drove away down the corridor.

Joe stopped our tank to ask somebody for directions. As soon as he left, the vehicle began rolling forward. Since I didn't know how to control it, I just stood impotently in the hatch until the tank crashed into the wall. The mine-clearing plow on front—like the cowcatcher on an old locomotive—punched through the wall. I got out of the tank and went a few feet down the corridor to the door leading into the room on the other side of the wall. I was afraid that the plow had killed a patient. When I found no damage in the room, I went back to the tank; it was gone.

The hole in the wall had been expanded into a doorway framed in wood, which opened up into an empty room made of cinderblocks. The walls had lots of windows that showed a theme park with roller coasters and Ferris wheels. An army of Muslim women in black abayas cleaned the windows and painted the walls pale green. Joe returned.

"I'm sure the maintenance staff took the tank," I said. "We have to find the garage."

He nodded, and we walked through halls, looking for the garage.

"I'll pay for the damage we did to the wall," I said.

"You don't have to do that," Joe said. "There's no way they can trace the tank back to me, so we don't have to worry about anyone charging us. If we find the garage, we'll just steal the tank. If we don't find it, we'll abandon the tank and nobody'll know who drove it into the wall."

It was dishonest, but I lacked the courage to confront Joe about it. I decided to come back on my own and confess to the hospital staff that I'd damaged the wall.

After meandering around the hospital for ages, we went out onto the street and saw a tow truck pulling a station wagon from the fifties. The car was about thirty feet long. Joe flagged down the truck and asked the driver if he knew where the hospital garage was.

"Sure," he said. "Follow me to *my* garage. It's only a few yards down."

He slowly drove along, and we trotted next to him on the sidewalk. When we arrived, the tow truck driver dismounted and gave us detailed instructions for how to get to the hospital garage. Joe wrote them down in a notebook, and then the tow truck driver lent us a car to drive to the garage, even though it was only half a block away. When we got in the car, I discovered that it had no steering wheel and no gas or brake pedals.

"How the fuck do we drive this thing?" I asked.

Joe shrugged, totally indifferent. "What's your phone number? When we get to the garage, they might ask where to send the bill for the wall, so I'll tell them to contact you."

Just a few minutes earlier, he'd said that we'd either steal the tank or abandon it, and now he wanted to make *me* responsible for all the damage his tank had done. That made me as angry as I'd always been before the Meniere's disease. It was an unhinged, operatic rage. Even so, I gave Joe my number. Our vehicle took off as he wrote in his notebook. We hurtled toward a line of cars at a stoplight ahead, but the lack of steering wheel and brakes meant that there was nothing I could do but wait for the inevitable. When we smashed into the back of a red convertible, Joe had no reaction and continued writing.

To keep from going completely out of my skull, I left the car and stomped into a nearby forest, where a crowd of well-dressed people emerged from a church after a wedding. The bride and groom beamed with joy. They made me furious with envy, so I kept walking until I came to a mall as big as Los Angeles International Airport. Inside, college-age kids danced to 1950s rock and roll. They were on top of tables and in front of all the stores; I had to elbow them out of the way.

After struggling through passageways and up the escalator, I came to a dance hall filled with hundreds of couples my age and older. When I tried to join them, jets of water sprayed up out of the floor, blocking me. I couldn't believe how unfair it was. It was the first time in almost thirty years that I wanted to dance, but I was prevented.

It was wrong for me to dance with the kids. I should've been allowed in where I belonged.

JANUARY 7, 2013

In the lobby of a luxurious Art Deco apartment building, a woman who was a dead ringer for the young Greta Garbo showed me her elephant gun. She was the most intelligent, beautiful, humorous, and interesting woman I'd ever met, with the kind of deep, smooth voice I like.

"Here's how you load it," she said, breaking it open at the breech. "You put the two shells in here. They're .600 Nitro Express cartridges. Shooting this is like wrestling an alligator. If you don't hold on as tightly as you can, you're done for."

"Please tell me you don't shoot elephants with it," I said. The thought of this wonderful woman shooting elephants made me depressed and sick.

She looked shocked. "Oh, no! I've never shot anything except targets. Besides, this gun is ornamental, not functional. Look."

It was completely plated in silver. Her refusal to kill made me so happy that I fell completely and utterly in love with her, even though I knew nothing would come of it. That didn't matter. I wasn't sad, and I didn't feel as though I'd miss out on anything by never actually being with her. Loving her was the important thing.

She knew that I loved her, and it gave her strength. I felt privileged that such a woman accepted my love without laughing or sneering. She put the elephant gun in a padded green rifle bag, zipped it up, and shouldered it.

"Would you excuse me for a second?" I asked.

"Of course." She smiled and touched my upper arm.

I turned around to find the bathroom and saw Carmen sitting on one of the lobby sofas. She was absolutely gorgeous, all slinky and enigmatic in her jeans and dark, long-sleeved blouse, her legs crossed and her arms stretched out along the top of the sofa back. I was shocked but so happy I wanted to cry.

She gave me her best, widest smile—the one that made her eyes into squinting little slits—and said, "I still love you, but now you're just some of the sad baggage I have in my life."

I could've died from joy. The last time she said she loved me was in 1992.

FEB 17, 2013

I made Scott Thunes a diorama of a sailboat navigating a choppy stretch of rapids. Instead of modeling or painting the water, I used a plaque of rough-hewn wood with swirly grain that replicated the current. It was extremely clever of me. I carved a waterline model of a boat from a single piece of wood, made a masthead, mainsail, boom, jib, sheets, and tiller from wood, paper, and thread, and I put tiny Victorian people on the boat to represent Scott, his wife Georgia, and his children Hazle and Virgil.

After waxing the wood, I sealed it with glossy varnish, creating a super-realistic, rushing-water effect, with the same yellow-brown color of the Orinoco River. It was the best diorama I'd ever made. When I presented it to Scott, I split into both a watcher and a participant. The watcher was the today-me, and the person presenting him the diorama was Jennifer Love Hewitt—the really young, hot version.

Scott graciously accepted the diorama, put it on the ground, and picked up a handful of dripping mud and Swiss chard.

"What would you do," he said with a smile, "if I dropped this on the diorama?"

The Jennifer Love Hewitt-me burst into tears. "I put so much work into it! I made it for you! Why would you *do* that? Why would you ruin it like that?"

He put down the mud and Swiss chard. "When you make art and give it to someone, it's not yours anymore. It's theirs to do whatever they want with it."

As he spoke, he was suddenly the Scott from 1981, with carrot orange hair, and then he was the today-Scott, with a black Betty Page wig.

The Jennifer Love Hewitt-me stopped crying and understood that the diorama wasn't mine. If I'd honestly made it for him, it was indeed his to do with what he wished. I realized that my motivations had been selfish and self-aggrandizing. Scott had shown me with elegant simplicity and directness how to let go. I felt deep gratitude. The watcher-me then began to interview him.

"During the period in which you stopped playing professionally, did you feel that way about your art? That once you'd created it and put it out there, it was no longer yours, and others could do with it as they wished? And if you truly felt that way, why would you be angry that you could no longer create art professionally?"

As he answered, he began dancing the Charleston and crying, but he also smiled.

"I didn't feel that way at first. The reason I was able to begin thinking of my art that way was because of my wife. As soon as I met her, nothing else mattered. My art became secondary to her, and it dawned on me that if I never made art again, it wouldn't make any difference. My wife and I *are* art. I no longer think in terms of *my* art, because it isn't mine. Nothing really belongs to us as individuals. It's everybody's or it's nobody's, but it doesn't belong to any one person, not even the person who created it."

FEBRUARY 23, 2013

Scott Thunes hired me to play bass in the 1988 Zappa band, which he'd reconstituted. I arrived at the studio carrying a gigantic leather gig bag for my electric bass; it was big enough to hold a double bass and had been reinforced with a metal framework inside. The band stood around watching me as I set my bag on the floor and unzipped it. Bryan Beller was there too. He seemed angry at me, though I had no idea why. I'd been nice to him for as long as we'd known each other. I thought maybe he took it personally when I cut myself off from the world in 2003.

My gig bag was full of junk: broken two-by-fours, old sections of pipe, water-damaged books, empty soup cans, and unidentified machine parts. I frantically rummaged through it, looking for my bass while everybody chuckled or walked away in disgust.

Scott laughed. "Did you think you could bullshit your way through *this* job too? Are you *insane?*"

Finally, I found a tiny Venezuelan *cuatro,* the purely decorative type made of light, cheap wood and strung with fishing line. I'd had one as a child. There was no bass guitar in the gig bag. I knew I'd utterly screwed up, but I showed Scott the *cuatro.*

"Look," I said. "I *did* bring my bass."

He roared with laughter, dismissed me with a flap of his hand, and went into a kitchen attached to the studio, where he sat on the floor in a lotus position and began to meditate. I knew this was all my fault, but I was also furious at him. Why had he hired me as bassist for the 1988 Zappa band when he knew I couldn't play anymore? After all we'd been through together, I couldn't believe he'd betray me that way. The fact that I'd agreed to do it made me even angrier. I went into the kitchen where Scott sat.

"What would you do if I did this?" I asked.

I punched him in the face as hard as I could. His head snapped back and forth in a blur, like a boxers' floor-standing speed bag. It even made the same spring-loaded sound: *rocketa-rocketa-rocketa-rocketa.*

He laughed and gave me a wide-eyed look of pretend fear.

"How about this?" I asked and punched him in the stomach. My fist sank into him well over a foot, as though he had no bones.

"Oof!" he said, just like in a cartoon, and laughed again.

I punched him in the head and stomach for several minutes. It was like hitting a pillow. He just kept laughing, and I did no damage whatsoever. I ended up so exhausted and dizzy that I fell over.

MARCH 15, 2013

As I stood at a podium and gave a reading for *Ghosts and Ballyhoo,* I broke wind continually and deafeningly. It sounded like a string of cannon shots in the large auditorium. I knew I should've left the stage, but I couldn't. Flop sweat poured out of me, and the audience laughed, groaned, or palmed their faces.

When each trembling, rumbling eruption built in my gut, I tried desperately to hold it in. This seemed to make the explosion even more violent. Some of my discharges went on for twenty seconds. I shouted to make myself heard over my own rear end.

People in the audience were hysterical—weeping and breathless, holding their middles, begging me to stop.

In reply I blew off the seat of my pants. It flew across the stage and hit the wall behind me, leaving my buttocks exposed. I felt cool air wafting over them as I thought of the lyrics to the song "The Music Goes Round and Round."

MARCH 23, 2013

This entry is formatted differently, since it's the only way I can describe what happened.

I fell asleep on the sofa, watching *Father Goose,* one of my favorite movies. I watch it when I want to lose myself in total fantasy. Carmen loved it too. We were great fans of Leslie Caron.

Watching movies is how I conquered my lifelong bouts of insomnia. My choices were generally sleeplessness or nightmares. I discovered that the sofa is less daunting than the bed, and my DVD collection is made up entirely of films can I watch over and over because they convey me. That's my only criterion for buying them.

Father Goose. Touch of Evil. Witness for the Prosecution. No Way to Treat a Lady. The Eagle Has Landed. Transylvania. Sleuth. Big Trouble. True Grit. The Big Clock. Dog Day Afternoon. Three Days of the Condor. Roman Holiday. The Taking of Pelham One Two Three. Dreamscape. The Transporter. Dead Calm. Against the Wall. The Gift. ReCycle. Crank. Crank 2. I'm a Cyborg But That's Okay. The Silent Partner. Rear Window. Oldboy. Fanny. The Pulse. Charade. Key Largo. The Craft. Designing Woman. Zulu. Intolerable Cruelty. The Man Who Would Be King. Up in the Air. A Very Long Engagement. The Quiet Man. 28 Days Later. Wait Until Dark. North by Northwest. Monster-in-Law. A Patch of Blue. The Crying Game. In the Heat of the Night. The Mothman Prophecies. A Little Princess. My First Mister. The Time Machine. Altered States. On and on and on, enough to fill a book. Film is my favorite art form.

It wasn't always that way. In fact, I used to hate movies.

When my father took us to movies, we arrived at the time he'd decided we would arrive. It didn't matter when the movie started. During our childhood, we never got to see a single movie from the beginning. We showed up in the middle of the film, watched it to the end, and then sat there through the intermission. Dad always chose the row behind us, the better to keep an eye on us and make sure we didn't move or speak. After fifteen minutes, the lights went down, and the movie began.

The second we got to the part we'd already seen, Dad stood and announced, "Time to go. Come *on!* Let's *go!*"

We left with him and rode home silently in the car. We never asked why we couldn't watch a movie from the beginning. It didn't occur to us. Sometimes Dad told us it was time to leave before we got to the part we'd already seen. There were plenty of movies I didn't watch in full, from beginning to end, until I was an adult.

On the night of March 23, 2013, I fell asleep on the sofa watching *Father Goose* and had a dream in which Leslie Caron danced for me. As I reached out to her, I heard Dad shout, "*Tom! Get in here!*"

I snapped awake, said, "*Yes,* I'm coming," and got up off the sofa. It was very hard to rein in the resentment and dread. His passing would never end, and it would just get more ugly and grotesque. I took five or six steps, bracing myself for what I'd see in Dad's bedroom, and then I remembered that he was dead. There was a moment of total confusion before I oriented myself: I was in *my* house, not his. He'd been dead for exactly one month to the day. I no longer had to take care of him.

The clock showed that it was 2:00 a.m., the hour he'd died. I climbed into bed, fell back asleep, and resumed my dream of Leslie Caron dancing. The dream picked up exactly where I'd left off, right as I reached out to her. She took my hand and smiled.

It was as if she'd waited for me.

MARCH 25, 2013

The songwriter-producer Matt Resnicoff took over Schiffer and told me that *Ghosts and Ballyhoo* wouldn't be published. Instead, they'd put out a book called *How to Busk,* a ghostwritten title with my name on it.

They sent me a copy. It was four pages long.

Each page was black and laminated in plastic, with neon-green line drawings and no text. The first page showed someone walking into a subway station with a guitar in a case, the second showed the person opening the case, the third showed him putting on the guitar, and the fourth showed him playing as money fell into the open guitar case.

A note was included with this advance copy:

> *Congratulations!*
> *Matt*

APRIL 12, 2013

It was a posh hotel that reminded me of the Columbus, where my family stayed in Miami during the sixties and early seventies. As I walked down the carpeted hallway, I saw a little blonde girl of about four, standing by the stairway that led down to the lobby. She wore a white sundress and shoes, and she was crying.

"Where's my mommy?" she sobbed. "I want my mommy!"

I hurried toward her, but before I could reach her, she went down the stairs. By the time I arrived at the stairway, she'd disappeared. It was a wide, curved, double stairway, heavily carpeted and fitted with brass railings; on the lobby floor below was a round marble fountain with a statue of a Greek or Roman woman. The twin stairways encircled the fountain like embracing arms. A crystal chandelier six feet wide hung from the ceiling of the second floor. It was low enough that I could look down on it from where I stood, my hands on the stairway railing.

"Did anybody see a little girl?" I asked the people going up and down the stairs.

Nobody responded.

"*Where's the little girl?*" I shouted.

Everyone ignored me. There was nothing I could do. The little girl was gone.

Sitting at the top of the stairs to my right was a woman bent double, covering her face with both hands and crying. She had long, dark hair and wore jeans and a gray hoodie. I sat next to her.

"What's the matter?" I asked. "Are you all right?" I touched her shoulder.

Sitting up, she spread her fingers so that she could peek at me with one eye. She was Asian, about sixteen or seventeen.

Though I felt guilty and deeply uncomfortable talking to her, I had to find out what was wrong. "Are you okay?"

She dropped her hands and laughed. It was all an act; she wasn't crying. Furious that she'd fooled me into being concerned for her *and* endangering myself by approaching a teenaged girl, I got up and went over to a picture window. On the other side of the glass were a lush garden, shade trees, and a well-kept lawn. The outside looked safe and inviting. I wished I could leave the hotel and wander the grounds.

There was a leather sofa with its back to the window, a coffee table in front of it. A leather armchair was at either end of the table, arranged so that a group of six or eight could sit in the three pieces of sumptuous, dark brown furniture and talk. It was a life-saving oasis of serenity. I plopped down into the right-hand chair, grateful for how soft and warm it felt. If everybody left me alone, I'd stay there all day. I stared at the purple carpet and tried to relax.

The legs of a woman in designer jeans came into view. She moved behind the coffee table to get as close to me as she could and sat on the sofa to my right. I looked up and saw that it was Carmen.

"*Hi!*" she said. "How *are* you?" It was her campy, unctuously perky persona, the one she used when she was a TV anchor and radio DJ. I didn't mind. I knew she had to speak to me that way now. The important thing was that she was there. I was struck again by how beautiful she was at fifty-two. She'd always been afraid of aging, yet she was even better looking now than she was in her twenties.

"I'm okay," I said. "How about you?"

"Not so good. Have you noticed that too many women have really big noses?"

Her campiness was phony. I could tell that she was very upset. She couldn't fool me.

"I *haven't* noticed," I said. "Pretty much every woman I see has a nose that's just right for her."

Carmen scooted forward and put her hand on my knee, the first time she'd touched me since 1992.

"Women's noses are too big, Tom!" she said urgently. "They're ugly and disgusting!"

"You're going to get a nose job, aren't you?" I said.

She looked away and nodded.

I sat forward and took her face in my hands, astonished that she let me. My palms remembered what it was like to do so eons ago. She hadn't changed. Her cool, pale, freckled skin was exactly the same. I traced the outlines of her nose with my fingers.

"Your nose is perfect," I said. "It always was. Now tell me the truth: Have you ever seen a woman who looked good after she got a nose job? Have you?"

She looked into my eyes, and I saw that she was crying. "No."

"We're meant to have the noses we were given," I said.

She clutched my wrists with both hands. "I know. You're right. You're right."

"So now you know what to do, don't you?"

"Yes. Thank you."

She smiled broadly, the tears running down her cheeks, and then she got up and walked away.

Completely at peace, I watched her depart, purged of my angst over the lost little girl and that sneaky, rotten teenager.

CHAPTER TWELVE
IT'S ALL GOOD

Some of my dreams have been fantastic. In fact, the very first dream I remember—which dates from 1968, when I was six—is still the best dream I ever had. It's in *Ghosts and Ballyhoo,* but I'll include it here in case you don't read the memoir. It would be a shame it you *didn't* read the memoir, since it's the main volume of the *Ghosts* trilogy and my best work.

I think you should read it. What could it hurt?

All these dreams are in their own individual ways almost as good as the one from 1968. Unlike in the other chapters, I'll include notes on each, since I think these are the most important dreams of my life.

*   *   *

1968

This—my best dream—is very odd for lots of reasons. When I was six, I didn't know what monks were, and I was petrified of heights. Yet this dream left me with a feeling of optimism that may have saved me. Things were already pretty awful when I was six. I can't say how this dream influenced my determination to keep trying regardless of how often I failed or how much pain was inflicted on me, but I think it was pivotal. At the lowest points of my life, when I thought it was best to just call it a day, I'd remember this dream and decide to stick around a little while longer.

I'm glad I did.

*   *   *

I walked somewhere up in very high mountains that had lots of jagged peaks and vertical faces, like the Alps or Himalayas. The mountains were covered with pillars shaped like giant bowling pins standing upside down. They were narrow at the base and flared out into a rounded bulb flattened at the top. There were thousands of them, each about one hundred feet high, covering the peaks like a dense forest. On the top of each pillar was a bald monk in an orange robe, sitting cross-legged in the lotus position.

I shinnied up the nearest pillar, and as I got to the top I realized it was made of rubber. It swayed gently on its narrow stalk, forcing me to hold on tightly. I was terrified. The monk sitting on the top of the pillar smiled.

"Don't be afraid," he said. "You have to jump off with me."

He began bouncing up and down, still in his sitting position, and then he leaped off. With the speed of a rocket, he careened all the way down into the valley thousands of feet below, his legs still crossed. He somehow maintained an erect posture, his hands folded casually in his lap as he sent rocks and dust flying in all directions.

An overwhelming sense of liberation and great fun hit me. There was no way I could get hurt. I jumped off after the monk, bouncing down the rocky side of the mountain, which was actually as soft and resilient as the mattress on my bed. Though I wasn't able to stay in a sitting position and rolled around violently, sliding first on my stomach, then on my back, then in a tightly curled ball, it didn't matter.

As I went over the edge and plummeted into the abyss, all the other monks jumped off their own pillars in an avalanche of orange. We fell into the valley and became fireflies, glowing with our own light, and then we all rose together and flew into the dusk, side by side, in our millions. I felt incredibly happy and excited, as if nothing bad could happen to me, ever.

MARCH 23, 1986

This is my second-favorite dream. Like the one from 1968, it's a reminder that complete peace is achievable. I've never felt such well-being, except for the three perfect years Carmen gave me. From the age of about four until July of 1989, I lived in chaos, fear, depression, self-hatred, and rage. Drugs and alcohol entered the picture when I was sixteen. My pre-Carmen state resumed—minus the drugs and alcohol—in August of 1993 and lasted until October of 2011. The three good years with Carmen are the apex of my existence.

In *this* cycle.

The symbolism of the Bic pen cap always eluded me, but I understand it now.

Is the dream prescient?

We'll see.

*   *   *

The flatbed diesel truck drove through the forest. I rode on the back, rocking gently on the splintered wooden deck. The sun shone through the bare trees, flashing intermittently in my eyes like a ship's signal lamp. It had to be winter, a hazy, yellow-gray January afternoon. Even so, I wasn't cold. I felt nothing, as if I were watching a film. Still, I was undoubtedly *there*, riding through a forest in the American Northwest, enveloped by immense quiet.

I gazed at the trees, experiencing the most profound sense of calm and contentment of my life. With me on the truck was an iron cauldron shaped like an upturned cymbal or Chinese wok. It was about ten feet across. When I crawled over to it, I saw that it was made of very thin metal, only about an eighth of an inch thick. At its center, the cauldron had a round, symmetrical depression about a foot deep, a smaller wok within a wok. It was scattered with branches and fragments of soft, rotting wood, and the mottled gray-brown interior was dotted with dewdrops. Some of the drops merged and ran down in trickles toward the center, like raindrops on a windowpane.

At the bottom of the cauldron was a tiny, bright orange fox kit. It was obviously a baby, because it was stumpy and had a compressed teddy bear's face with big eyes and ears. It pounced like a cat on pieces of wood, turning its little head avidly, its ears cocked forward.

It saw me and scampered up to the lip of the cauldron, stopping about six inches in front of my face and holding on with its small white paws. Its tongue hung out of its mouth, and it seemed to smile as it stared directly into my eyes with complete trust. Then it turned and ran back to the bottom of the cauldron, its nails ringing on the metal like rolling gravel.

Down among the fragments of wood, it sat and looked up at me. I took a Bic ballpoint pen from my breast pocket, pulled off the missile-shaped cap, and dropped it into the cauldron. The cap shot into the bottom as though jet propelled and sped past the fox. It flew out of the depression into the air, where the slipstream hit it and flipped it over the fox's head back at me. The fox craned its neck to follow its flight, and I caught the cap with my left hand. Since the fox seemed amused and fascinated, I dropped the cap into the cauldron again. It rocketed past the fox, ascended, and blew back into my hand.

I did this over and over, feeling love and respect for the fox, as well as a powerful desire to protect it.

JULY 21, 1996

At the risk of embarrassing him, I have to confess my admiration for Gene Simmons. Interviewing him was a life-changing experience because not only did he let me know that he didn't consider me a fraud, he also understood and appreciated my goal, which was to create unforgettable performance art. He took a great professional risk at a crucial moment in his career, and he did it with self-deprecating humor and a fearless sense of adventure.

Interviewing him was *fun*. Incredibly fun. If circumstances had been different, it would've assured my place in the world of music journalism.

A critical failing of psychiatry is the notion that being affected by the opinions of your fellow humans amounts to "seeking validation from others."

I disagree. It depends entirely on who's expressing the opinion, how it's expressed, and the circumstances of the interaction. If you're standing on a street corner and a homeless lunatic come out of nowhere and screams, *"You suck as a writer,"* it won't have the same impact as one of your heroes saying you're an abject joke as a human being.

Why tell people that they should never care what anybody thinks of them? If you're utterly indifferent to how every single person alive thinks of you, it means you're a psychopath. Your entire sense of self-worth shouldn't be based on how others feel about you, but it's nice to get praise from people you admire. And when people you admire think you're a clod, it hurts. That's just reality, and there's nothing wrong in copping to it. The secret is not letting the opinions of others chart the course of your life.

Still, it did me a boatload of good as a writer to have Gene Simmons tell me that he really enjoyed his time with me and that he hoped I'd become wildly successful.

So sue me.

*　　*　　*

A woman and I walked together on a beautifully kept estate at sunset. Though I didn't know who the woman was, I didn't turn my head to look at her. She was beside me, at the periphery of my vision, about three feet away. I felt compassion for her, an unaccustomed emotion. For the first time in my life, I was in control. I was proud of having given up a terrible trait that I'd nurtured for years. Being there with her relaxed me and made me the happiest I'd been in decades.

The gravel path circled a lake. As we strolled along, something disturbed the surface of the water. It was Gene Simmons, emerging like a sea monster from the depths. He splashed toward the shore and smiled warmly at us. It was a strange expression for such a brutish face. He wore a black leather jacket that poured off streams of water. Seeing him comforted me, the way I felt when among my closest friends. He trudged up onto the shore, and we walked past him, not stopping because it wasn't necessary. I now knew that we were on his estate. He'd always be there, and we'd always be welcome.

We left the gravel path and walked across a lush lawn. The ground felt incredibly soft under my feet, as if I were walking on a thick shag carpet. We entered a small copse and continued on, my feeling of peace increasing the further we moved in among the dark trees. They were beautiful—ancient, strong, and protective.

A weapon was half-buried in the ground at the base of a tree. I recognized it as a French M29 light machine gun, a large weapon with a pistol grip, a wooden butt, a long barrel, and a magazine mounted on the top. I picked it up and realized that it was just a toy, that the butt and grip were made of purplish-red plastic. I took it with us as we moved into a clearing in the trees, where a folding stepladder had been set up. Gene Simmons stood on one of the steps, stringing Christmas lights on tree branches and giving directions to unseen minions in the brusque, frightening manner he'd used when I first met him. I felt the same gratification as when he'd come out of the lake. He was the answer to all my questions.

I handed him the machine gun. He took it with one hand, the other hand gripping one of the ladder steps. Scowling at the gun uncomprehendingly, he held it by the pistol grip, the barrel hanging down.

"No, no," I said. "You don't hold it like that. You hold it like *this*."

I rearranged his hand on the grip, took his other hand from the ladder step, and placed it on a handle that protruded from the breech in front of the magazine. He leaned back against the ladder and allowed me to manipulate his hands. I appreciated and respected him for submitting without protest.

"You see?" I said. "Now you can use it for antiaircraft work."

He nodded and hefted the weapon experimentally, understanding that my way was better.

I watched with a sense of complete fulfillment.

NOVEMBER 26, 1997

In November of 1997, the new editor at *Bass Player* killed most of my articles that were in the can when he took over. Everyone in the entire organization promised me that this wouldn't happen, but they lied. When I told the editor about the promises, he laughed.

"Tom," he said jovially, "that's what they always say, and the new editor always kills the leftovers from his predecessor. That's just how it's done."

I knew then that my career was over, but I refused to accept it. Denial and all-consuming rage prevented me from trying to find a different job. I stopped keeping my dream diary because the nightmares reached a crescendo. They were so intense that they became a form of mental illness. To imagine what it was like, just take any one of the nightmare clusters in this book and distill them into syrup, like fine balsamic vinegar.

Since my life consisted solely of failure and being at the mercy of unreachable rinky-dinks who wouldn't know quality if it latched onto the end of their nose with razor-sharp piranha teeth, writing down all the mayhem inside my head just made my presence in this world even more unbearable. So I stopped.

A clarification.

When I say "quality," I mean strictly as an interviewer. I never wanted to be an author. It took me years to teach myself how to write books, and I'm still not happy with the results. My novels were awful, and my dream diary required weeks of polishing to make it readable. I'm not a natural writer. The only real skills I had were playing the bass guitar, interviewing, building scale models, and drawing cartoons. I can still do the fourth. Tim tells me—insists, really—that I should publish a book of cartoons. I love B. Kliban, Gary Larson, Dr. Seuss, and Charles Schultz in his surreal period, when he produced *Speak Softly, and Carry a Beagle.* Maybe I'll give it a shot.

Anyway, this is the last entry of my dream diary.

*   *   *

As I lay in my bed at night, a fissure opened up in the wooden floor. One second it wasn't there, and the next it was. Shaped roughly like a diamond, it released a cool blue light that filled the room and awed me with its beauty. I got out of bed and cautiously approached. The hole revealed a vast underground city—skyscrapers, monorails, elevated freeways, and flying machines like ornithopters. The blue light came from the sky, which was below my floor.

Two women appeared on either side of the fissure, gazing up at me. I saw solid ground beneath their feet, and I realized that they stood on a mountaintop. It was as though my house floated above their heads. They were dressed in sleeveless, thigh-length white tunics, with cloth belts and leather sandals, the straps of which criss-crossed up their calves to their knees. Both women had dark brown eyes and long, wavy, dark hair with loose buns on the backs of their heads. They smiled at me the way Carmen did when I told her I loved her. It took me a second to recognize their outfits: They looked like Artemis, the Greek goddess of the hunt, the wilderness, and wild animals.

"Come on down, Tom," one called, holding out her hand.

I sat on the edge of the hole, woozy with happiness. When I turned over onto my stomach and lowered myself, the women grabbed my legs. I dropped down, holding on until I hung about two feet above the mountaintop, and then I let go. The women caught me in their powerful arms.

Standing on the mountain, I looked at the beautiful city. A gentle, refreshing breeze blew. It smelled of the ocean.

"Are you ready?" one of the women asked.

"I don't know," I said. "Where are we going?"

She pointed to the city. "Down there. We've been waiting for you."

"Are there any men there?" I asked.

The other woman touched my forearm. Her hand was hard with callus built up from extensive training with swords and quarterstaffs.

"Yes," she said, "but we won't let them hurt you."

I was home. When they set off down the mountain, I followed.

APRIL 10, 2013

This is the only dream I've ever had that exactly recreated an event I'd actually experienced.

Some background.

Although I'm not religious, I believe in a Planner, and one of my heroes is Saint Michael the Archangel because he fearlessly confronts evil. After my father died, the hospice chaplain told me that Saint Michael is also the Angel of Death. He's so ferocious because his job is to protect the souls of the departed on their journey.

The real-life counterpart to this dream took place on Easter Sunday, March 31, 2013.

*　　*　　*

Using an ATM in a bank vestibule, I tried to transfer funds from my savings account to pay for my health insurance. My father had picked up the tab for it without me asking. He'd just told me one day in the mid-1990s that from now on he'd write the checks. I didn't argue.

Though he'd had ample time to do so, he didn't make the last payment, his impending death from cancer having driven him mad with terror. I discovered this in many ways, one being when I got a notice telling me that my insurance would be canceled unless the carrier got its money by April 4.

In the bank vestibule, the transfer of funds wouldn't go through. I tried three times, and it kept giving me the balance instead of making the transfer. I got angrier and angrier, and suddenly every horrible development of the previous three months came crashing down on me, making me nearly hysterical. It's the closest I've come in my life to pitching a stupendous tantrum and just trashing the place, like a gorilla doing one of those smash-it-all-up displays in the jungle.

The door behind me opened, and someone came in. I turned around; it was a young man in tight jeans and a form-fitting white T-shirt. Tall and olive skinned, he was the most physically fit person I've ever seen, with immensely broad shoulders, a V-shaped torso, extremely muscular but not large arms and legs, and spiky black hair. His face was perfectly androgynous; it was literally and completely without gender. I knew he was a man only by his body. He struck me—and I have no idea how I got this impression—as incredibly kind and utterly dangerous, a fierce warrior calmly holding himself in check. I didn't feel a threat directed at me but rather at anyone who messed with him and those he cared about. He exuded supreme confidence and peace, as though nothing could possibly anger him. If he resorted to violence, he did so without malice and only when necessary. His expression was complex, a faint smile and what I can best describe as concerned impartiality. He was intensely present yet detached.

"I'm really sorry about this," I said. "I can't get this thing to do what I want."

"Don't worry, sir," he replied. "It's all good."

His voice was very strange, eerily musical and neither male nor female. There was something distinctly hornlike about it. And what a bizarre choice of words for the situation. Even so, I felt deep gratitude toward him, way out of proportion to his polite patience. He made me almost want to cry. I relaxed, the urge to destroy gone in a flash.

After one more try, I gave up and went into the bank. As I passed through the door, the young man advanced to the ATM. Inside the bank, I turned left toward a teller, and when I looked over at the ATM again, only two seconds later, nobody was there. The young man had vanished.

APRIL 29, 2013

Here's the first such dream I've had since 2002, the year I lost the ability to play the bass guitar. I didn't realize that in eleven years, I never once dreamed of what once meant so much to me. It was a form of self-protection, I suppose. I wasn't ready to revisit.

*   *   *

On the crowded sidewalk in front of a Scottish pub, I was about to play my bass. I wanted to demonstrate that the Bryan Beller hooked-fingers-as-a-pick technique really works, even though I'd never tried it before. My old Carvin amplifier was set up, and all my effects pedals were plugged in. I'd learned Bryan's technique from watching his instructional video.

Scott Thunes and my bassist friend Mark McCann were there with glasses of Guiness. Glancing around, I also saw Joe Cady, Bryan, and most of the *Bass Player* staff from 1995 to 1997.

"Look," I said. "It's easy."

I held up my left hand, the index and middle fingers curved.

"All you do is just go up and down on the strings. It's a completely natural motion."

They all looked skeptical. Even Bryan, inventor of the technique.

"Just *watch*," I said impatiently.

My thumb resting on the edge of the pickup, I began playing a blizzard of notes, the bass line from a Volkswagen commercial that I've never been able to get out of my head. The Carmen bass—the right-handed MusicMan Sting Ray she bought for me and had converted to a lefty version—sounded spectacular, with the grinding, deep treble I love. I'd added distortion and a slight amount of flange, making it absolutely killer. I could've been Klaus Flouride, fellow recipient of an autoimmune disorder.

It was the first time I'd played since 2002, but I hadn't lost any of my abilities. When I laughed in sheer gratification, my audience joined me, especially Scott, Bryan, and Mark.

They were happy that I could still play and that the first time I tried this new technique, I pulled it off without a hitch. It was amazing to feel the strings against my fingers again and to curl my right hand around the neck of a bass. The only missing element was Carmen herself. Her bass would have to be enough.

I'd won everybody over. And yet as grateful as I was for their support, I knew the second I picked up the bass that I could do it.

EPILOGUE

My hope was that I'd have a dream that would provide an elegant, logical ending to this book. What I've discovered is that accepting and letting go has not only liberated me from the past, it also seems to have opened a magical door that leads directly to the fulfillment of wishes. Not wishes for material gain; I'm not "manifesting success" or any of that garbage. Instead, I keep being granted wishes that lead to personal improvement. My aspirations to become a better person seem to have caught the attention of someone or something. These aren't prayers, though. I haven't once asked, "Could I please have...?" I've simply thought to myself, *Wouldn't it be great if...?*

Since I junked my rage, I was able to reconnect with one of my music idols, Scott Thunes. We became friends, and I was finally able to see him play live, from no more then ten feet away. I could closely study his technique on the bass, which led to several "Eureka!" moments. Though I can't play anymore in the physical realm, I play in my mind and in my dreams. Scott's techniques have been very useful.

Since I junked my rage, my friend Rolf Schamberger—head of the German Firefighter Museum in Fulda—found the memorial and death book of the Guard Reserve Pioneer Regiment, the German flamethrower regiment of World War I. It disappeared in 1983. I gave up looking for it in 2007 after a two-year quest. Rolf sent me an e-mail titled, "We have found it!" The photos of the memorial that he included were literally a dream come true. One of my dearest wishes had been granted, and I can tell you that it was everything I could've hoped for and more. I realize now that I tried to find the memorial as a way to connect with my father, a man cast in the same mold as the commander of the flamethrower regiment, Major Bernhard Reddemann.

Since I junked my rage, I no longer have nightmares that make me think I've died or gone crazy or committed some horrible atrocity. I still have bad dreams, but they're different from the ones I recorded on and off for ten years. They've lost their power over me.

Since I junked my rage, I don't fear the night. I don't fear the day either. In fact, I don't fear much anymore, except for flying. And cauliflower.

Since I junked my rage, I had this dream, the perfect ending to *Hallucinabulia* and the *Ghosts* Trilogy. I don't need Joe Cady to interpret it for me, even though he's an expert. It's the first dream I've had of my father since he died.

I couldn't have asked for a better way to close so many books.

*   *   *

MAY 12, 2013

Most of my mother's relatives, my immediate family, and I were on a wooden covered bridge somewhere in New England. It was winter—sunny and cold— and all the trees were bare. I was both watcher and participant. The watcher-me was my present age, while the participant-me was about thirteen, wearing the red jacket that was my trademark at the time. I had my long hair and big glasses again; I looked like a middle-aged Latvian spinster, the style I cultivated in the eighth and ninth grades.

The scene became very blurry, as though suddenly I were looking through a sheet of ice. Then I found myself at the Department of Motor Vehicles. Tim and my father were with me, as were hundreds of people I've known my entire life. Some were from the oil camp in Venezuela, some from Texas, some from the Netherlands, some from Norway, some from college, some from Japan, and some from San Francisco. We all had appointments at exactly the same time.

We were directed to a large room where there were no seats. The first people into the room sat on the floor. When the floor was filled, the rest of us simply climbed in and lay on top of the others. It was a ceiling-high pile of humanity, all tangled together. Nobody spoke.

As I lay there, different people did weird things to me. Someone tickled my sides and went, "Cootchie-Cootchie-Cootchie!" Then someone else put the top of her head—I knew it was a woman—in the center of my back. Someone else rubbed the upper parts of my arms up and down with both hands.

Several hours went by. The lights went off intermittently, leaving us in total darkness. Finally, Carmen pulled my hair and blasted her donkey laugh into my ear.

"Okay, that's it," I said. "There has to be a better way. This isn't working."

Everyone agreed. We untangled ourselves and went out into a waiting room full of leather-covered armchairs and sofas, enough for us all. I couldn't figure out why we hadn't seen it before and why the DMV employees hadn't told us about it. As I looked for a place to sit, I saw Tim and Dad leave through a side door. This upset me so much that I ran after them into a twisting hallway with a low ceiling. Framed maps and old, faded advertisements for oil companies hung on the walls.

I found Tim and Dad in a foyer, standing in front of a set of double swinging glass doors like at a 7-Eleven. Dad looked exactly like Barry Goldwater. He wouldn't acknowledge me.

"I don't have any more time to waste," he said to Tim. "You guys got more time than I do, so you can stay and wait, but I can't."

He went out the doors and disappeared.

"Where's he going?" I asked Tim.

"He's going home," Tim said. "He wants to work on his bicycle."

That made me extremely sad because I knew Dad would never ride his bicycle. It was just more busywork, the type he did to keep from thinking and feeling, but there was nothing I could do about it. He was unreachable.

Tim vanished and a group of soldiers came through the swinging doors, wearing berets and the obsolete Class A Dress Green uniform replaced with Dress Blues in 2008. All the soldiers were black or Latino.

"As you know," the young noncommissioned officer leading them said, "we try to recruit as many coconuts and Oreos as we can."

I couldn't believe that someone would say such a racist thing to Latino and black soldiers. It was even more surreal because the guy who said it was Latino himself. The last soldier held open the door for me. He was a heavily decorated, middle-aged black man with a short gray beard shaved into snazzy, futuristic points on his cheeks. I went outside and found that it was raining.

As I walked along a tree-lined path through a large green field, I heard a kitten meow. Looking around, I saw a ball of mud beside the path. The meowing came from it. I stooped and began stroking the mud ball, which meowed frantically, the way kittens do when they're lost or when they're about to be fed. The mud fell off in globs, exposing an orange tabby. It stretched and purred loudly. As I stroked, its fur dried and puffed out. I realized that I had to adopt it. The prospect terrified me. There was no way to safely get it home, and my house was a shambles. I'd have to keep the cat inside to protect it, but I simply wasn't qualified. My illness, tiny home, indeterminate future, and solitary lifestyle made me unfit to have a cat.

A cat carrier materialized on the path beside us, and the kitten jumped into it. There were blankets and toys inside. I thought the decision had been taken out of my hands until I saw that there was another kitten already inside, covered with mud. It growled at the orange kitten and attacked it. They rolled around inside the carrier, screaming and biting each other.

I went into a total panic, not knowing what to do. In front of me, a small stream flowed down the gentle hill and fed a brook of clear water that rushed along beside the path. At the top of the hill was a pergola full of plants, gardening tools, and terracotta pots. I took the carrier up to the pergola, trying to find something that would make the cats stop fighting. There was nothing. I'd have to do it myself.

The cat carrier had two layers, like bakery trays stacked on top of each other. I lifted off the top layer; the two cats were locked in combat, scratching and kicking. Since there seemed to be no alternative, I tipped the cats out of the carrier, and they rolled down the hill. By the time they got to the bottom, they were both adults. Although the cat that had attacked the orange cat bled from one eye—which nearly made me faint from horror and guilt—the orange cat was unscathed.

The cats separated and sat several feet apart. They didn't seem interested in fighting anymore. I felt such relief that I had a rotational vertigo attack. To keep from falling, I slammed down in a lotus position on the flagstones that made up the pergola floor. It hurt my tailbone, but I didn't care.

After a few seconds, the bleeding cat walked away. The orange cat then looked up at me and spoke. Its voice was high-pitched and feminine, and I knew that speaking was a huge effort for it.

"Thirsty...mister," it said. "Not...hungry. Thirsty."

I wanted desperately to save it, but I was also annoyed because it sat right beside a brook of clean, cold water. All it had to do was move forward less than two feet, and it could have all the water it wanted. It was obviously manipulating me, playing on my sympathies and vulnerabilities.

Aware that the whole situation was phony, I leaped up and began looking for a container to get the cat its water. I found a little pot with a blue-green glaze, filled it in the stream, and took it down to where the cat sat beside the brook. By the time I got there, the pot was empty. Instead of simply scooping water out of the brook, I ran back up the hill again and dipped the pot into the stream. When the pot was filled, I raced back to the cat, and by the time I got to it, the pot was empty again.

"So...thirsty...mister. Thirsty," the cat said in its feminine voice.

This time I crouched next to the brook and submerged the pot. It filled to the brim with cold water. When I lifted the pot out of the brook, all the water ran out the bottom, even though there was no hole anywhere. In a rage that was as fake as the cat's helplessness, I threw the pot down on the path, shattering it into a million pieces. Then I ran back up to the pergola to find another pot.

"Thirsty...mister," the cat called after me. "So...thirsty." I turned and saw that its eyes were half-closed. It looked very content.

It's true, I thought. *I'm absolutely insane.*

I continued my frenzied, bogus search for a container to give the cat water, when all it had to do was get up and walk four steps.

BIBLIOGRAPHY

Crane, Stephen. *The Black Riders and Other Lines.* Boston: Copeland and Day, 1896.

Cunliffe, J.W. (Ed.). *Poems of the Great War.* New York: The MacMillan Company, 1918.

Wictor, Thomas. *Ghosts and Ballyhoo: Memoirs of a Failed L.A. Music Journalist.* Atglen, Pennsylvania: Schiffer Books, 2013.

ABOUT THE AUTHOR

Thomas Wictor is the author of the *Ghosts* Trilogy:

Ghosts and Ballyhoo: Memoirs of a Failed L.A. Music Journalist.
Chasing the Last Whale.
Hallucinabulia: the Dream Diary of an Unintended Solitarian.

Other books by Thomas Wictor:

In Cold Sweat: Interviews with Really Scary Musicians.
German Flamethrower Pioneers of World War I.
Flamethrower Troops of World War I: The Central and Allied Powers.
German Assault Troops of World War I: Organization, Tactics, Weapons, Equipment, Orders of Battle, Uniforms.

His physical essence is situated in Southern California.

www.ingramcontent.com/pod-product-compliance
Lightning Source LLC
LaVergne TN
LVHW051501080426
835509LV00017B/1861